IN THE NAME OF LANGUAGE!

IN THE NAME OF LANGUAGE!

EDITED BY
Joseph Gold

MACMILLAN OF CANADA
MACLEAN-HUNTER PRESS

CONTENTS

PREFACE

In the spring of 1973, teachers from all parts of Ontario gathered at the Glendon campus of York University to discuss the fate of literacy in the Ontario educational system. They were invited by two organizations, the Chairmen of English Departments of Ontario Universities, of which I was president at the time, and the Ontario Council of Teachers of English, then under the able leadership of Brian Meeson. The topic of our conference was chosen after careful thought and given the deliberately melodramatic title, "The Survival of Literacy". In spite of the calculated provocation in so naming our subject, most participants saw nothing strange or satiric about it. For those actually working in the schools the threat to language is real enough, for they saw and still see alarming inroads made on the most central of all the educational areas. It is teachers who know the inadequacies of their own training, who can see the time once given to mother-tongue learning eroded by civics, home economics, social studies, film-making, and the dozens of other activities that demand the student's time. Teachers have seen in English studies the disappearance of compulsory practice, and, in the place of reading and writing, something called Communications, which may involve, for instance, the study of computers and film, or model-making. English has been rendered optional or frequently by-passed by an alternative and less-demanding surrogate. Classes have been allowed to grow, hours have been reduced, school library budgets have been cut; those who specialize in machine-shop instruction or in other skills frequently end up teaching English without enthusiasm, and children can reach twelve years of age, and sometimes even enter universities, never having written a single piece of formal, extended prose in their native language.

That this situation strikes many as profoundly alarming is not surprising; that governments of civilized democracies should view it with equanimity must be. Since governments and educational authorities are, in the present decade, insensitive to the consequences of this sad state, it remains for practising teachers to see if they can somehow restore to its focal position in the curriculum — a position both natural and vital — the intensive, exacting, and joyous practice of coming to grips with language.

Our Glendon conference heard several papers, and from what was said there grew the idea for this book. These essays are now published for the first time, although four of them are based on earlier oral presentations. For too long we have given our discipline into the careless hands of "educationists". It is with the deepest gratitude, which must be shared by English teachers everywhere, that I am able to gather here the contemporary thinking of some of Canada's leading practitioners in the discipline of English. They are people who have devoted their lives, like so many others, to the sharing of their experience and expertise in the language, and who have given a professional lifetime of thought to their subject. It is my conviction that these essays constitute a statement of profound importance in the struggle to find a lively and vigorous role for language in our educational system.

There is no doubt that the ideas expressed in these pages are traditional and that they have for a decade at least been unfashionable, but it is my belief that fashion is a blight on education and that common sense and the experience of teachers is what should prevail. The price for fads and completely unfounded theories has been enormous. It is the view of these essayists that teachers should have in their hands an authoritative, well-expressed, contemporary defence of the centrality of language study in education, and it is our hope that this book is such a statement.

The theme that runs through these essays, which were written completely independently of each other, is that language is inseparable from our humanity, that literature is its highest expression, and that the study and practice of writing, speaking, listening, and reading must once again become the central, nucleic, irreducible mainspring of our culture and of its formal educational system — that is, if we are to sustain the humanity of learning.

It is a pleasure to acknowledge the practical and moral support

I have enjoyed at every stage from Patrick Meany of Macmillan of Canada, whom I here wish to thank. He has helped me, encouraged me, and strongly endorsed the concept of a book of essays on literacy since the earliest broaching of this idea. I am grateful also for a University of Waterloo grant in aid of preparation of the manuscript for this book.

JOSEPH GOLD

DEDICATION
For English Teachers, Especially Now

Here's the end, then, of the first word on Education. Idealism is no good without fearlessness. To follow a high aim, you must be fearless of the consequences. To promulgate a high aim, and to be fearful of the consequences — as our idealists today — is much worse than leaving high aims alone altogether. Teach the three R's and leave the children to look out for their own aims. That's the very best thing we can do at the moment, since we are all cowards.

Away with all smatterings. Away with the imbecile pretence of culture in the elementary schools. . . . Teach a boy to read, to write and to do simple sums, and you have opened the door of all culture to him, if he wants to go through.

Education of the People by D. H. Lawrence

If we think of it, all that a university, or final highest school can do for us, is still but what the first school began doing, — teach us to read. We learn to read, in various languages, in various sciences; we learn the alphabet and letters of all manner of books. But the place where we are to get knowledge, even theoretical knowledge, is the books themselves! It depends on what we read, after all manner of professors have done their best for us. The true university of these days is a collection of books.

Heroes and Hero-Worship by Thomas Carlyle

NOTES ON CONTRIBUTORS

GEOFFREY DURRANT was recently named Master Teacher at the University of British Columbia, and since he is the most effective public speaker I know, I was not surprised. His eloquence, conviction, and learning make his lectures memorable events. I have had plenty of opportunity to observe that his colleagues in various places seem naturally to become also his students. Since his first degree from Cambridge, he has studied and lectured at a dozen universities, and has served on numerous examining boards and as chairman of the High School English Committee of Manitoba. He saw a good deal of active service with the allied army in the North African campaign of World War II. He has headed English departments at the University of Natal, the University of Manitoba, and the University of British Columbia, where he still teaches. Among his hobbies, Professor Durrant can boast unusual patience and skill with a fly-rod. Among a very long list of publications, I should mention *Wordsworth and the Great System*, published by Cambridge University Press in 1970.

MAURICE ELLIOTT was born in London and educated at Cambridge, and has taught at the universities of Manitoba and Toronto; he now teaches at York University, where he is an Associate Professor of English. He speaks French and Russian, the latter learned in the R.A.F. His colleagues and students describe him as a teacher of rare talent and a most sensitive reader of and respondent to poetry. He has for six years been Visiting Professor at the Yeats International Summer School at Sligo, Ireland. His doctoral dissertation is a pioneering work on the prose of Coleridge, and his views on the force of imaginative perception and its embodiment in language undoubtedly owe much to the influence of that greatest of English critics. Fishing and gardening take up what hours are left from a vast amount of reading.

MICHAEL HORNYANSKY heads the English Department at Brock University, where he has taught since 1964. Born in Brussels, of non-Belgian parents, he arrived here at the age of two. In 1950 he was Rhodes Scholar to Merton College, Oxford, and became the second Canadian to win the Newdigate Prize for poetry. He has taught at Carleton University, published verse and fiction and the occasional scholarly article and what he calls a book for children of all ages, *The Golden Phoenix*. Gardening, wine-tasting, and as he puts it, making speeches about the teaching and learning trade, seem to take up much of his "spare" time. Readers of this book would almost certainly enjoy his essay "The Enemies of Light" in the *CAUT Bulletin* for 1970.

F. E. L. PRIESTLEY recently retired from his professorship at the University of Toronto. His students now teach in every part of Canada, and he himself has taught at every educational level in this country. Students remember him with affection and respect as a man of precision in and passion for his subject. In 1975 the Association of Canadian University Teachers of English honoured him at a banquet so that his colleagues could pay homage to his lifetime of dedication to their discipline. To meet Felp, as he is called by his friends, is to discover a warm and courageous man, though one could hardly know from such a meeting that he was once third chef on a CNR diner, built bridges for the CPR, or played jazz in the Twenties (and still does in the Seventies). He has been a Nuffield Fellow and is an F.R.S.C., F.R.S.L., Hon. D. Litt. (etc., etc.) and has recently published *Language and Structure in Tennyson's Poetry*.

PHILIP SMITH, who heads the ARTS computer group at the University of Waterloo, took his first degree at Harvard, with a major in biochemistry. He knows English, Spanish, Czech, Russian, and German, and has worked in Germany, Brazil, Colombia, Venezuela, and Czechoslovakia, and was a student of East European languages at the University of London. He can lay claim to international stature as a specialist in language and the computer, and is a pioneer in programming computers for language handling. Among his publications are translations of the novels of Egon Hostovsky (Czech) and *A Concordance to Beowulf* (with J. B. Bessinger).

GEORGE WHALLEY was born in Kingston, where he still resides, and teaches at Queen's University. He was Rhodes Scholar for Quebec in 1936 and took his first degree at Oriel College, Oxford. He served throughout World War II in the Royal Navy and retired in 1957 with the rank of Commander, having seen an extraordinary amount of action and excitement, and with the medal of the Royal Humane Society for saving life at sea in 1941. No more humane man of letters exists in Canada to speak for the profession. He is currently the holder of a two-year Senior Killam Research Fellowship to complete the huge task of editing Coleridge's *Marginalia*. A long list of publications includes *Poetic Process* and *The Legend of John Hornby*. He is an F.R.S.C. and F.R.S.L. and for five years was Head of the English Department at Queen's. Professor Whalley is known to his colleagues as a man of deep and quiet wisdom and eloquence and an indefatigable fighter for the best in teaching and learning. When he does find time for the non-academic he likes to ski or play the piano.

Editor

A Word to the Wise
JOSEPH GOLD

*"Lord, there were a lot of lovely books once, before
we let them go."*
Ray Bradbury, *Fahrenheit 451*

"I believe that the country demands from us that we should at least try to do two things . . . namely, cover the country with good schools, and get the parents to send their children to those schools. I am aware, indeed, that to hope to arrive at these two results may be thought Utopian." So said Mr. W. E. Forster, vice-president of the Privy Council, on February 17, 1870, when he introduced into the British House of Commons the first public education act in the English-speaking world. It is hard for us to imagine controversy surrounding education, once a blessing and a privilege, now one of the most readily assumed basic rights of a tax-paying public. Yet controversy there was, for what was called "the principle of direct compulsion" to schooling was approached with extreme caution, lest it infringe upon the basic freedoms of a proud people. The freedom to be ignorant is no longer available to us, not merely because the government has taken it away, but because being informed has become a social law of survival, a necessity of our inheritance.

A mere one hundred years, and countless billions of pounds or dollars later, we have a country, Canada, covered with "good schools" and filled with children enthusiastically sent there by their parents. The buildings are excellent, centrally heated, replete with equipment, well-staffed by professional personnel, humanely managed with little or no physical violence, and integrated smoothly into their environment. The schools free the parents for most of a day and by and large the great majority of

1

students do not find their schooling fearful or stressful. What goes on inside? Are today's schoolchildren bored? Are they imaginatively excited? Given that the most formative thirteen or fourteen learning years are surrendered to this willing or unquestioned captivity, do the children fully realize their capacity for intellectual discovery? Do they learn and discover there what, if left to adulthood, would be ten times harder to learn, sometimes impossible to learn?

Certainly we have done something. Jane Eyre gives us a bleak picture of her village school in 1850: "This morning, the village school opened. I had twenty scholars. But three of the number can read: none write or cypher." Write, cypher, and read: the three R's we have just barely mastered 130 years later. Where do we go from here? Mr. Forster, in 1870, could go on to say that, "upon the speedy provision of elementary education depends our industrial prosperity." We have that prosperity now. We have a population in Canada that can read to vote, read to buy, write a letter, and fill in tax forms—no small feat given the complexity of the task. Is it enough? Does it take thirteen years to produce these skills? After the basics, after the survival-learning, what is left? What is the *objective* of our expensive, compulsory schooling? What can schools do, beyond acting as baby-sitting centres and unemployment safeguards?

One must suppose that after all the rhetoric is put aside—after the claims about whole men and women, beyond the requirements of good citizenship, and aside from work-training—we glimpse a tiny, ineradicable light that glimmers at the centre of our educating process. This light, without which we could hardly justify what we do, is the faith we have in the self-realization of the individual, in the humanizing experience that will make our living richer, more personally satisfying, make us more aware and alive. In this belief that the child is capable of awesome feats of learning, feeling, thinking, and creating we insist on the right to keep the child in school for 20 per cent of his allotted seventy years, and we enforce this right by acts of law; we make it a civil offence to be persistently and wilfully absent from our schools. This is worth emphasizing. So strongly do we believe in the medicine we administer that, while we argue about how to make it more palatable, we never seriously question its indispensability.

This dispensing of learning nostrums is an awesome responsibility. If a free people gives up its freedom in exchange for schooling, it had better be receiving something of undoubted value. Time is precious, costs are great—there must be no shilly-shallying about the quality of the offering.

Nothing less, then, than what I am calling self-realization, for want of a better term, can justify the demands we place upon children and their parents. To put it another way, *the only decent exchange we can make for surrendered freedom is greater freedom.* This greater freedom may be acquired through learning; *the heart of this learning and self-realizing process is language.* It is through the acquisition of language that human beings realize themselves as human. Language, and the greater freedom it brings, is acquired through discipline—the discipline of learning. The paradox that freedom comes through control and practice is obvious enough in areas of physical activity, for no one doubts that to ski down a steep slope, fly a plane, or play Mozart sonatas requires arduous discipline, training, practice, desire, knowledge. Why is it not equally obvious in the matter of language? I suppose it is because most people do not ski, fly, or play the piano, but everyone has some language; since they have enough to work, eat, shop, and procreate, that seems to be enough. But is it adequate that after decades of schooling, our citizens should be no better equipped to lead a richer life of the mind than they are, no freer to find out who they are, what they can do, and how they might order and enjoy their world and their perception of it?

Why should language be vitally central to the acquisition of individual freedom? The first great discovery, indeed the first event of being-in-the-world, is the experience of aloneness. This aloneness is both realized and partially overcome through the senses. To see something, to touch it, and finally to grasp it is the earliest expression of extending ourselves, increasing our power, and overcoming our separateness. Sound and language are then bridges to the Other, to the not-me. Language is the most natural and sophisticated self-extension. The fact of language is human, that is, human beings are linguistic; language is a defining characteristic of humanity. Since we have no choice but to be "language-animals" as George Steiner puts it, we had better be as language-developed as possible, for the language is there to be acquired and used. The infant learning of language remains a mystery, but it is clear that the desire to speak is normally intense in children. The physical utility of speech is obvious. Psychologically, language renders the human being less alone, he gains attention and *he hears his own voice*. The discovery that naming things produces power over them is not only of the most ancient and primitive origin, attested to everywhere in folklore, it is also rediscovered by every infant. The mother is brought running at the shout of her name; but even more amazing is that her being and influence, her person and presence, come to reside in the name itself. The very word will come to have this extraordinary power for all the remaining life of the child. Out of sight, out of mind, could not be further from the truth of language, for the mind brings the reality into being by the mere mention of a name.

The most vivid account of the psychological and political power of language was rendered by the Genesis poet millennia ago. God brings the animals to Adam "to see what he would call them". It is revealing that the omniscient God of the Hebrews should want to watch this extraordinary entertainment and that, knowing everything else, he should want to know what Adam would call the animals. Clearly the ancient poet is asserting here what poets have observed ever since, that language is a human phenomenon. It is Adam who invented it, while God watched in fascination the fulfilment of this innate and unique power inherent in man. Nor is there any question but that "whatsoever Adam called every living creature, that was the name thereof, not excepting his wife." The naming of things defines both Adam's supremacy, and his responsibility, since, if naming has such power, it requires his earnest observing of whatever there is and his response to its qualities. This power gives him both control of and responsibility to what he forms into its graspable finality by naming.

Let's face it. We shape and order our world through language. By naming things we embody the essence of the thing named and transpose it into the manageable, the graspable, the placeable. Later, in fact very recently, when writing was invented, perhaps by the Sumerians, one thing became immediately apparent: permanent retention, the record of language, was now possible. It is surprising how we have forgotten that this quality of permanence is the outstanding characteristic of *writing*. It should follow that this difference between speech and writing ought to produce considerable respect for language *written*. If it is worth retaining it should be worthy of great care in its composition.[1]

A considerable degree of confusion has been generated by discussion of print as a medium without a corresponding discussion about what it mediates. Print, in other words, has become a substitute word for language. My own view is that print is a much more manageable subject for commentary than language is. If I am right, and print has become a word sneaked in the door while language goes out the window, the effect is to lead us to forget that film, play, advertisement, and television programme are language-centred. It is a cheating evasion to discuss the media as though language were peripheral to any or most forms of communication. If a head of state, in emotionally charged rhetoric, declares war on another state, and that declaration *in language* is simultaneously heard on radio, seen on television, read in the press, put to music and sung, placed on billboards, or repeated with film accompaniment on the national television news, *the language message remains*, as those about to suffer the bombing will shortly discover.

I am conscious of treading familiar ground here and I know that these general and metaphorical propositions have become intellectual assumptions, even clichés, of our culture and should therefore not need restating. Even more dismaying then, is the obvious need for their reiteration, for in the face of a new contempt for language, everywhere in evidence (in our press, in our broadcasting, in our schools), what can one do but insist that, if we fail to see how profoundly language is woven into our humanity, we will inevitably dehumanize ourselves. It is curious, for instance, that we take our political freedoms so for granted that we can forget how hardly they were earned, how delicately they are maintained, and how dependent they are on a population possessed of a sophisticated knowledge of language and endowed with the freedom to express that knowledge. George Orwell shows us, in *1984*, a totalitarian government whose most important ministry is that one controlling language. *Orwell knew that reality was made by the human account of it*. To call people slaves is to make them slaves, but black may "be beautiful";

Jews may be a "problem" to which the Nazi party can propose "a final solution"; children can be turned into "per capita units", learning into "grades", villainy into "misjudgment", bombing into "air support". We know that totalitarian governments always alter history and control language, and we know that any evil may be disguised by careful rewriting, yet we have failed to retain language, our best and possibly only defence against modern forms of tyranny, as the indispensable centre of our schooling.

Part of our problem stems from the widespread notion that form and content in language are separable. We seem to believe that language is a vaguely decorative shape conveying some other, truer "reality" which can be extracted from it, as one takes a pearl from an oyster. In this process the oyster dies; we are likely to find that we have become real swine rooting for false pearls. By the same token, a contempt for language will naturally derive from the belief that it conveys "information" rather than that it shapes reality. It is no accident that *Reader's Digest* produces the most forgettable material, since everything is reduced by it to as neutral and undifferentiated a précis as possible. If "content" is inseparable from the texture of its embodiment in language, then its unique content disappears along with its unique form. If, on the other hand, *Reader's Digest* were right, then language would be to all intents and purposes dispensable.

What we want for our children is a learned respect for the power of language and the freedom to choose how to use it. Nothing is more disheartening to a sensitive English teacher, or more challenging, than to see a student struggling painfully to find the words in which to express a response to experience. What would one not give to have students who might choose from even a modest list of words or expressions to embody their response to, say, a novel or a film they have read or seen? To see only a primitive sampling, let us look at a short list of words available to any reasonably literate person: was the book, or any part of it, intriguing, perplexing, alarming, comforting, provocative, evocative, fascinating, bewildering, depressing, offensive, liberating, reminiscent of, allusive, challenging, soothing, complex, obscure, confusing, laughable, oblique, amusing, ludicrous, absurd, obscene, sentimental, compelling, disturbing? Was its import arguable, indefinable, untranslatable, impenetrable, accessible, redeeming, disgusting, inspiring? Or in metaphor, was it off course, near the bone, off the track, on the mark, meaty, heavy, light, racy, spicy, up to scratch, hard to digest, tough, tortuous, touching, outside the pale, in a nutshell, up to par, down to earth, deadly dull, like a maze, a tangled skein, hard as nails, a recurring pattern, closely woven? Is it asking too much that our children should have the easy and ready use of thousands of words beyond their basic material nouns or that they should go beyond the contemporary and incomparably vague jargon on which they depend with pathetic desperation? I think it is not too much to insist that, above all else, our children must emerge from their compulsory schooling having read much, having written often and at length, having spoken in public under careful and patient correction, and having learnt respect for the precision and the flexibility of the truly articulate. I have seen university graduate students unable to read aloud a passage of prose without faltering after every few words. The man who sent his wife a cable from the convention and whose marriage was ruined by a telegraphic error, "Having a wonderful time, wish you were her," learnt in dramatic fashion that words alter cases. I recently had the interesting experience of directing adults in a mime drama based on early silent film, a kind of short, domestic melodrama. They were lost as to what to do at first, so I provided a kind of verbal running commentary to accompany them. Finally, the only thing that could induce them to act with genuine precision and conviction was to teach them how to create spontaneous silent dialogue in their heads in order to see what actions and gestures would be appropriate. They were paralysed without language. There is a language for the street, the barn, the game, the hustings, the school, the bedroom, the fight, and the church, and they are all right. To be fully articulate is to have freedom to choose among them and this means submitting to the discipline that is necessary in order to acquire a mastery of language; this mastery must be founded on reading, for literature is the source of a multitude of models.

But there are other, equally important reasons for stressing a wide experience of literature. We should never forget that the primary case for encouraging the habit of reading the best that has been thought and said is that it gives almost unbounded pleasure—when it is possible to read with facility born of practice. Experience shows that those who have acquired the habit of reading widely enjoy a peculiar blessing, given to few, but surely the right of all. Further, and perhaps I am here touching on the source of pleasure, is the invaluable psychological freedom gained through the reader's identifications in literature. We escape our limitations and inestimably extend our psychic experience by reading. Flora Thompson, in her description of English rural life in the late 19th century, gives us a glimpse of this power of the story for unsophisticated readers, and we can see how their range of sympathies was imaginatively extended.

> The children brought home from the Sunday School Lending Library books about the London slums which their mothers also read. This was then a favourite subject with writers of that class fiction; their object apparently being not so much to arouse indignation at the terrible conditions as to provide a striking background for some ministering lady or child. Many tears were shed in the hamlet over *Christie's Old Organ* and *Froggy's Little Brother*, and everybody wished they could have brought those poor neglected slum children there and shared with them the best they had of everything. "Poor little mite. If we could have got him here, he could have slept with our young Sammy and this air'd have set him up in no time," one woman said of Froggy's poor dying little brother, forgetting that he was, as she would have said at another time, "just somebody in a book."
>
> *Lark Rise to Candleford*

The genuine power of literature to alter the world by altering the consciousness of readers is obviously incalculable. Little wonder that books and widespread literacy frighten those with a leaning to tyranny or a need to control. If horses could read, they would eventually read Book IV of *Gulliver's Travels*, and the Royal Winter Fair might have a lot of trouble on its hands.

There is no path to self-realization so pleasurable, exciting, available, or sure as that through imaginative literature. Most children cannot go around the world or above it or under it; no one can play enough roles in life, follow enough careers, meet enough people; no one can experience the extremes of all emotional situations, marry many women or men, experience great danger, hardship, luxury; no one dies or is born more than once. How may we extend our experience endlessly, and how may we free ourselves to play many parts except through our reading? The child not only deserves those experiences, he vitally needs these encounters for his emotional wholeness, for his imaginative growth, and for his intellectual freedom. He needs to know how it is possible for a reader to cry when a book is ended, an expression very much akin to genuine grief and perhaps explained by the loss of a priceless temporary experience—one that was gained through perceiving the utterly new, the magic and freshness of a reality ordered by someone else's language rather than his own. It may be that only language will permit us to be actually, if briefly, someone else, and it does this by virtue of its unique power to shape and create new realities in time. Where are the child's heroes, his models, his enemies, and his lasting friends if not in books! Today's television provides no alternative to the repeatable, reliable experience of fiction and poetry. The desolation of Oliver Twist as he settles to his first night under the counter at the funeral parlour; the discoveries made by Huck Finn of a black man's humanity on a raft in the Mississippi; the imperturbable exactness of Sherlock Holmes' deductions; the persuasive deception of Milton's Satan as he vows to use man in a war against God; the doubts and hopes of Christian Pilgrim as he plods towards his destiny—these are not merely recognized by the reader but are realized and experienced and then absorbed into a genuine extension of his personality. They become a framework of referential experience. The roles we play in imagination are not only fun, they are discoveries of ourselves and we are never the same afterwards; we are violated, remade, and renewed, our understanding of humanity incomparably deepened by our imaginative life in literature. We should remember that a picture remains itself and while it may inspire and influence us, we cannot use it as our own, cannot transport it either literally or metaphorically into a new living order of one's own making. It is words, not pictures, that have altered the history of action. Remember also that film is a collection of "stills". Give a child a picture and you have a child with a picture. Give a child a word or two and you have someone who may create his own new worlds with them.

Pleasure and psychic freedom are, then, the rewards of reading. We realize who we are by encountering what we are not. Through the best literature we may even find that we encompass and transcend all that we meet. The third inescapable consequence of informed reading also relates to our need for identity. Each child is part of a culture, and his culture, since Babel, is peculiarly the product of its language. A child must read widely the literature of his particular past if he is to see how he comes to be himself in time and place. There is no one source of the liberal education as sure as that in literature. For this reason, if for no other, the Canadian student must encounter the writings of his own country—the familiar names, the peculiar preoccupations, the unique climate, so to speak, of our national perception of terrain, history, and climate. The case for reading Canadian writing should not depend on the "greatness" of it, and those who insist on inflating its claims in order to justify its inclusion in curricula do a disservice to both students and literature. But even more necessary is an awareness of the background to these perceptions, the long, rich tradition of literature that precedes North American experience and which flowered by no accident into the colours and shapes of Canadian and American literature and language. In English, for instance, we must discover that Chaucer and Shakespeare, Milton and Blake, Jane Austen and George Eliot, Donne and Dickens, speak to us about our own forming culture, our history, our religion, our economy, about what it has been like to be part of the long story that made our minds. We may then come to see what we have inherited in our very language, the language we speak, and in our very perception of the shape of things. We do not really see the woods in winter, the daffodils, the lamb, until the poet shows them to us. Ours is a Judeo-Christian culture that has produced particular men and women of genius who have distilled the essential and otherwise invisible features of their culture. Our children have a right to know the tale of their tribe. Pleasure, freedom, and identity may not be guaranteed by reading, but they may be unavailable without it. We may yet have the dubious privilege of finding out if this is so.

What will happen to us and to our world if we become leisured but uncultured, rich but uncultivated, powerful but insensitive?

Let me quote the conclusion of a speech by A. Whitney Griswold, the former President of Yale University, at the National Book Awards in 1952. He has been speaking of his dismay at the discovery that an American university has announced a course for ghost writers.

But what if present trends continue? Since reading maketh us full men, when we stop reading we shall be empty men. Since men who do not read have no use for writing, and in any case empty men have nothing to write about, we shall stop writing. We shall then be empty and inexact, though presumably we shall still be able to confer and conference will still make us ready. Ready for what? For some technological *deus ex machina* to finish the plot we have forgotten how to write? For some graduate of the school for ghost writers to whisper to us from the prompter's box?

They will not serve us. They cannot promote the more general diffusion of knowledge essential to a democratic society because they are mere transmitters; they cannot inform the statesmen to whom that society must look for the preservation and renewal of its charters because they are themselves uninformed. During the past century the average working week of our industrial and white collar workers has shrunk from seventy to less than forty hours. The millions of man hours thus conserved form the new Colossus. This Colossus has more leisure at his disposal than all the captains of industry and kings of enterprise. What will he do with it? Will he read? Will he make himself a full man and an exact man, or will he be content to be merely a ready man—a measure of muscle and a shout from the mob? The choice lies before him. Who will help him make it?

Fellow citizens of the world of books, as an academical superintendent I make common cause with you. I hope *we* will!

It is no great step from ghost writers to ghost exam writers. The truly alarming condition we have reached is indicated by the existence of a business which flourishes by selling essays to students. The student indicates the topic, pays a fee, and someone writes his essay. If the course can be thus circumvented, and if the student has no interest in learning, how can we justify continuing the charade?

Writing and Reading must remain the irreducible ingredients of our educational system, the heartbeat of the body politic, and the life force of our learning process. In the last several decades various fashions have come in the shaping of our schools and their curricula. We have particularly witnessed the growth of double jeopardy in the shape of two monsters which joined to form a hydra-headed dragon guarding our schools. These two powerful shapes, which united in one decade, may be referred to as the Child-centred Syndrome and the Relevance Retreat.

The child-centred syndrome sounded humane and friendly enough and took its force from a swing of opinion among educators against rigid curricula, bad instruction, and inflexible methodology. The new fashion was intended to contrast with, rather than rejuvenate, subject-centred and teacher-centred instruction. This new panacea was given added urgency by the cry for greater student freedom and the desire for increased course choices. Students knowing nothing of the ingredients were to write their own recipes. Government alarm at rapidly escalating classroom costs, inevitable if instructional excellence was to be maintained in small classes and in traditional curricula, further augmented these changes. A highly educated and literate population can be achieved only at enormous cost.

It should be obvious that in a "freer" system, one in which there is greater student choice, no matriculation, and less subject insistence, the most highly motivated student will educate himself and achieve most. Such students almost invariably come from intellectually privileged homes, already well-supplied with books, records, musical instruments, journals, and reasonably articulate parents. Teachers themselves, for instance, would presumably have such homes and so would many professional people. Children from these backgrounds have seen parents read as a matter of course, have been given library cards at an early age, have frequently heard informed conversation, have been taken to plays, and have already encountered a profound respect for learning. In other words, in any system the child who is *already educated* learns the most, but especially in a system without clearly stated subject-goals, without intensive individual instruction, and without strong teacher leadership, the intellectually underprivileged suffer most. In other words, the cost of what is called a "free" educational environment is the imprisonment of the majority inside their own inadequacies. Do we believe that an elite is inevitable, that a truly literate populace is an unattainable dream? We have not had the courage to say so. We want to eat our cake but we want to have it too. The production of an elite ought to be cheaper, and a disguised system for producing an elite seems politically possible. Yet the disguise itself is enormously costly and humanly wasteful. In actual experience the child-centred system produces a vast paraphernalia of equipment, tapes, slides, films, and hardware that quickly loses value while gathering dust and boring everybody to inertia. Education costs have accelerated dramatically, especially in the areas of administration and materials, while teachers face ever-increasing workloads; *there is no substitute for the inspired, informed, and not over-worked teacher*. Can anyone in Canada honestly say that our educational system has produced a more informed and interested, and, most importantly, a more literate body of students in the last ten years than in the preceding twenty? If not, surely we must conclude that all talk of forsaking "subjects" is pure cant? What will happen to "subjects" if they are not transmitted? Children are born with the capacity to learn and with a variety of talents to be discovered, but they do not come from the womb trailing skills and learning. These await them on earth and are part of their civil and social rights.

There are already some signs of protest against the abandonment of English studies in education, but the "official" response seems to be more lip-service and humbug. To use Ontario as an example, the Ministry of Education reduced the number of high-school English periods from seven to five, greatly increased the number of classes and students per teacher, and then, in the face of widespread concern, turned around and re-introduced this undermined structure as a requirement.

The Relevance Retreat was intimately connected with a passing hysteria for quick social solutions to seemingly insoluble problems and a desperate desire for education to do everything, make good and useful people, and render the world good and happy as before the Fall. Relevance was blithely discussed by students, teachers, and educators who had probably not read anything worth recalling and certainly not the works and thoughts they rejected. Thus we have witnessed the spectacle of students, who had once been bored by *Macbeth* in an ill-taught, overcrowded class, telling us that Politics was everything and Shakespeare was nothing. They gave us indeed a "tale told by an idiot, full of sound and fury, signifying nothing" and had not the wit to know who foretold it. Relevance in fact became the new euphemism of the last decade for intellectual vandalism, a kind of poorly disguised mental book-burning. The irony of this should be apparent, as though a man in a drifting boat should throw away his oars in anger.

The net result of all this has been a weakening of the educational process that has had no parallel since the Public Education Act was introduced in 1870. Since then and up to the end of the Second World War we had seen a persistent and vigorous growth in schooling and learning for ever-growing numbers of people. Recently we have seen the first major reversal of this trend. Having worked for universal education we are now working to make it not worth having.

Writing essays and marking them is hard work. Preparing people for degree status is exacting. Without inner compulsion or external pressure the temptation has grown to let anything pass. The passion for the greater status and earning power traditionally bestowed by education, coupled with a moral failure of the system, losing as it has all conviction, has produced the situation in which neither completion of high school nor the acquisition of a degree in Canada is a guarantee that the student has even a fraction of what would once have been called learning; worse still, it is very likely that the student will be barely literate, inarticulate, faulty in reading, and inaccurate and insensitive in writing. It is not strange that this should all take place in a compulsory system? So I go back to my earlier question: given the present pass, what is the compulsion for?

Imagine that a mother, shopping in a food store, encounters her child in the company of forty others, escorted by a teacher and supposedly learning the nature of commerce! Is it not bewildering in its absurdity, this kind of school activity, pursued at great and unnecessary cost: the transportation, the teacher's time, the child's energy, the empty classroom, the disrupted store, all to be accounted for? This takes place, remember, in a society drowning in consumer-oriented advertisements for worthless products, amidst which the child spends its waking life and from which even the school is no longer a refuge. We force children out of their homes and away from television, into the school and in front of the television, with supermarket visits from time to time for variety.

Ignorance feeds on itself. Children asked to choose, as indeed they sometimes are, between a visit to the library or a visit to a shopping mall, will and do undoubtedly choose the latter. Are they in school, by compulsion, to make such choices? There are entire worlds closed to them which they have a right to encounter, but these are left unrealized. One could understand non-compulsory, non-educative, play-oriented babysitting centres. One could understand compulsory, subject-oriented, learning centres where skills and information are presented to be mastered and measured. But surely one cannot understand compulsory attendance that was designed for the latter applied to the former. Schools should be seedbeds of intellect, but in our time they are often sterile nurseries.

Universities are, of course, not merely accidental or secondary culprits in this process. Often guided by singularly uninspiring and visionless administrators, they have too frequently acceded to a process urged by governments which has seen universities become undifferentiated degree-factories. Far from being exempt from blame, universities have fostered mediocrity where they were obliged to excellence. They have suffered the fate of all expansion leagues and, in the scramble for box-office receipts, have diminished the spectacle, disenchanted the spectators, defrauded the promoters, and earned the contempt of the participants. English study in a university has traditionally been directed towards the acquisition of the critical faculty, the reading of a large body of material of unquestioned and lasting excellence. Reading is a life-game of supreme importance, of commentary, conversation, response, linguistic selection, respect for precision, sensitivity to nuance, delight in diction, and of the discovery of metaphor, pun, rhythm, and wit. Today we are reduced to accepting the shoddy, the approximate, the vague, and the jargon-ridden, and to handing out barrelfuls of degrees for a measure of competence that cannot possibly be subsequently productive. The English curriculum and the English teacher's standards in many Canadian universities today testify to incompe-

tence and moral abdication. For this state of affairs we blame
television, parents, governments, and everyone but ourselves.
Television is not in itself the enemy of literacy any more than
rivers are necessarily the carriers of pollution and disease. Indeed, television may be the ally, as certain BBC series, based on
work by Galsworthy and Trollope, have shown, if one is to judge
by the enormous sales of novels following their presentation. The
truly frightening force of television is in its power to produce
conformity. It is worth remembering that literature is our surest
defence against Disneyland and Forest Lawn—that is, if we can
prevent the same marketeers from taking over publishing and
authorship.[2]

No, neither television, nor film, nor the atomic bomb may be
blamed for a declining literacy. What is certain is that we, the
teachers, are contributing to it by a loss of faith, a lack of moral
conviction, a failure of rigour, the too-ready awarding of degrees
at all levels, especially in Arts and Social Sciences, and by the
underlying decadence that wants quick, cheap results from as
little effort as possible. We seem to be in the grip of rationalized
expediency. I am convinced that our system will be judged in
time by the degree of literacy it produces. During the long debate
on the Elementary Education Bill, which lasted, on and off, the
best part of seven months, Mr. Winterbotham, the member for
Stroud, said of the people of England that, as regards their attitude to education, "Ignorance made them indifferent, and indifference left them ignorant." Could it be, is it possible, that the
same will come to be said of us? And worse, will it come to be
said that when they forsook their language they also surrendered
their freedom, yielded to boredom, were content with mindless
passivity?

The essays that follow affirm the belief that it is not too late to
restore language to its rightful place in our culture.

NOTES

1   Perhaps the tape-recorder is a greater enemy of language than the television
image, for speech has now been given a kind of permanence without writ-

ing. Speech has not thereby acquired greater precision, but it has become more voiced by more people to more listeners than ever before. The standards for speech have now assumed a new authority as writing is practised less, and the immediate and occasional is preserved more.

2   And let not intellectuals comfort themselves with the soothing thought that a few dedicated literati can keep literacy alive. Libraries, publishers, and poets depend on a large audience. There is an economics to literacy that must not be forgotten, and if publishers switch to audio-visual kits and libraries close for lack of borrowers, or change to "information centres", the knowledge of our rightness will be cold comfort.

English: An Obsolete Industry?
F. E. L. PRIESTLEY

My title attempts to put in a nutshell what I take to be the kernel of implication in the whole question of the future of literacy. English is taught by a body of professionals, trained to certain procedures and techniques for the pursuit of certain aims and the production of certain results. They are organized into managerial units within a large complex system with a strongly hierarchical structure: in short, the teaching of English is very much like a large industry, running small or large factories with a limited amount of autonomy under the general supervision of top management. The product is describable in very general terms as "literacy", and until recently, although the *nature* of the product may have been veiled in varied layers of confusion, its value was almost universally accepted. Literacy was well worth having, even if few knew what it was or who had it. The subject of this volume suggests that the situation has changed drastically, and that we teachers of English are now conferring, almost like a concourse of managers of buggy-whip factories, to wonder if we can keep the industry going through the sale of whips for flogging dead horses.

Having been summoned to give evidence as an expert, I propose to start with an analysis of the industry and of its situation, in an attempt to see what has gone wrong. We can then see if it could be put right. This will involve some comments on happenings over the past fifty years which I expect to be challenged by all those who were not there at the time. I was.

Fifty years ago I was teaching English language and literature —along with every other subject in the curriculum—to students in rural Alberta, grades six to eleven (junior matric). Before that I had taught grades one to eleven for two years. The next year I moved to a high school, and taught high-school English for the next ten years. I mention this to establish the fact that I am not speaking from hearsay. By the time I retired, I had been a professional teacher for fifty-two years, had taught for some years every subject in the curriculum in every school grade from beginners to university entrance, in every kind of school from the one-room rural to the city high school, and had taught English at every level from the infant to the Ph.D. student. From very early in my career I took what I considered to be a completely professional view of my craft: my function was to teach, as a doctor's is to heal, and, like a doctor, I very soon discovered that the rule-of-thumb methods taught in training gave limited success in practice. Teaching, like medicine, is more art than science. And, like a doctor, I learned from my failures, which in my profession were at least less immediately disastrous. I held firmly to the belief that a perfect teacher ought to be able to find a way to teach anybody anything—the problem was to find the way. No two classes, no two students, no two things to be taught are exactly alike, so that what works here and now will not necessarily work elsewhere and tomorrow. As a result, teaching is perhaps the least boring and most challenging of all occupations; I can honestly say that I have never spent a boring day in the classroom.

I can still recall very vividly the excitement of teaching beginners to read. The very intelligent offered no problem; they would suddenly see how the system of the printed word works and become fluent readers almost overnight. The slow ones offered one of the most fascinating problems, giving a real insight into the artificiality of a written language. They gave me my first training in patience and hopeful persistence, and the first real test of my ingenuity in trying to discover how their minds were working (or not working), and how to induce their minds to give that sudden click of recognition when the light dawns. One dear puzzled and anxious little face still looks up at me—he would now be nearly sixty years old and has long forgotten me—I smiled at him and patted his head, and bless me! the next week he suddenly saw how c a t, kuh ah tuh, compressed itself into cat, and began to read. No successful Ph.D. thesis ever gave me more satisfaction.

Professional success or failure in teaching infants to read is very easy to recognize; in many of our other activities it requires a good deal of careful investigation and thought to find out what results we are getting, and there are lots of surprises. One I recall with grim amusement was the student (in his case, I am afraid, a courtesy title) who remarked to a colleague of mine, "Priestley and this guy Milton and me seem to have the same idea about women." A more pleasant surprise, and a more complete one, came to me some years after I left high-school teaching. In the last school, I had had two brothers in my classes for three years or so, both extremely nice boys, sons of a local butcher. The one, the small one, was extraordinarily brilliant, obviously destined for an academic or professional career; the other, the large one, was very willing but decidedly slow—once he got something he had it, but he did not learn easily. I had not kept in touch with anyone in the town after I left, and had no notion of the fate of either brother. Then one evening in summer, my brother and I, coming back from a photographic trip to the mountains, stopped for coffee at a highway café. Sitting next to me at the counter was a huge figure in a black leather jacket, and, as we drank our coffee, I saw out of the corner of my eye that he kept turning and looking at me, so I turned to look at him. "Aren't you Mr. Priestley?" he said. He was the large brother, now driving an oil truck. Then came the surprise. "A year after you left," he said, "I suddenly saw what you had been talking about all those years. And you may find it hard to believe, but since then I have read the whole of Shakespeare every year, and intend to go on doing so." I did find it hard to believe, but knowing his absolute honesty I believed him, and I have no doubt that if he is still alive he is still reading all of Shakespeare every year. I have had several surprises of this nature; one of the glories of teaching is our inability to be certain which ground is stony.

Even where the ground is indubitably stony or stonyish, the challenge to find the right kind of seed and cultivation is fascinating. Every teacher naturally rejoices in the first-class student, the born scholar and thinker, who responds to every hint and suggestion, and whose horizons broaden visibly at an astounding rate as the riches of the realms of gold are laid out in front of him. And the teacher must use special techniques for the brilliant student, guiding and collaborating and suggesting, rather than directing and driving. But the unacademic have also always had for me a special kind of attraction, perhaps partly as problems for me to solve. I have always remembered with particular affection a class I had at Toronto in the last year of the war. They were all RCAF aircrew members, demobilized from the European theatre and offered a one-year course in business by the government. I was asked to give them a course in literature, which I was to design. They were not academic—many had not completed high school—but they were mature and had seen a good deal of life; most of them had seen a lot of action, and many had multiple decorations. There was no need to talk to them of the relation of literature to life; if they read the literature they would see it. What I suspected they would not have thought about was literature as an art, and the kind of problems and choices the author faces in constructing a work of art. I chose three tragedies, two comedies, three or four novels, and a few poets, to illustrate widely different kinds of structure and technique. I spent my first lecture talking about the problems of aircraft design, particularly the design of an aircraft wing. This was something they knew about, and they saw readily the impossibility of designing a universal wing suitable for every kind of aircraft and every kind of function. They knew the limiting relations of lift and drag, the competing virtues of high aspect and low aspect, of swept and non-swept, of thick and thin, of degrees of camber, and so on. They grasped readily the principle that all design is a matter of choice, and that every choice offers certain advantages and with it certain limitations, and that choice has to be related to what the design is intended to do, what it is for. I then moved on to art in general, what it was for, what broad possible designs are open as choices to the painter, to the musician, to the literary artist. Then to why one would choose to write a play, a novel, or a poem, the basic differences between these as art forms, what the artist can do with each that he cannot do with the others, and *vice versa*. And so on to tragedy. This approach worked surprisingly well, and when I got to poetry I started them off with Hopkins, as something they could not possibly think of as prettied-up prose. When they had successfully wrestled with their first two Hopkins poems, I said to them bluntly, "Why the hell couldn't he have said all this in a plain straightforward fashion?" They showed me precisely what he would have lost if he had done so. The class generally was one of the most interesting and exciting I have ever had, and my experience with it confirmed very strongly my conviction that the study of art *as* art, of literature not primarily as something that is being said but as a special kind of structure for saying something, is the proper study.

I apologize for all this reminiscence; it is one of the penalties of calling upon the aged for their opinions. It is difficult for me to avoid it, since, as I have said, I am casting my eye back over the past fifty years to see what has happened to the study of English. Let me go back again to the Alberta high school in which I was teaching the subject half a century ago. The curriculum was a very broad one: in literature there was a good representation of English, American, and Canadian poetry, one text being the admirable bilingual anthology of Canadian literature in English and French by E. K. Broadus and his wife, Eleanor Hammond Broadus. Grammar, composition, and literature were given separate places in the curriculum and separate examinations. The composition texts (from Ontario) were passable, offering passages for analysis from a wide range of literary styles, so that a good teacher could get the students' ears tuned to various types of writing and train them to notice how effects were being obtained. The grammar texts (also from Ontario) were very bad, and I soon learned to do without them altogether, using my own approach and examples. The formal separation of the three subjects had considerable advantages. The aim of the grammar course (not realized in the textbooks, unfortunately) was to get the student to understand how the English language works, how it can be manipulated, how it can be honed to a sharp edge, how delicately and precisely it can express minute differences of meaning or of emphasis. The aim of the composition course was to train and exercise the student in the use of the language, to teach him how to order it into structures and shapes, how to get life into his writing, precision and economy, how to arrange his ideas, and how to proportion the parts of an essay. His final textbook in composition in his senior matric. year even had an excellent chapter on logic and the common types of fallacy. Composition also aimed at developing a wide and precise vocabulary, and included exercises in discriminating between so-called synonyms. The course in literature, although it naturally drew upon the other courses in grammar and composition, was relatively free to concentrate on its main aim, the study and enjoyment of literature as an art. Few rural students, for example, had ever seen a play, and it was important to get them thinking about what gestures and business could be given to a speech, what emotions a speaker should be expressing, what tempo each scene should have, and so on. It was also important that they should get some sense of the flow and pattern of the play as a continuous performance. Nor had many of them much experience of hearing poetry read aloud, and, consequently, of the shape each poem has.

You will recognize from this analysis of a curriculum of fifty years ago that its different parts had different aims, and different techniques for achieving these aims. The aims are, of course, not unrelated—eventually they all come together—but there was a great deal to be said for pursuing them to some extent separately. The first breach in this triple pattern came while I was still teaching school, and occasioned one of the savage quarrels I often had with inspectors. As I have said, the grammar textbooks were very bad, and many teachers followed them mechanically, turning grammar into the dull set of mechanical rules that gave the subject a bad name. It is one of the fundamental principles of Canadian educational systems that if a subject is being badly taught, the simple remedy is to abolish the subject. Then no-one can complain that it is badly taught. So grammar was first drastically reduced. I had at that time a grade ten class that was fascinated by grammar, by parsing and analysis, so that we played a regular game in which I would concoct sentences of increasing subtlety for them to parse, and they would unravel them all triumphantly. The inspector caught us at it and forbade it. I must not give them problems like that, it was too hard for them. But they were all doing them successfully. No matter, they were not to do it. They were actually at the stage where they could have read Milton's prose not merely with ease but with delight at its architecture, but Authority would have none of it. Of course I ignored him, but not all teachers would or could, and soon grammar virtually faded out of the curriculum.

It seems by now to have come to be widely accepted that grammar is a Bad Thing, and even relatively conservative teachers of English are often diffident or apologetic in suggesting that a little grammar does no harm. The traditions established by the generally very bad textbooks, and by teaching inevitably shaped by the textbook, were, as might be expected, very bad traditions. The main purpose of the study of grammar came to be presented as the inculcation of "correct" usage; the method was to learn the "rules" and to apply them for the correcting of "incorrect" writing. There was a narrow circularity in the process: the "rules" were drawn from a narrow definition of "correctness" while "correctness" was defined by the "rules". Grammar was thus reduced in large measure to a set of rule-of-thumb regulations to be memorized and applied without much notion of why they were there or what they were for, and all the regulations, major and minor, seemed to have equal sanction. The effect was to be seen in what came to be known by the derogatory term of "school-ma'am's English", with its hauling out of bell, book, and candle to excommunicate the split infinitive and "It's me".

The natural, if ill-advised and illogical, response to this totally inadequate conception of grammar was, as I have said, to abolish the subject, and to deny the validity of any notion of "correct" usage. It should have been obvious that the proper response would have been to re-examine carefully the reasons for teaching grammar, the methods of teaching it, and the definition of both "rules" and "correct usage". It was rather curious that at the time I am speaking of, half a century ago, when the textbooks of grammar were so deplorable, a very good textbook for composition was prescribed for senior matriculation in Alberta, with the title *Effective Expression*. It was not concerned with grammar —grammar finished in junior matriculation year; but as its title suggests, its whole approach was concerned, not with the "correct", but with the "effective". It is of course true that in the grammar books the "correct" was often the "effective", but this was given little emphasis.

As far as I was concerned, the "correct" was only "correct" in so far as it was "effective", and the "effective" is that usage which makes the language serve best as an instrument of communication, the usage that allows the user to say what he wants to say as clearly, as neatly, as persuasively, as attractively, as unambiguously, as the language will allow. Since language is a very complex and subtle medium, to use it effectively is not easy, and involves first of all some knowledge of how the language is built and how it functions. The proper study of grammar is directed at providing this knowledge. It is of course true that some degree of "communication" is possible with a minimal knowledge of a language, and that the majority of speakers of all languages convey to each other, by means of what we could call the vulgate, a range of rough ideas, sentiments, and feelings adequate for everyday dealings and occasions. This fact has never seemed to me to provide a good argument for letting the vulgate be the ultimate standard; for ordinary affairs most people need no more mathematics than suffices to count their change, no more knowledge of mechanics than how to start their car, turn on the TV, toaster, washing machine, or electric light. Not much perhaps depends on their knowing more in many areas, but the effects of a limited grasp of language have wide and important implications, of which I will say more later.

What I was trying to do with my grade ten class, when so rudely interrupted by the inspector, was to get them interested in the structure of the language, excited by its potentialities, and fascinated by the way in which it worked. They had been subjected for some years before to the textbook "grammar", and I can still remember how I started my first class with them. I wrote on the blackboard the word "iron", and said, "What part of speech is that?" When a number of them promptly called out "Noun", I wrote after "iron" "my shirt". When they called out "Verb", I rubbed out "my shirt", and wrote "is hard", then, still leaving the original word in place, made other sentences round it, including "His head is iron hard", which gave them some trouble. I then rubbed all out and wrote up another single word. "What part of speech?" They refused to bite. It was then possible to consider what functions were indicated by each of the "parts of speech", agreeing that "parts of speech" is a misleading name for them. I then went on to double functions, verbal nouns, predicate adjectives—and triple, like adverbial predicate adjectives, showing always the shades of meaning and emphasis produced by various structures—the difference, for example, between saying "A walk in the country is pleasant," and "Walking in the country is pleasant," and "To walk in the country is pleasant." They were asked to contemplate groups of little sentences: "He looks at a book," "He looks at ease," "He looks carefully," "He looks capable," "He looks a likely winner." I gave them sentences bringing out the different functions of each "part of speech". Then I began taking a simple sentence and modifying it by substituting phrases for single words, then expanding to clauses, always asking them what difference the substitution made. We shifted the order of elements in a sentence, or expanded first one element, then another, to show how a shift of emphasis produces a shift of meaning. We took lines from poetry like Gray's "And all the air a solemn stillness holds," in which his habit of inversion allows either "air" or "stillness" to be the subject, and discussed the two meanings possible. *Paradise Lost* provided other good examples of passages with a choice of grammatical interpretation, and hence of meaning. The students came to recognize the close relation of grammatical structure and function to meaning, and also the delicate shades of emphasis and precision the language is capable of. Sorting out difficult and complicated sentences also became something of a game for them and for me, and I would sometimes lie in bed at night making up new ones to tax their ingenuity. I have forgotten all my grammatical brain-teasers, and remember only a sentence I invented for them to punctuate, punctuation being taught to them as a device to illuminate structure: "Smith where Jones had had had had had had had had had been right." The two important things about that class were that they learned through grammar the relation between structure and meaning, and became closely observant readers and flexible and precise writers, and that they got great enjoyment out of it as a game. It seemed to me, and still seems, a great pity to discourage so innocent and profitable a study.

Grammar having been banished, and with it the kind of close analysis of language essential to a real grasp of composition, the next blow was struck at the literature. I happened for a time to be a member of the provincial committee on curriculum, where I was consistently out-voted. The first cry was based on "what you could teach" to students. Most of the classics (with the peculiar exception of the universally revered Bard) were apparently unteachable to high-school students, although I had never found them so. I think Scott was the first to go. I had taught *The Talisman* to a grade ten class by pretending I had only had time to read the first two chapters, which I outlined and partly read to them. I was full of curiosity about events, characters, motives, but simply had no time to read on—could they tell me what went on in the next two chapters, and the next? They were not only eager, but expert, and as I speculated at the end of the lesson on what was likely to happen next, or what So-and-so was up to, they were bursting to get at the next chapter to fill me in. I have often wondered how my colleagues on the committee who agreed that Scott was unteachable had tried to teach him. Of all the great novelists in English, Scott could with some plausibility be considered the most relevant to us, closest in general theme to recent Canadian concerns. What preoccupied him was national and cultural character or identity, and the clash of two cultures. This accounts for his enormous influence in Europe, and particularly in Russia. Apart from his skill as a writer, the Russian novelists saw in him an ability to analyse national identity, to sort out the elements in a national history, the events, the habits, the temperament that made the Highlander what he is as distinct from the Lowlander, the Scot as distinct from the English, the Saracen as distinct from the Western European, the Norman as distinct from the Saxon. It was Scott who induced the Russians to show what it is to be Russian. Canadian novelists, concerned with defining the Canadian, and with our two cultures, are, consciously or unconsciously, following where Scott led. Nor is his recognition of the role of history in creating a national consciousness any less relevant to Canadian than it was to Russian novelists. I suspect that the teachers who could not teach him saw in him only a superior G.A. Henty. Milton was another early casualty, and even Shakespeare was chopped down from two or three plays a year (four in senior matric.) to one.

After "teachableness" came "relevance", which is still with us. The age-old theory of literature had indeed always insisted on its "relevance"—the greatest works were the most universally relevant. Shakespeare was not for an age but for all time. In this context, the term "relevant" is obviously very different in its significance from the modern usage. The ephemeral—the fashions, modes, customs, events, and issues belonging only to a particular place and time—belonged to literature in what were accepted as minor and transient forms: to "occasional" poems, to lighter forms of comic drama, to periodic essays, to specifically aimed satire. The greatest kinds of literature—tragedy and epic, lyric and even the most valuable forms of occasional poem, comedy, or satire—owed their higher importance in large measure to their universality, to their wider extent of relevance. Dryden's *Absalom and Achitophel*, for example, which is from a superficial point of view an "occasional" poem, relevant specifically to the situation in England at the time of the Popish Plot and the Exclusion Bill, endures as a work of permanent relevance, not merely because of the excellence of its execution, but because it in fact deals with a number of recurring and permanent problems of political stability and of political power in the state. The classical theory of universality, of relevance to men of all times and places, assumes certain permanences in human character and in human situations which are illuminated by the best literature. It is taken for granted in this theory that the illumination is assisted by the power given by this literature to see characters and situations presented from a large variety of perspectives, unhampered by the biases and confusions introduced by contemporary particularities. This is why great literature is seen as having the ability to broaden, deepen, and sharpen the reader's perception and understanding of life, of men, and of their habits and problems. It will be apparent that this theory also assumes that the reading of literature makes demands on the reader. It was Wordsworth who perhaps explained these demands most clearly:

Aristotle, I have been told, has said that Poetry is the most philosophic of all writing; it is so; its object is truth, not individual and local, but general and operative . . . Poetry is the image of man and nature . . . The Poet . . . considers man and the objects that surround him as acting and re-acting upon each other, so as to produce an infinite complexity of pain and pleasure; he considers man in his own nature and in his ordinary life as contemplating this with a certain quantity of immediate knowledge, with certain convictions, intuitions, and deductions; he considers him as looking upon this complex scene of ideas and sensations, and finding everywhere objects that immediately excite in him sympathies . . . To this knowledge which all men carry about with them, and to these sympathies, . . . the Poet principally directs his attention. . . .

(Preface to *Lyrical Ballads*, 2nd ed.)

As for the reader:

> Is it to be supposed that the reader can make progress . . . like an Indian prince or general—stretched on his palanquin, and borne by his slaves? No; he is invigorated and inspirited by his leader, in order that he may exert himself; for he cannot proceed in quiescence, he cannot be carried like a dead weight. Therefore to create taste is to call forth and bestow power, of which knowledge is the effect.
>
> *(Essay Supplementary)*

The reader, having in him qualities of imagination, feeling, and thought of the same nature (but not of the same degree or liveliness) as the poet's, must apply to the poetry and to his own experience something like the long and hard contemplation the poet has applied to man and nature. Knowledge—that is, the relevance—will derive only from power called forth by effort. Such knowledge will transcend the bounds of his own experience.

This, then, is the classical doctrine of relevance; to what does it tend now to be reduced? I would venture to say to what is virtually its antithesis. Relevance now is defined in terms of the particular, not the universal; it starts in fact from the assumption of the irrelevance of the past, the uniqueness of the present. At its worst, "relevance" in the present popular sense invites the reduction of literary works of art to embodiments of the current journalistic clichés and headline topics, in terms of which the student interprets his own narrow and superficially defined experience. It invites the student to measure the significance and value of great works of art with the dubious yardstick of his own callow and naive immaturity.

Emphasis on particular and topical "relevance" has often reduced *Hamlet* to a modish example of current "hangups". Some producers of Shakespeare, obviously feeling that the poor old Bard needs his incompetence to be aided by a scaffolding of novel gimmicks, have worked hard to give him this sort of "relevance", apparently scanning the headlines eagerly for fashionable twists and distortions to impose on the text. A further danger has always been present in all the doctrines of relevance, even the classical, as Wordsworth's prefatory essays indeed show. This is that relevance is conceived simply in terms of content. It is significant that the feeblest part of Wordsworth's major essay is that in which he explains why he has chosen to write in verse rather than in prose. Emphasis on content, and on content seen as didactic, tends to obscure, if not to ignore totally, the importance of form and the fundamental truth about works of art: namely, that art is its own way of expression, that art speaks through the idioms of art, through its own "language", of which formal structure is a major component. It becomes too easy for the "relevant message" to be reduced to non-artistic definition and then to be accepted as the equivalent of the work of art from which it has been extracted.

Thus, emphasis on "relevance" as contemporary topicality can easily lead to a total, or virtually total, blindness to the quality of a work of art, topicality becoming the one virtue looked for. It is difficult for critics, and almost impossible for untrained readers, to discriminate when faced with expressions of their own familiar and strongly-held sentiments. Offer them twenty would-be poems deploring Viet-Nam, or pollution, or any other current emotionally charged topic, and their stock response, as I. A. Richards called it, will render them unable to make any artistic judgment.

What are some of the implications of what I have said so far? The first is clearly that the aims and structure of the old curriculum have dissolved. The second is that no clear conception of aims and hence of structure has emerged, or at least none has gained general approval and consent. We have now, in fact, our vast organization of departments and teachers, of classrooms and equipment, with no very clear or agreed idea of what we are doing with them or what we ought to be doing. Yet we must get clear and agreed answers to certain fundamental questions before we can give any coherence to our activities. It is futile to argue about whether English should be a compulsory subject in schools or universities before having a precise idea of why it should be a subject at all. The first step needful is to face the question, "Why teach English?"

It would be quite easy to make out a case for not teaching English at all, at any level except the primary. One could argue that the English of ordinary communication, the English our students in fact use, the Canadian vulgate tongue, is picked up naturally by the usual oral processes operative in all societies, primitive or sophisticated. Any attempt to teach the language merely interferes with a natural process. Young children need to be taught to read and write, since these skills are necessary to extend the range of the vulgate in place and time. This is an entirely reasonable position, given the assumption that the functions of language performed by the vulgate are and ought to be the only functions worth preserving.

Again, if the vulgate is the only form of the language that matters, and is a sufficient means of communication, there is no case for a study of literature written in anything but the vulgate as a way of examining modes of exploiting the resources of the language. The study of English literature as an art then has to be considered separately. As far as literature seen as something written in another language than the vulgate is concerned, its study would have to be justified in the same way as Latin or any other literature written in a related but foreign tongue. The argument for making a study of literature compulsory, given this context of attitudes, would be little if any more persuasive than the argument for making the study of Latin literature compulsory again. In short, given the premises on which the foregoing arguments are based—the primacy of the vulgate, and its sufficiency as a mode of what current jargon likes to call "communication"—ours is indeed an obsolete industry, and there is a strong case for abandoning all but primary instruction in reading and writing. If we are not prepared to accept this conclusion—and I certainly am not—then we must find another set of premises to draw *our* conclusions from.

Let us start by examining the question of language and "communication". No age, to my knowledge, has ever talked so much about "communication" and shown so little aptitude for it as has our own. We are always hearing about the "media" and their mass communication, but little emphasis is placed on the fact that apart from the visual element in television and the limited use of photography for illustrations in printed media, the dominant medium for conveying information and ideas is language. Even the pictures can convey little without the commentary or caption;

the range of visual communication by picture is very limited, even if one grants the power within that range. Any regular and thoughtful watcher of television soon becomes aware of how little the visual element contributes to "communication" in newscasts, interviews, discussions, and various kinds of analyses and expositions, apart from the projection of "images" of personalities. We are told that "the medium is the message"; insofar as the "message" is emotional or non-intellectual, it is powerfully conveyed perhaps by the visual, but the intellectual must be conveyed dominantly by the heard or read language. If you try the experiment of watching television for an evening with the sound turned off you will soon appreciate the extent to which the "communication" depends on language, and will find yourself relying heavily on the photographs of printed messages and titles to know what is going on. It is no exaggeration to say that the failure to recognize the dominant function of language in all "communication", and to understand what the so-called "visual" (which seems to exclude the visual act of reading) can "communicate" and *not* "communicate", has led to an almost total neglect in the use of language. Any television cameraman who produced nothing but blurred, out-of-focus, and incorrectly framed pictures would have a short career, but an announcer or commentator can pour out endless hours of blurred, out-of-focus, and incorrectly framed English with total impunity, indeed with honour. Worn clichés, malapropisms, mangled idioms, dense thickets of inexact jargon, and clouds of woolly vagueness interspersed with windy and pompous expressions of the obvious, are all too characteristic. It would be difficult to find in any of the "media" half a dozen individuals who were chosen for their job, not on account of their charm or personality, but on account of their real command of the English language, their ability to express what they had to say in clear, simple, direct, and precise English—or, for that matter, for their ability to find something worth saying.

There is no public outcry over this state of affairs, partly because most of the public have little realization of what they are missing, of how little they are getting of what there is to communicate. They are also accustomed to the same inept use of the language by their politicians and other public figures, who have little interest in mastering the art of language for precise communication. To some extent, this is because in this, as in many other matters, the age is also bedevilled by an *esprit simpliste*, and an eagerness to reduce the complex to the simple. It consequently has little love for precision, since precision depends on the observance of fine distinctions. Our age insists on precision in scientific measurement, in defining a second in terms of the vibrations of this atom rather than that, but has virtually abandoned all precision in vast areas of thought and language. Since language is the medium of thought, imprecision of language and thought accompany and reinforce each other. Any people reduced to measuring with lengths of string with knots, with sandglasses or sun-dials, or with thumbs, fists (or hands), and knuckle-to-elbow, would soon lose all conception of really precise measurement. As it is, we now all have a *conception* of precise physical measurement, although few of us know how it is done. On the other hand, a similar few have a conception of precise expression of ideas and how to achieve it, but there is no generally accepted recognition of the possibility or need of precision in the areas of thought and language. Scientists who would be horrified if you offered them a tape-measure will write English no more precise as language than "a handful" or "a good dollop" would be as mathematics. Some scientists have the notion that reducing the language to something like mathematics, or feeding a vocabulary into a computer, will make it precise, showing at once their ignorance of the nature of language, and their unawareness of the limited power of communication inherent in mathematics.

Our first task is to try to create a wider sense of the real nature of language and of "communication". There is a tendency to talk of "communication" without paying much attention to what is communicated, to whom, by whom, and under what conditions. Communication can in fact range from communicating a sense of goodwill and neighbourliness by saying "Good morning", or raising a hand in gesture, or communicating genial sociability by a discussion of the weather, to an attempt to explain problems in the design of variable-pitch fans for turbo-fan engines, or to clarify the Thomist doctrine of Essence or Leibniz's doctrine of pre-established harmony, or to discuss the validity of Keynesian economics or the probable future of the Common Market. In between what I have chosen as extremes lies a vast spectrum of situations calling for an infinite number of modes of "communication". The vulgate will serve only a small number of these modes. The full range of modes demands all the resources of the language. No-one would deny, of course, that for most of the ordinary man's ordinary conversation very little precision is called for, and the vulgate is perfectly adequate to exchange loosely formed and uninformed opinions, which constitute the bread-and-butter of social conversation. No-one insists on weighing butter with a laboratory balance or slicing bread with a microtome. But there are occasions when the vulgate, or rather the unsophisticated and unanalytical use of the vulgate, leads to a lack of precision where precision of thought and utterance would be valuable.

At this point I will drop the use of the term "vulgate", since I disapprove of it, and disapprove of all the attempts to split English into a number of competing and mutually opposed languages. I also disapprove of the term "standard". I know that craftsmen divide tools into two categories, rough and precision, but they do so with the full knowledge that in the hands of a real craftsman a hammer becomes a precision tool, while a botcher can make a mess of a job with an expensive lathe. Craftsmen also know that the tool is selected for the job, not from an innate categorical superiority. Similarly, it is possible, even common, to botch a job of communication using so-called standard English, or to make a precise job using the so-called vulgate. I prefer to think of the language as a vast kit of tools, suitable for every kind of job. What is essential is to know as many tools in the kit as possible, how they work, and what they are for. One learns about tools from craftsmen, and from watching craftsmen work. Anyone can see something of what a chisel is, and of its marvellous range of function, and its precise power of expressiveness, by watching carvers of wood and stone at work, or by looking closely at some work of Grinling Gibbons or at the Elgin Marbles. No-one will learn much by watching his neighbour doing rough but serviceable carpentry.

So I see the real justification for teaching the English language, not in the attempt to enforce a standard of "correctness", still less in an attempt to foster a new standard of slovenliness, but in trying to make students aware of the possibilities of precision and to start them as apprentices in the practice of it. This can be done only by a study of the language, to find out how it does what it does, to find out how you choose the precise rather than the loosely-fitting word, how you choose a lucid grammatical structure rather than an opaque one. This calls for studies of grammar, vocabulary, and composition, and a close consideration of a variety of styles, modern as well as past, with emphasis always on the craftsmanship, the kind of effect aimed at and produced and the technique for producing it—and all studies as far as possible freed of preconceptions about the absolute superiority of one style to another: all aimed rather at finding out what language will do and how you make it do it. At a later stage, as the student's approach to language becomes more sophisticated and analytical, he can be made aware of various types of elegance and beauty, of classical, romantic, and baroque virtues of language structures, of the function of various types of form and structure. At this stage, too, he will be ready to consider artistic problems of form, and the nature of formal choice as it presents itself to the artist in language.

The proper study of the language as a versatile instrument or set of instruments is inseparable from a study of precision in thought, and training in the precise use of language is inevitably training in precision and order of thinking. This ought to need no justification as a compulsory form of training. The old composition texts used to talk a good deal about unity, coherence, and emphasis. It is true that they often tended to treat these in a purely mechanical fashion, but this should not obscure the fact that these qualities are important. They are qualities of ordered language, that is, of composition, and hence also of ordered thought. It is evident to any teacher of English that language and thought are embodiments of each other, and that the student's main problem in writing any but the simplest composition is in sorting out loose and disordered and half-framed thoughts into some sort of logical and coherent pattern. It is natural for the student to wish to believe that only the technical problems of language hinder the transmission of his clear thoughts, and that the muddle is on the paper, but not in his head. The teacher must convince him that few, if any, are born with naturally clear minds, that the techniques of thinking, of logic, of ordering ideas, of shaping them to clarity, of giving them the exact shades of emphasis they require, have to be learned. I used to assign myself a subject for an essay in front of the class, rapidly write down a number of ideas suggested by the topic, think up two or three possible approaches, start ordering the ideas for each approach, chatting about the advantages and disadvantages of different arrangements, suggest different ways of starting each possible essay, different types of logical order, how much emphasis each part should get, and so on. I also found the preparation of class debates very useful, putting the emphasis not on scoring points but on trying to sort out the essential issues involved in various topics. It was useful to have students prepare both sides of a debate. Debates also allowed a discussion of the common types of fallacy. As the students acquire a sense of precision in thought, they acquire simultaneously, since they are thinking in language, the same sense of precision in expression. There are, I suppose, natural limits to the degree of precision each can attain, but very ordinary minds can acquire a very satisfactory level if given the right training. Close reading of good prose that deals with ideas also provides useful exercise, and a good many students learn the pleasure of getting an idea, driving it into a corner, tying it up, and pinning it down neatly.

Now, finally, let us consider the study of literature and its justification. Since literature uses language as a medium, and language conveys facts, ideas, and emotions, literature inevitably has what is commonly called a "content". As a consequence, there is a permanent temptation to reduce it to its content, to translate the content into a matter-of-fact paraphrase, to inquire into the significance and social function of this content so paraphrased, and from it to argue the importance of literature. This approach is even more fatal as a justification for literature than treating it simply as an amusement and pastime. There is a profound truth in the remark made by Coleridge about the *Lyrical Ballads*, that his task was to make the strange familiar, while Wordsworth's was to make the familiar strange, "to give the charm of novelty to things of every day, and to excite a feeling analogous to the supernatural, by awakening the mind's attention to the lethargy of custom, and directing it to the loveliness and the wonders of the world before us.'' Loveliness is not here to be confused with prettiness, as I perhaps need not remind you. Elsewhere Coleridge describes the qualities of Wordsworth's poetry, which in essence are the qualities of most great literature; he found in it

> the union of deep feeling with profound thought; the fine balance of truth in observing, with the imaginative faculty in modifying, the objects observed; and above all the original gift of spreading the tone, the atmosphere and with it the depth and height of the ideal world around form, incidents, and situations, of which . . . custom had bedimmed all the lustre. . . .

To this description it is essential to make some additions. Coleridge has given us only part of what we need always to remember. Art presents (or, if you wish, ''communicates'') this union of feeling and thought, this fine balance of truth and imaginative modification, this fusion of the ideal world of the imagination with the common world of everyday, by its own unique modes, its own structures, its own idioms. These are not translatable into the idioms of non-art; no discussion of a poem, no commentary on or exposition of it, is the poem. Nearly everyone recognizes the impossibility of successful translation of a poem from a foreign language into English; it is equally impossible to translate an English poem into English. This means that all discussion or exposition or ''interpretation'' must constantly be recognized as a very limited aid, useful to a reader only until he has learned the idioms and structures of art. To a great extent, this is equally true of novels and plays; I sometimes suspect that where novels or plays use what looks like ordinary prose as a medium, it becomes even more difficult for the student to recognize the idiom of art.

It is only because the idioms of art are *not* the idioms of other forms of discourse, and because they are untranslatable into other forms—because art has its own unique ways of speaking to us —that we can justify its importance. If it said nothing that could not be said in other ways, it could be dispensed with. Everyone accepts the importance, the necessity, of music and of painting and sculpture, of the dance, knowing that they mean something to us, and that their meaning is not otherwise to be conveyed than through their own forms and idioms, an idiom being a unique way of saying something. Teachers of literature, particularly those concerned with arguing "relevance" by translating literature into discussions, interpretations, and comparisons in terms of non-literary exposition, have lost sight of the uniqueness of literature as an art, and hence of its one justification.

The idioms of an art can only be learned, like the idioms of a foreign language, by becoming familiar with them. One can only learn the idioms, or patterns, of hockey by watching enough games, noticing what different shapes games assume, what varied tempos arise, what patterns of plays, and so on. Those who pack the arena merely to watch their side win, satisfied with victory or outraged by defeat, carry home what might be considered the "content" of a hockey game. They learn nothing of the art of hockey, nothing of its real meaning. By comparison with hockey, or with any sport, any true art is infinitely complex in its variety of patterns and of idioms; and of all the arts, literature is the most complex. This is its glory and its perpetual challenge.

Within the period assigned to formal education, it is possible to begin with reading aloud to small children until their ears get attuned to shapes and forms. They very soon develop a sense of beginning, middle, and ending—of the rhythm of literary designs, of shapes of poems, of the different melodic and harmonic patterns of poetry and of prose, of the various dances of words. Their imaginations respond and expand, not only to the "content" but to the artistic structures. A teacher who learns the art of reading can profitably continue reading aloud through every year up to the Ph.D.

I would put great emphasis on reading aloud, by the teacher and by the student—many students lose interest in reading because their own reading sounds so dull to them. I have had Ph.D. students who found Pope's couplets mechanical and sing-song; when they were asked to read some lines aloud one understood why. The very great importance of reading aloud, an importance which I think can hardly be over-estimated, carries with it by implication the necessity of giving a like importance to the study of the art of reading, to which little attention seems to be paid at more advanced levels of education. I found it symptomatic that one of my last and best classes of senior graduate students asked if I would give them some instruction in reading eighteenth-century poetry aloud. It was even more symptomatic that they were already much better than average as readers; most graduate students who are rather incompetent as readers seem unaware of their shortcomings.

Reading aloud is, as a performing art, perhaps less difficult than singing opera, but not vastly so. It demands almost equal control of voice, of breathing, of delicate gradation of pitch, of attack, of sustaining, modulating, or breaking off a tone. It calls for the same sort of sense of phrasing as a singer's, the same ability to choose the right tempo, the same placing of accent and choice of proper strength of accent. It demands the same kind of practice and exercise, the same working over and over of phrases and sentences, trying various patterns of tempo, pitch, and phrasing, finding out by experiment how long to sustain this syllable or that, how lightly to glide over another, what shape to choose to bring out best both the meaning and tonal pattern. Just as the singer or the violinist works over a piece of music, so the reader must work over a text. Practice brings a trained ear and a developed art, and eventually decisions can be made almost instantaneously; but a trained reader, like a trained musician, keeps an alert and critical ear and eye on his own performance. Good recordings of reading can be useful to teachers and students alike, but it is a sad fact that these are rather scarce—some very eminent actors read poetry quite badly, through an insufficient grasp of the meaning of the lines they are saying. It is a valuable though chastening experience to use a tape-recorder to allow a play-back of one's reading. This gives a prompt revelation of grosser faults, and encourages comparison of various trial versions. A tape-recorder would also be a useful tool in the classroom for training the students' ears and developing their powers of self-criticism.

Poetry is obviously written to be heard, and is read not only with the eye but, if not aloud, with the mind's ear, which is only as good as the external ear: if that external ear is untrained, and if the reader's voice is untrained to read, what the mind's ear hears will be something far inferior to the poem. Nor can we ignore what Milton called "that other harmony" of prose. Many of those who read aloud without giving much thought to how they are reading seem not to grasp how slight a difference of pitch or of stress can reveal or obscure the meaning of what is being read. I am constantly astonished by great readers or actors reading passages of poetry long familiar to me.

A few years ago, at a performance of *Twelfth Night*, I sat up with special alert anticipation to hear Viola's "Make me a willow cabin at your gate," one of my favourite passages in the play. To my delighted surprise the actress gave the whole speech a new pattern, new tempo, new accents, new melodic phrasing, which changed the dominant mood, and with it the dramatic significance, of the scene. It was all exactly right in its execution, and added another possible meaning to the speech. Another familiar example of the importance of verbal treatment from Shakespeare is Macbeth's "Tomorrow" speech. This is often given a sad, elegiac effect, by using a very slow tempo and a *piano* and *legato* delivery. It may, with at least equal dramatic plausibility, be rendered in a *staccato* and *forte* mode, the explosive "petty pace", "day to day", "dusty death" emphasized. Each reading, each sound effect, obviously creates a different dramatic effect, involving a different view of Macbeth's state of mind and situation. Sense and sound, in short, must operate as a unity: neither can be neglected or even thought of as subordinate. This means that the study of literature is inseparable from the study of how to read it aloud.

The problem of the curriculum, of what works of literature students at various levels should be asked to study, is by no means a simple one and has often been a vexed and contentious one. No other problem in the teaching of English is more confused, more bedevilled by conflicting theories. As I see it, the conflicts arise from inability to reach agreement on two matters: on the purpose or purposes of teaching literature, and on the kind of works of literature suitable for each purpose. As to the first, the purposes, the reasons why literature ought to be taught, the confusion is by no means merely recent. The old curriculum which I have praised was certainly not faultless and was based partly on tradition, on the feeling that the great works of English literature were essential elements of our cultural heritage which we must preserve, partly in the belief that the study of literature improves us by cultivating the imagination and the understanding, partly on the conviction that good literature develops proper moral attitudes. Some concession was made by the inclusion of Canadian (and American) works, to the theories that literature helps to create a national spirit, and the modern doctrine of "relevance" was evident in the selection of some contemporary writing. What was good about the curriculum was not so much that it was coherent and unified in purpose, but that it was comprehensive—by present-day standards, vast—in the amount of material it included. It introduced the student to a very large range of great writing, and allowed the teacher a great deal of scope. But the vague definition of its purposes, reflected in the official introduction to the published curriculum, left all those teachers who did not really know why they were teaching English literature (except that they were paid to do it) with little sense of what to aim at in their teaching. Many of them at that time had themselves had little training in their subject: they would be faced with the Tintern Abbey lines without having read any large volume of Wordsworth's poetry, without any notion of what Wordsworth thought about poetry, its function, the way in which it should be written. They taught Shakespeare, many of them without ever having seen a Shakespeare play on the stage. It is small wonder that many taught mechanically, going through Shakespeare with emphasis on the footnotes and glossary, killing the poetry by reducing it to a bad prose paraphrase, and reducing the action and shape of the play to a discussion of the psychology of the characters and the morality of their behaviour. The old curriculum perished, having demonstrated some home truths: that with good and well-trained teachers a rich and comprehensive curriculum offers immense opportunities; that with inferior and badly trained teachers it is necessary to know clearly what it is they are being trained to do, and how to train them to do it.

The obvious fact that literature can and does do a great many different things to and for different readers no doubt explains why there is such a problem of purposes in teaching it. But the only thing that fully and uniquely justifies the teaching of literature is that it is an art. Since it is an art practised by an artist who is, as poets remind us, a man among men, looking with human eyes at the world of humanity, the world of human occupancy and human affairs, and since it is an art using as its medium a language not, like the languages of music and of the pictorial and plastic arts, specific to it as an art, but used also for other modes of communication, it can seem to operate as if it were another mode than art. I have had students in psychology and in sociology, for example, who read novels as if they were case histories in their own discipline. But the simple and important and unique fact about a novel is that it is a novel, a work of art, and not a case history. And the simple and important and unique fact about a work of art is that it is worth studying *as* a work of art. Not all teachers are sure how to study a work of art *as* art; many know how to study it as social comment, as case history, as political document, as an elegant arrangement of thoughts to be made intelligible by a prose paraphrase, or as an interesting tale of events involving people just like us. But emphasis on art seems to them to suggest a study of that dubious thing called "technique", which, in poetry, means counting syllables, trying to find "feet", and carefully tabulating rhymes, alliterations, metaphors, and so on, and, in novels, hunting for symbols.

What I mean by studying a work of art as art centres on trying to understand art as a process, on trying to understand how the artist worked, what he was trying to do, how he has done it, and why. Years ago I used to suggest to high-school students different arrangements of scenes in a Shakespeare play, or, in the historical plays, other scenes he could have written. With university students, I have set Dryden's *All for Love* against Shakespeare's *Antony and Cleopatra* as a study, in two great plays on the same theme, of different principles of structure, different choices of dramatic scene and action, each with its advantages and disadvantages. The vital thing is to get the student to understand art as an activity, made up of choices—the choice of a *genre* to begin with, then of a large variety of kinds and of techniques within that *genre*; then of medium, since the language offers a tremendous range of styles, tones, tempi, and flavours of association. The writer has to determine from the start the general shape he wants, and why—his choice may be a mixture of current fashion and personal preference; he may be trying to beat his rivals at their own game, or he may be wanting to try an experiment of his own. At all events, he must start with a rough sense of what he wants to do, knowing the effects he is after, and choosing a structure and techniques to get that effect. If he succeeds, he will have built a structure not quite like any other work of art before, and it all depends on his choices and his skill in execution. This is the real excitement of the study of art, an inexhaustible excitement. And when, having seen something of how he did it, the reader senses, along with the skill, the power and the life of the work, he is learning a bit about what makes literature an art, and of the greatness and living quality of the art. What must be brought home to the student is the recognition that literature is not a *datum*, something that is there, could not be otherwise, and is a dead thing to be dissected; rather that it is something conceived, shaped, hammered out, by a living artist with a vision, struggling to shape his medium into a lasting work that will rejoice men for ages with the beauty of its shape, the power of its vision, and its complete harmony of matter and form, of what it says and how it says it—a body and soul which in great art become inseparable.

Given teachers with the right taste and training, the choice of curriculum comes down to two questions. First, what works must be chosen to introduce the student to the main kinds of literature, and to some varieties of each kind. The second, and more difficult, question is what to introduce at what levels of education. As to the first, it should be noted that good, and even great, literature need not be solemn. We should remember that Milton wrote *L'Allegro* as well as *Paradise Lost*, and that he thought Spenser, who wrote *The Faerie Queene*, as sage and serious a teacher as Scotus or Aquinas. The fantastic, the light-hearted, the comic, even the frivolous, are part of great literature. The imaginative is the essential part of it, and should be emphasized. At an early stage children should be asked to make pictorial illustrations of what they have read; at a later, perhaps to design stage sets or depict a particular moment of action on the stage or in the story. At all levels it is important to get them to exercise their own imagination, to try to ensure that what they are reading comes vividly alive. The young child is by nature a Romantic, with an appetite for adventure, for swift action, and for settings dear to the Romantic heart—wild scenery, castles, and magic forests. He also has a special liking for beast-epics and fables. He has an innate sense of dramatic form, with its beginning, middle, and end, its dramatic conflict, and its ironic surprises. These are the qualities Dickens wished to see cultivated in education and which he saw being crushed and stifled by Gradgrind and McChoakumchild. Dickens was profoundly right, and our first concern should be to select a curriculum, and to foster the kind of teaching of it, that stimulates the natural faculties by which literature is apprehended. As I have said, the sense of form is partly innate. It is also partly developed unconsciously through growing familiarity and widening experience gained through much reading and being read to. In elementary and early high school, I used to select one or two works on the curriculum, longer works —one, I remember, was Dickens' *Christmas Carol*—which I would read aloud to the class, setting aside an hour every Friday afternoon. I am in favour of having a rather large body of prescribed literature, some to be read aloud by the teacher, some to be read privately by the student and talked about in class, some to be "taught" and also read aloud by the teacher and by students in class.

This inevitably means limiting the number of long works, and I would willingly restrict the number of novels in favour of more poetry, short stories, and essays. The student's sense of the immense variety of forms and techniques in the novel could be developed through an anthology of extracts like those in Broadus and Gordon's *English Prose from Bacon to Hardy*, now, unfortunately, long out of print. The essay used to have a prominent place in the old curricula; I suspect it was dropped because it was difficult to ask examination questions on, and because it seemed to offer obsolete models for modern prose-writers. Since the essay retained its popularity as a literary form from the seventeenth century until at least the 1930s, and is not actually dead yet, it provides a richly varied *genre* of small-scale structure with an immensely wide range of subject matters, techniques, styles, and tone. Next to poetry, it is perhaps the best form for training the student in close and attentive reading. Short stories provide an excellent and easily managed form for the study of many of the techniques and structures of prose fiction. Poetry should have an increasingly large share of the curriculum. As the most imaginative, most subtle, most formal kind of verbal art, with the widest range of structures, techniques, and conventions, it demands the most concentrated study, the longest and most patient familiarity with its virtually infinite varieties, and ultimately the greatest maturity and subtlety in its readers. Only a curriculum that exposes the student to increasingly large and varied bodies of poetry, as he develops more and more sense of how the poet uses language and shapes it, can bring him during the period of his education to a sufficient degree of mastery to serve him for the rest of his life.

As will be evident, I define literacy in terms of an education in the English language and in the art of literature which uses that language as its medium. The future of literacy is ultimately in the hands of the teachers of English. If they are well enough trained, determined enough, and dedicated enough to the cultivation of literacy, no-one can actually stop them from making their students literate. Not every student can be educated to the same degree of literacy, though my own long experience taught me what a great deal can be achieved with what might seem to be unpromising human material. But the teacher must have a clear notion of what he is trying to do, and of how to do it, and be constantly imaginative and inventive in his methods. English is by no means an obsolete industry. It is an industry which has been suffering from a good deal of confusion about what products it is trying to make and about what its workers are supposed to be doing. Its genuine and proper products should be as valuable and as necessary as ever.

Picking Up the Thread
GEORGE WHALLEY

Much could be said about threads, apart from their use as material for nest-building. We can, for example, get so wet that we haven't a dry thread on us; there is the thread of life which Lachesis, her cloak encrusted with stars, snips with her shears when the time's up, so that our lives can be said to hang by a thread, and our fortunes too; there is the thread of an argument which is always more tenuous than we hoped it would be; and there is the thread that led Theseus out of the labyrinth after killing the Minotaur, the thread having been laid out from inside information by his lover Ariadne. Any of these threads could serve my purpose, but it's the last one I have especially in mind—not for Ariadne's sake (though I think she deserved better from Theseus than she got on the island of Naxos) but because of the labyrinth; and not because the thread would lead us out of the labyrinth as it did Theseus, but because it could lead us back into the labyrinth where we belong. We may take heart from reliable witnesses who tell us that there is not always a voracious Minotaur at the heart of the labyrinth. I wonder whether the Delphic Oracle (who knew a thing or two about double-talk) had something labyrinthine in mind when she caused to be carved over the entrance to her cave the command: "Know thyself." At least Coleridge and Yeats guessed that it might be so.

Three or four years ago a fashionable phrase emerged—"The Survival of Literacy". It was put round, I suppose, by those exponents of envious egalitarianism who make it their business to accelerate the decline of any aspect of life that cannot be shown to contribute directly to the gross national product. Although it's always a mistake to meet the enemy on his own terms, a conference of teachers of English from schools and universities met —our composure a little ruffled—to discuss this theme and its

implied conclusion: that "literacy" is holding on by the skin of
its teeth for the moment but probably won't last long. It is difficult to accept the phrase "The Survival of Literacy" very seriously, recognizing it as belonging to the same rhetorical family as
"The Death of God" and "The Two Cultures", whose poor
relations are "The Pursuit of Knowledge", "The Just Society",
and "Peace with Honour". But there we were, members of a
vanishing species, fellows of the duck-billed platypus, the whoop-
ing crane, the sperm whale, and those delicately poised pelagic
birds of the Pacific Islands that were driven from their own
natural homes by pigs and rats. We addressed ourselves to the
theme on the supposition that—at least for purposes of serious
discussion—it was not a trendy catch-phrase, loaded and
equivocal, beloved of weekend journalism and debating
societies; we tried to overlook the patronizing insolence of the
phrase; we tried in all charity to see if we could make some sense
of it, and quickly came to the conclusion that the phrase was
meant to imply something of this sort: "The age of authorized
misrepresentation has dawned. 'Communications' and 'the
super-8 revolution' have taken over. Let there be noise above the
threshold of pain. To discriminate is to be economically anti-
social. Verbal is out, visual is in. Literature is not 'relevant'."

We are inclined to bridle a little at such a declaration: we had
thought that, since "literature" is our business, "literacy" was
perhaps our peculiar business. If "literacy" goes, our business
goes. (Note the subtle but familiar shift in the word "business".)
The more resolute among us could say: "*Professional* survival
matters very little. The 'great work' is all. I can, like the deposed
leader Zatopek, drive a junk cart and be content—nobody can
stop me humming." The more wary among us might be puzzled
that in societies allegedly civilized the ear should suddenly be
superseded by that abstractive organ the eye. Reflecting a little
(which is difficult to do without words), the rather limited intellectual and emotional life of the dragonfly and the owl might
suggest that to be able to see well may not be quite enough; we
might even wonder whether the waters prophetically described by
McLuhan are more muddy than profound, and whether the confident declarations that go with the discovery may be more collu-
sive than illuminating. Nevertheless, there can be no doubt that

the threat is aimed at us, and I think it would be well to consider whether there is any substance to the threat, and also what connection there is between "English" and "literacy". What with aggressiveness on the one side and a saintly ineptitude on the other, idle rhetoric could produce an actual killing. If it did, the killing would be a suicide.

To begin with, "literacy" is not identical with either "the teaching of English" or "the study of English". I should like to move in two directions. First to look at the term "literacy" in the hope of bringing the word to some agreeable definition. Then, if the only purpose of "English" is to make students "literate" (as seems to be assumed in most schools and universities), I should like to affirm the traditional view—never more poignantly relevant than it is now—that the purpose of "English" is not simply to provide a "literating" regimen, but to fulfil a civilizing function that has been renounced by virtually every other "subject".

The evolution of the word "literacy" shows an interesting shift in emphasis: it began by referring to a quality to be admired, and has ended by becoming a low-order fact to be entered in census statistics. "Literate"—from Latin *litteratus* (lettered) —was used in mediaeval times to refer to a person who not merely knew the letters of the alphabet but particularly who made good use of that knowledge: it meant "learned" or "educated". "Illiterate", also directly from Latin, was originally the negative form of "literate", meaning a person who was *un*learned, *un*educated. The positive and negative forms of the same word often follow different semantic paths. By the middle of the sixteenth century "illiterate" was sometimes used of a person who could not read or write; not until 1894 do we find "literate"—the opposite of the negative word "illiterate" in its new sense—used of a person who *could* read and write: it took about 250 years for that particular meaning of "literate" to develop out of a special and limited meaning of the word "illiterate". The history of the nouns formed from those adjectives endorses the history of the adjectives. The noun "illiteracy" occurs in 1660, referring to the state of being unlearned or uneducated, and in the late seventeenth century only occasionally in the special sense of the state of one who could neither read nor write; "literacy" first occurs in 1883 as the state of being literate, presumably in all senses, but particularly in the sense of being learned or educated.

It is worth noticing that the word "literate", coloured from its earliest use by the respect and reverence paid to those who (through being able to read and write) were learned or educated, carried over into the abstract noun "literacy" (when it came to be coined) assumptions about the *potential* implied in the ability to read and write rather than the mere fact of being able to manage the letters of the alphabet intelligibly. Yet the word "illiterate" is now seldom used except to refer to a person who either cannot in fact read or write, or else is so grotesquely uncivilized that you can't believe that he can do either. The abstract noun "literacy", however, suffered no such reversal of meaning: it was coined at a time when the assumed benefits of universal education were first being advocated on a national scale in most civilizing countries.[1] The undefined emotive word provided a convenient rallying-point—a procedure now well known to us from the propaganda and advertising industries. It is melancholy to reflect that the soft-sell that drew tens of thousands of guileless but bemused young people into universities in the sixties said nothing about literacy or civilization, but much about economic self-improvement and the gross national product; the word "education" (equally undefined and emotive) promised a painless initiation into the mysteries of "the good life", as specified in full colour with the molar grin of confident affluence.

Unfortunately high-mindedness does not always go hand-in-hand with a profound sense of reality. To be able to read is indeed something worth attaining; but we all know that there are different levels of reading, as there are different levels of writing; we also know that to be able to voice printed or written characters in a semblance of intelligible speech, or to be able to job together written or printed characters into a semblance of coherent writing, is a rather compassionate test of literacy. Those who say "I *only* want you to teach my people how to write simple plain English" never seem to understand that that is precisely what any serious writer would give his eye-teeth to be able to do.

If we place the test of literacy (of being learned or educated) at a rather high level, as I am sure we should insist, the definition of "literacy" can be seen to vary according to the size and homogeneity of the group that can be called learned or educated. If the group is homogeneous and sizable, a knowledge of certain authors and writings can serve as indications of how learned or educated any individual is. In the first half of the eighteenth century, for example, we could assume for a literate person a reading knowledge of Horace, Cicero, Vergil, and Ovid, and some Martial or Juvenal (according to taste); Greek would be desirable but not imperative; in English, Milton and Shakespeare could be assumed, with perhaps a little Spenser. Prose fiction (as far as it existed) would be regarded as a pleasant diversion but not worthy of serious regard, yet a literate person would probably know that very civilized and dotty book *Tristram Shandy*. Certain contemporary English poets would be well known—Dryden, Pope (not least his ingenious translation of Homer), and when they came along, Gray, Collins, James Thomson, and the like. But there would also be included certain philosophers, preachers, essayists, historians, and biographers, and much literature of travel. The locus of literacy was limited pretty much to capital cities and the few university towns. The very strictness of definition and uniformity of taste gave a peculiar blend of zest and urbanity to the literate class—what Coleridge, about the time of the Reform Bill, was to call "the clerisy", by which he meant all educated professionals. The zest of that literate complex was transplanted to North America in the early years with a sense of responsibility; unhappily little of the urbanity has survived, and not much of the zest.

In the Canadian House of Commons it is a long time since anybody quoted Horace or Martial—or even Milton or Clarendon or Swift or Harrington. I am not aware that in the last twenty-five years our elected representatives have ever quoted anything except each other's more hasty and exploitable utterances, though it is true that Mr. Trudeau, a very cultivated man, has once or twice chosen phrases from *Desiderata*—which was a comfortingly democratic thing to do. In 200 years circumstances have altered in many ways, not only in the House of Commons. The number who can read and write has increased immensely in this century, and the number who can read well and write well must be rather larger than it was a century ago. Yet journalism, becoming increasingly pervasive, has on the whole set a rather low and uniform level for staple reading and everyday speech; the best-seller market (already lively 200 years ago) has turned into an organized industry that circulates a large volume of commodities of variable quality that are sometimes read and usually, for a short time, talked about. The *Reader's Digest* has, I suppose, taken the place of the *Quarterly Review*, and Andrew Tooke's *Pantheon* has been superseded by the comic strips; distinctions of class, in speech as well as in dress and deportment, have been heavily eroded; for some years the schools have been teaching methods of reading that ensure shallowness of impression. All these considerations (and many more) prevent us from conceiving of "literacy" with the precision that could have been achieved even as late as the onset of the Second World War.

Whatever "literacy" means now, we are forced to recognize that we must look for it under a number of different manifestations, with a large variety of indicators, and in a much more heterogeneous group than ever before—not least among those who are self-taught. The concept of literacy is now very difficult to define, and statistical surveys won't help much with a definition because we don't know what questions to ask to identify a *quality*. But that does *not* mean that "literacy" itself has declined or that it has been dissipated or even that it is in danger of disappearing. A term that was in the first place very imprecise, though for a short time stable enough to be definable, has become much more fugitive in the ninety years since it was coined. But the blurring of the field of search need not affect the fineness of the search. If we are looking for garlic in a pig-sty we can still know quite clearly what garlic looks like and smells like. It may be difficult to find a needle in a haystack, but the difficulty doesn't prevent us from knowing what a needle is and what it is used for; and if it's a needle we want, it would be more intelligent to look for one in a pin-cushion than in a haystack.

The word "literacy" was never intended to imply anything but a desirable or admirable *quality* of intellectual cultivation. The word was coined and borne aloft by the assumption (now largely disappointed) that given the *means*—to be able to read and write—the *quality* would naturally follow; that a person who was "lettered" (knew his letters) would tend (other things being equal) to become *literate*, learned, educated. But the process can work very slowly. John Berryman, when he was a brash young American undergraduate before the Second War, discovered a curious instance of provinciality in Cambridge—Cambridge being, one would have thought, a fairly civilized place, and its undergraduates moderately literate.

> These men don't know *our* poets.
> I'm asked to read: I read Wallace Stevens & Hart Crane
> in Sidney Sussex & Cat's
> The worthy young gentlemen are baffled. I explain

> But the idiom is too much for them.
> The Dilettante Society here in Clare
> asked me to lecture to them on Yeats
> & misspelt his name on the invitations.

This refers to a matter of elementary literacy that we run into more and more as more and more students come from a relatively unlearned background—and some teachers too. It can of course happen to anybody. How could anybody be expected to know by instinct that the name Bagehot is pronounced "Bajut", or that Elia is pronounced "Elīa". Louis Arnaud Reid, studying aesthetics at Oxford about sixty years ago, thought for a whole undergraduate year that Bosanquet was two people—Bowes & Kett—like Liddell & Scott, or Lewis & Short, or Samson & Delilah. I have met students who thought that "jesting Pilate" was a seafaring metaphor. I usually think it advisable at the end of a course in literature to say: "These are some of the names we have been bandying about. This is how they are spelled; this is how they are pronounced. I can't insist that you *read* them all; but if you want to give the air of having read them, it is well to get the spelling right, and the pronunciation. It goes ill in a billiard saloon to chalk the wrong end of the cue." But we must be patient. Some of my students still say "Colleridge" even though I point again and again to Coleridge's own epigram on the various mispronunciations of his name (including this one). We must indeed be patient.

"Literacy", in the historical view, means to have read or heard or seen some things that made the heart leap up because they seemed to have been made especially for you; to have encountered some things that "with the swift composure of a fish" (Virginia Woolf's phrase) entered the fibre of the mind and stayed there; to have some feeling that literature is a living tissue spread out in time, a spider's web that can, at a light touch, tremble right back to the beginnings of recorded speech or far below the levels of individual memory or experience. Literacy in that sense cannot be *taught*; but the possibility of it can be made available. To teach children—a little roughly if need be—to read and write and do sums has always been the staple of schools; this is how it all begins and this is how it all should begin, and the sooner the better.

But the formal study of "English" in universities is a quite recent development, which began, roughly speaking, when classical studies ceased to be the central humanist discipline and the torch was handed to "English". Until that time—say the first quarter of the twentieth century—it seems always to have been assumed (in England at least) that a firm acquaintance with the literature of one's own language was what—given a salutary shove at school—civilized people achieved, somehow in the dog-watches, when nobody was looking. You didn't have to "take courses", you were taught your own language at school and made to read a certain amount of "what everybody reads"; after that you were on your own. (Those who clamour for a strong diet of courses in "Canadian Literature" should give a little thought to this.) Oxford considered "English" hardly a matter worthy of serious study, compared with the classics; and when an English School was eventually established late in the nineteenth century, the emphasis was placed on philology and Anglo-Saxon (a foreign language), and after Anglo-Saxon the advance towards Milton was tentative and grudging. It was not supposed that in such a study you were meant to *enjoy* English: that was your own affair, not the university's. Cambridge was a little less stuffy, and recognized that there might have been some writing in English after 1800 that would, in educational terms, reward study.

When Classics was finally edged out of its commanding position, through the neglect of those who could best have profited from those studies, "English" found itself landed with the responsibility that Classics had borne ever since the thirteenth and

fourteenth centuries. Such arrangements are never made formally
and are never openly acknowledged; after a decorous delay professors of English found themselves carrying the ball. But to have
to turn the study of language and literature into a prime civilizing
instrument is rather a tall order, and nobody knew quite how to
do it; and anyway matters of this sort seem to go better when
there is no apocalyptic purpose openly in mind. The New Criticism, begun in Cambridge and turned into a paedagogic technique in the United States, threw the emphasis very firmly upon the
integrity of literature and single works of literature; this greatly
extended the precision, depth, and comprehensiveness of literary
studies, and seemed for a while to have provided a way of
"teaching English" that would engage a fine range of discern-
ment appropriate to the heart of humane studies. That was in the
Thirties and Forties. But by about the time the last veterans of the
wars had left the university and Cleanth Brooks was beginning to
look theoretically a little thin and Ivor Richards' hope of a
psychological calculus for literature looked more like a piece of
science fiction than a real possibility, signs of fragmentation
began to appear, mostly in the promotion of broad dogmatic
schemes of interpretation and the representation of literature as a
form of social history.

It seems to me that, at present, "English" is not in general
carrying out the function of a central humane discipline. I speak
of the run-of-the-mill work both in schools and in universities
—which I suppose is what most "teaching" is.

The back-wash of the New Criticism, reinforced by the nihilis-
tic abstractions of behaviourism and scientific analysis, and fostered by a desperate desire to get in on the power-game, is to be
seen in the wanhope of short cuts and technical gimmicks. There
is talk of teaching "skills" and "techniques" (rather than of
making people skilful); of the "tools of research" and the "tools
of criticism"; of identifying "approaches" and "views" and
"problems"; Faculties of Education and Institutes of Education
(who seem in an odd way to be busy with something other than
education) refer confidently to "the learning experience" and
"the educational process" as though those actually existed, and
urge us to establish "objectives" and "goals" and "to evaluate
performance by objective criteria" or by "behavioural output",

and to "quantify the results". This is a godforsaken and desolate zone, as deadly as uranium 235, to be avoided at all costs if what we have in mind is the civilized study of "English".

Yet I suppose this sort of thing is inevitable in times of desperation. Our minds are by nature idle; faced with a taxing circumstance we hope for a simple solution, an easy answer, and clutch at anything that looks "viable"; with the instinct of a cat-burglar we try the back door first; we look for a key that can be turned in one motion of the fingers rather than a clue to be followed or a thread to be patiently unravelled; and if we can manufacture some high-sounding jargon to cover the case, rationalization and self-deception go decorously hand-in-hand. We insist that we must *understand*, and so avoid the grace of showing that touch of respect that would make us determined *not* to *mis*understand. To insist on understanding is to be most unreasonable. Not that all that loose jargon, with its crude analogies and empty abstractions, is utterly useless; but it doesn't happen to serve our central purpose, which is to illuminate, to come upon the vigorous complex reality of language and literature and grasp it for what it is. Yet with all the beating of drums about innovation and audio-visual technology and "communications" and Canadianism, the noise can get a little confusing, and the urge to conform can become almost compulsive if we get nervous and are afraid that we might miss a trend or a new vogue and be thought old-fashioned—and think that we might wake one morning to find that for a whole generation most people had been talking in Arabic and we hadn't even noticed.

Thinking of language and jargon and the wide uncritical currency of catch-phrases, I should say that in my view there is no such thing as a *language* of film, or a *language* of music, or a *language* of dance or painting, even though, as loose metaphors, those phrases may not be utterly useless. The only language is the language of what we call "words". A true language has a grammar—that is, a description of intrinsic functions; music, painting, film, and the like have only *syntax*—that is, principles of putting together. Anybody who has ever attempted criticism of music or painting or film will know what I mean. Words alone have intrinsic "meaning" (as we call it for lack of a better word); and words alone have the intrinsic functions that shape syntax.

Visual images can have quite strong implications: a smiling face is not usually an unhappy face (though it may be an empty one), a male and a female figure disposed in a certain configuration can imply an amatory, erotic, or filial relation; but not everybody finds a toad ugly, or a mouse frightening, or a snake repulsive; and not all of us "read" the bee or the goldfinch as a symbol of chastity. The minor mode seems to close a sad relay in our emotional circuitry; a descending interval or scale is less elevating than an ascending figure. But these emotional resources, although they can in context be controlled with fine and intricate precision, cannot be articulated with the specific definition that words at a much lower level of accomplishment are capable of.

I say that words have "intrinsic" meaning and function in order to make the point that language is not a "medium"; it is not simply a neutral "carrier-wave" (although under certain conditions it can be); we can push it only so far; it plays on us as much as we play on it; language even affects the physical structure of our faces. We have somehow to come to terms with it, because language—no matter how conventional it sometimes seems—is not merely a conventional notation in which we record thoughts, wishes, and feelings. We spend several of the early years of our lives trying to find out how, in a rudimentary way, to use language; and since language in its very nature is always complex we often do quite well at the beginning even though we may get clumsier as we go on. Some of us spend the whole of our lives trying to use language, and only in occasional moments of elation are we confident that it is possible to advance much beyond the level of finger-pointing and vague gestures.

The implied threat to literacy is the barbarous assumption that language has decayed to such an extent that it is no longer useful for human purposes, and that a substitute must be found —anything visual or noisy (it seems) will do: film, artificial fog, fluorescent plastics, disorienting confusion of indiscriminate sound. Which brings me back to "literacy". The word bears in its bones the implication of "letters", the record of what is spoken or written; it may even carry with it some feeling for the unfathomable gap between what is written and what needed to get said. As far as "literacy" means being learned or cultivated, we should want to extend the word to include some acquaintance with (say) music, painting, sculpture, architecture, dancing, acting; but the indissoluble element of "literacy" is language, and the use of language, and some recognition of the manifold and variable functions of language. We need to pay attention to *what* is written, but even that is difficult to pick out because of the bond between the *what* and the *how* in any writing other than semi-mathematical discursive prose. A "literate" person is, I think, what we mean by an "educated" person (however he comes by it). I think not of *expert* knowledge but rather of the honest and comprehensive appreciation of the keen amateur who has a reasonably well-developed and well-informed taste. His mind is not so much "filled" or "stocked", as ready, alert, responsive, having something to respond *with*.

Particularly, to be literate is to be sensitive to language in all its manifestations. Reading—that is, actually reading lots of books—is perhaps a specialized activity, like skiing or rock-climbing or engraving on glass; for writing there is no other way of "Studying monuments of its own magnificence." Short of that—but not really a substitute for it—is to speak articulately, preferably with a touch of rough and improvised eloquence; and to be able to listen to speech attentively, grasping it as the dramatic unfolding of a necessary improvisation. The breaking up of isolated social groups, and the pressure to conform to "standard speech", may now have deprived us almost completely of dialects, and so of impromptu virtuosity in language. But the old instinct quickly returns if we decline to ape the formulated patterns.

This, I suppose, is the keystone or knot or nucleus of my argument—if it is an argument: that "literacy" is radically to do with language, and that the heart of any genuinely educative activity is to be found in language; not language as a phenomenon, nor as an object of inquiry; not language considered merely for what it says or "means" or contains; nor even literature as examples of the use of language and ways of living; but everything that is engaged by language and in language—the thinking, the feeling, the activity of mind, the reality of experience that, in the wording of it, can be as solid as an inconsolable grief; the reality that language constantly confronts us with, of *making* as a necessary and natural human activity; language as an inventive mode of inquiry that can disclose ourselves to ourselves, discovering to us what we wanted to say; above all the language that allows us to make and utter things that are not simply extensions or expressions of ourselves.

It is conceivable that the sense of language may go on decaying, that the finely articulate and modulated poetic speech that English is capable of could collapse into a mutter-tongue. But language is always decaying; and also language is always renewing itself. The renewal is brought about not by tight-lipped academicians standing pale (and almost speechless) at the barricades, nor by the stern schoolteacher who has a ruler for every knuckle; it occurs through the sheer exuberance of invention and delight in invention. For language is not only the specific and distinctive mark of man, but his most naturally inventive resource. Nobody knows how we do it; and probably nobody ever will.[2]

Literacy, whether arising from formal or private study, is a by-product rather than a definable end, a spin-off rather than a product, a responsive and discerning habit of mind rather than a possession or an accomplishment. If, in our teaching, our concern is to encourage literacy, we might do well not to assume that it will come only to the most talented students. The most talented will find it anyway, somehow or other. Our concern should be to provide at every level a starting point from which individual development and vitality can begin to discover and affirm the gift of language. Yet the literate will always be a minority because literacy depends upon a gift for language; there is no law that says that everybody must be fascinated by language (though I wish there were a law, particularly among people in positions of influence or authority, about using language in a responsible manner). The only mistake is to suppose that it could be otherwise. The ideal of teaching everybody to read and write was probably inevitable; but the risk almost outbalances the blessing. It is now very clear that universal literacy (in the elementary sense) is in danger of producing universal illiteracy (in the qualitative sense), by breeding disrespect for language and whatever can be finely spoken or written; by submerging our sense of wonder at the most remarkable of our endowments, the gift of inventive speech; by throwing doubt upon our discriminate perception of the *why* of anything that is spoken or written.

I can't remember when I last met a person who could not read printed words—except for very small children and perhaps a few psychopaths. That disability is surely much rarer now than to have only one leg, or two eyes of different colours, or to bear scars of incontinent motor-driving. Speech is a marvel enough in itself; we are perhaps most often reminded of it when we hear a five-year-old child speak fluently in a language not our own —Dutch, Hungarian, Russian. To be able to convert written characters into speech, or to render speech into written charac- ters, is yet another and different marvel; it demands a flair for imaginative projection more studied and artificial than the act of speaking. One ideal of written language is that it should sound as though spoken, even though a direct transcript of actual speech will seldom do the trick. Yet many who have "done well at school" are (we find) utterly deaf when they read; content to "get the message" or to "pick up the information", they fail to hear in the writing the very qualities that in speech they would welcome and even rejoice in.

We know that in real life if we do not *listen* we miss not only *what* is said but also *why* it was said. Yet, for reasons mysterious to me, children have for many years been taught in school to "read by eye", thereby systematically suppressing the ability to listen to what is written. This may explain why we find so many students—even some "good" university students—who stiffen at the sight of a pen, the hand scrunching up like an arthritic old bird's claw; the writing then goes clumsily enough, often with a deadly pedantry or uncouth pretentiousness that we never hear in their speech (unless they are trying to talk like an article in a learned journal or are engaged in student politics). No doubt it's a good thing to have a quick way of getting through large quantities of printed material that "isn't worth listening to"; but if that is our only way of reading we ensure that nothing we read will be worth listening to—that is, worth reading.

A large part of my energy and ingenuity as an instructor of English in a university goes into encouraging people to read attentively and to write as well as they can. The first is not too difficult because some have survived their early training scot-free and few have suffered irreparable damage; the second is more taxing because few are endowed to write as well as they speak, and even fewer are willing to accept the risk of discovering that language is not so much a "medium of expression" as an instrument of inquiry.

To direct students towards competence in writing is a laborious and discouraging task. No wonder most instructors find that they have so much else to do that they have no time for it. Yet there is no substitute for learning to write. Speech will not do as a substitute because it lets us off the hook too easily—both speaker and listener—through the persuasive shorthand of gesture, facial expression, and intonation, and every *bêtise* in public tends to be endearing even if not always pardonable. Hence the great importance traditionally (and correctly) placed in humane education upon writing. There really is no other way of coming to terms seriously with language than by trying to write well. To accept the proposition that writing is outmoded, that society is no longer "verbal" enough for the skilful conduct of writing to be "relevant", is to arrest the development of those who—though confident that they can in some sense "read"—are unaware how easily—by "reading badly"—they can be made mute victims of cynical manipulation (social, commercial, and political), and could become emotional cripples and intellectual dwarfs.

To be not-illiterate is to be able to recognize the unity of the *what*, the *how*, and the *why* of anything that is spoken or written. If we cannot recognize by the ring of it that an argument is specious, or that it is no argument at all, being merely a reiteration of emotional catchwords and sophisms; if we cannot tell by the ear the peculiar *timbre* of a third-rate mind fumbling with matters that he neither understands nor respects; if we cannot sniff out the shiftiness of doublespeak, of gross dishonesty and bland self-deception dressed up in jargonish togs of the latest design; if we cannot by ear detect the poverty of dull earnestness or the ponderous tautologies of degenerate abstraction; if we can do none of these things, then we are indeed illiterate, no matter how extensive our vocabulary, no matter how many improving magazines we subscribe to. Illiteracy of that sort thrives, I regret to say, not only among students who might (at their risk) be momentarily pardoned, but also among many who profess to "teach".

We must recognize that there are now, and long have been, forces in society that make it their business to induce illiteracy, and that strive to persuade us (often in the name of "truth", "objectivity", and the benefits of programmed conformity) that there is no point in listening while we read, or in judging while we listen. It is the duty of schools and universities to keep alive these capacities and to nourish them as fully as may be in every individual who will let us. We can do this by reminding ourselves continuously of something that we know perfectly well and that we live by every hour of the day: that we can tell what people are saying to us and that we can usually judge pretty accurately why they are saying it. To fulfil this duty is of course to be subversive: by seeking to establish the autonomous discrimination of the individual (within reason), we threaten to undermine the programmes of power, authority, and abstraction that at present dominate our society. To be subversive in a "free" society is always sternly punished sooner or later, partly by having a submissive claque called "the public" organized against us, partly by the betrayal of waverers and opportunists from within. William Tyndale, the first translator of the *Bible* into English, was exiled from his country and was eventually strangled and burned; there were complex grounds for Henry VIII's displeasure, but one of them was not treason. We no longer burn people in public; we roast them in private—by withholding essential funds, by intrusive legislation, by demanding so much reporting-in-detail that no honest work can be done, by putting about misleading propaganda, in short by cutting off telephones (the approved method of destruction in big business). It is strange that in our society we tenaciously insist upon preserving the authorized conspiracy of trades unions, yet spend much effort in trying quietly to destroy the benign conspiracy of education that we ourselves have authorized by choice.

Human nature being what it is, the direction of wilful human ambition is always degenerate. Yet there is a certain wisdom of the body that can secure our integrity against all the sly tricks from without—and even from the sloth from within that would make us complacent, unwatchful, destitute of delight. Long after the last polar bear has been driven from the last garbage-tip, we shall go on *listening*, unless we destroy our ability to do so. It is of our nature, a habit of growth and preservation, a source of responsive power and refining attention—to listen, not for the sounds of danger only, nor only for the sounds of delight (bird-song, running water, music), but for voices: voices speaking, voices that speak intently to us, one by one, voices that we can recognize and put a name to.[3] This is not a matter of policy, and is therefore unassailable. As instructors, our business is not salvation or programmes for salvation, but simply with helping people to discover their capacities, their intrinsic nature, their selves.

Now for the "thread"—the bond, that is, between the formal study of "English" and the quality of "literacy". What is the thread we suppose ourselves to be unravelling or following —deliberately or absent-mindedly—and where does it lead us? Let us recognize two things: (*a*) Our discussion so far has taken the work of school and university as a single continuum, but I have spoken perhaps as though the emphasis fell mostly on the university. As we trace the thread we shall need to pay closer attention to different levels of function, to make some distinctions between the work of primary school, high school, and university. (*b*) In schools, and also (but to a lesser extent) in university, education is not directed exclusively towards the training of experts or the cultivation of highly endowed intelligences. We need to recognize that (for a number of various reasons) a certain number of people are uneducable beyond a very modest level. Nevertheless, we hold as an aim that each individual should ideally be trained to a high level of his own capacity, whatever that may be; and we also wish to arrange the quality of our work in such a way that (as with some artists) the "picture" in a real sense is complete at every stage; if a person has to stop before reaching the end of a programme (say Grade Nine or Grade Thirteen or an Honours B.A.) his education to that point will be coherent and at that level self-consistent. Education is not only for "experts"; a literate or educated person is *not* an expert, but he does approach in some way the ideal of the "generally educated person". Intense and specialized training can assail the integrity of that ideal, and pedantry or the closed mind can destroy it.

If "English" is to assume from Classics the function of *the* central humane discipline, it must be not only learned but substantial, earthy, physical, subtle, and far-ranging. The earthiness, subtlety, and range are to be found by concentrating on language. And "English", though certainly not devoid of "content", is to be regarded not as a "subject" but as a discipline in the true sense: a certain way of mind, a habit of mind, a quality of perception—from which all other kinds of study can radiate and in which they can be seen to be rooted. This is an axiom, not an argument. In no other terms could "English" take on the general educational responsibility that Classics traditionally held. Classics had always been a study, not of language and literature only, but of the history, philosophy, and social institutions of two complete, highly developed, closely related, and strongly contrasted cultures; a study not only (say) of comparative philosophy and history, but of the origins and growth to civilized stature of philosophy itself, and of historiography; a study not of two foreign languages but of two languages representing two contrasting mentalities, each very different from our own mentality, despite the profound effect both languages have had on our own.

Lacking that complex perspective, and lacking the strong intrinsication or *inward* pull exerted by the study of such flowering-at-the-source, and deprived of the otherness, the sheer strangeness of those two languages and cultures, "English" has always had to make a deliberate effort not to relapse into a narrow and myopic study of "English language and literature" as a "subject". In my view such a relapse has largely occurred; and I applaud the challenging proposition of my learned colleague Felp Priestley that perhaps English has become an obsolete industry—that is (I take it), that English has become obsolete by being turned into an industry; that "English" has become a worn-out shorthand omnibus term, an omnibus (to change the image) in which we long ago stopped checking the oil and haven't noticed that rust has afflicted the steering mechanism.

It is not enough, I suggest, to say that we are going to teach people to read and write and gain a knowledge of literature; nor is it enough to say that literature embraces just about any study you can think of—history, philosophy, politics, psychology, semantics, etc., etc., etc. We need to be continually following a thread that leads us back into the origins of all these special kinds of study—even our own; to be finding in the ways of language, and in literature (as language superlatively realized in any form of expression or in any subject), a continuous discovery and affirmation of the nature of language and of the inventive and integral activities of the whole person that we call "mind".

We need to take into account, though, that—as teachers—we are thinking of a continuous process covering usually (without much serious interruption) a span of sixteen to twenty years in the life of a potentially literate person; and also that within such a span, and within the working span of any single teacher, the vision will be blurred from time to time and that declared purposes will be deflected by waves of irrational fashion, by ignorant intervention, and by crass methodological doctrine. Therefore, in a matter at once complex and elusive, subject to erosion from within by fatigue and languor—or simply by losing the thread—we need some strong and single focus of attention.

We need to recognize that within the field of "English" there is an almost infinite number of things that we can "do with" literature, but that not all—or even many—of these have much to do with the central paedagogic value of studying literature. There is a very small nucleus of activity where the going is very hard indeed because what is sought is of the utmost simplicity; and there are a host of peripheral activities that grow up from using literature and language as evidential material for quite other interests. Much of the time and attention of our students is consumed with these peripheral interests. Those interests are legitimate enough in their own way; but, in comparison with what a central educational discipline can be expected to do to us, they offer little more nourishment than lists of irregular verbs or columns of stock exchange quotations. The nucleus I speak of is not, of course, the exclusive prerogative of "English"; it is the nucleus of all humane study. But literature and language give a peculiarly direct and penetrating entry to that nucleus, and, although the chances of deflection are abundant and debilitating, it is usually easier in the study of English than in other humane studies to tell (if we are honest with ourselves) whether we are being deflected or not.

I suggest that the nucleus is accessible along a single thread that is composed of two strands—as is the case (I suppose) for all things and states imaginative. These strands are a sense of wonder and a sense of language. Plato said that wonder was the beginning of philosophy—and by "philosophy" he meant the affectionate pursuit of wisdom. Without a sense of wonder the mind remains closed, or irritably aggressive, or morosely fear-ridden. Wonder is a respectful way of mind, a grace that we seem to be born with; by discipline we can nourish it; it brings with it the exhilarating release, the sheer delight, of discovering living things that are not projections of our selves, and that liberate us by their exuberant vitality, their unaccountable otherness and rightness. By "a sense of language" I mean a feeling for the physique, the nerves and muscles of words, and for their textures; a feeling for what language is *doing* almost more than what it is saying or "meaning", for what it is tracing out, acting out, gesturing forth, embodying; a feeling for the *intrinsic* qualities of words, their origins and transformations, their minute particularities as they establish themselves by context, by location, by rhythm; a feeling for their ability to declare, in precise configuration and ordered hierarchy, multiple meanings, often contrary; a feeling for the inner shaping energy that comes to the ear as shapely rhythm, as a tune often so subtle that it might seem to be on the fringes of silence. To follow this thread—a thread that leads *back* into the mind and into the source of our most inventive endowment—is to move toward the centre of articulation and initiative both in ourselves and in what we are studying.

We can pick up the thread at any time, as long as the last vestiges of innocence and candour have not been destroyed, and as long as we are not finally convinced that the mind is a clockwork orange constructed on the principles of Newtonian physics; but the earlier we pick it up the better, while the sense of wonder still naturally supervenes upon the fascinating effort of learning to speak. To discover the transfiguration that language is capable of, to come upon the imperishable substance of things-made-in-language that are no more than sounds on the air or marks on paper yet are sometimes as deep as life, often as commanding as a presence—this is to experience the synthesis that language flows out of and can bring us to. So to concentrate on dynamics, *dunamis*, energy, the originating and shaping forces that are carried in the bones and nerves of anything well made, is to find a nuclear centre of a minute critical mass. The rest depends upon what, individually, we can do with it.

There is not time, nor is this the occasion, to specify in detail what can be done by picking up this thread and taking the courage to go back into the labyrinth. But I can make a few hints. At the very beginning, writing is making shapes that will evoke sounds; the correlation of sound to shape is seldom very exact, but the letters have shapes interesting in their own right, and they have histories; and when it comes to spelling, that is a good way of beginning to get a feel for the shapes of words as physical entities. (It is recorded that J. A. Smith, a Wynfleet Professor of Moral and Metaphysical Philosophy at Oxford, came to breakfast after a sleepless night saying what a dreadful thing it would be for a learned Chinese to go blind: some of the ideograms that make Chinese so beautiful when written have no sounds attached to them and can therefore only be read by eye.) The study of grammar, essential I should have thought, but now, I understand, largely neglected in the school as a matter of policy, is to study the intrinsic functions of words, how they "work", what they have to be to "work" at all—the static noun that for an adorning or refining touch calls adjectives to itself but won't have more than one at a time (usually) or they will quarrel; the range of functions of the verb from passive and impersonal inaction and neutrality to the vigorous forward thrust in search of an object that imparts such impetus to an utterance that the words have to fall into place because they haven't time to do anything else. Syntax is another matter—the way words actually go together in utterances; and given the terms of identification we can find out by analysis (that is, by unravelling) how in actual cases the words do work together.

Here it is that considerations of "style", the unique "this-ness" of anything, come to conscious attention, though we had long ago caught the tune of it; under the spell of wonder we may well have taken it for granted. Here we come upon the peculiar nature of language—the fact that we discover our meaning in the wording of it; for it is persons, not words, that mean. In matters of spelling, in identifying parts of speech, and even in classifying figures of speech, we may be able to speak of "right" and "wrong" (i.e., correct and incorrect), but as soon as we are dealing with syntax and style we are dealing with the judgment of what "works", what is "exactly right", in an actual context. There are many grammatical difficulties that are insoluble except by complete reconstruction; "rules" are indications, navigational instruments, not immutable imperatives. Here the only test is whether in fact a certain wording "works", whether it is the best words in the best order—and perhaps nobody can say that for sure except the writer. Hence in "teaching" writing—if we want to encourage a sense of the dynamics of the language—it is important to reserve "right" and "wrong" for the few cases where "correct" or "incorrect" can be determined beyond question; elsewhere a scale runs from "right" to "not quite right" to "not right at all"—but neither of the last two is "wrong" in the sense of "incorrect"; when we say "no" to the choice of a word, the position of a phrase, a grammatical construction, we have located a *symptom* that something has gone adrift, slightly or seriously. What has "gone wrong" has still to be discovered; it is usually in the conceiving of it. What we have to do is not usually to tinker with the words but to reconceive the exact mental action or gesture that we had in mind. I don't know how anybody who does not have a refined sense of language and the patience to weigh minute verbal values in other people's writing can ever hope either to write well or to induce anybody else to write well.[4]

All this places an almost intolerable burden upon the teacher, not least because little of it can be learned by rote. To teach the minutiae of grammar and syntax is a rigorous and exacting matter; yet it is refreshed and reinforced by reading works of literature, to begin with—and perhaps always—for the sheer enjoyment of it, deliberately looking for a spell to fall under; as teachers, explaining as little as possible (because explaining is almost invariably explaining away), and yet encouraging our students as best we can to grasp the multiple activity that goes on in good writing, the many implications that are set in motion and sustained with fine precision. When we are studying literature as a way of finding out how to write well, "criticism", "explication", and all the alleged "tools of research" are to be handled with the utmost delicacy and restraint; if they are really used as "tools" they will certainly dismember what we seek to grasp whole and intact. And so for all the fascinating details of prosody and versification, the principles by which, in verse, the words have in fact been set in the right order so that they resonate and are transfigured—we need to conceive these principles in dynamic terms, as the disposition of energy in relation to chosen constraints and limits; for a study of prosody can immensely heighten the sense of verbal *drama*—exactly what the words are *doing*, how they are acting (as actors act).

And if, with the advance of self-consciousness, students suspect that the sense of wonder was only a paedagogic trick, it can be restored by examining how poets and artists actually work, how they deal with their need to go to the labour of making things in words, what the relations are between the historic person of the poet and what ends up in his poem. This needs to be handled delicately too, and is probably slippery ground except for those who have practised the art of poetry a bit and are familiar with its forthright and craftsmanlike axioms. A study of artistic making will not *explain* much, but it can restore wonder by clearing away inappropriate assumptions about "communication", and "information", and "messages" and "media" and "audience-appeal" and "the poet's Philosophy" and "motivation" and "social commitment". These drift into the background as too crude to help us, or as totally irrelevant to the poetic matter in hand. There are also questions about "fact" and "value", about the alleged "subjectivity" (unreliability?) of all personal judgments—as though any judgments were anything but personal; about ways of knowing and recognizing; about seeing and observing, describing and symbolizing and naming; about the enclosed integrity that some poems have and how others are more discursive and open; about the distinction between what is merely actual and what is actually real (the two being concentric); about the relation of feeling to thinking; about the poetic ordonnance that works through metaphor, and how this is different from "logic", though more intricate, and yet embracing logic (as language must); about the peculiar reality of fictions over against the unreality of descriptions of the actual. Above all we should choose carefully works of such strength and complexity that they force our attention into the symbolic mode and hold it there. Lesser works do not deserve our full attention: they will cheat us by letting us have our own way too easily. Acquaintance is easy enough to arrange, yet the shock of personal discovery must somehow never be destroyed.

This is really a labyrinth, but that's where the thread leads. In such a pass, at the present time, I'm not sure what sort of results we could guarantee—if any; except that we can be reasonably sure that there will always be a few innocents and crackpots to follow Tom Piper's whistle. As instructors we can at least take stock of our individual resources and decide up to what level we can work with confidence, without doing serious (i.e., erosive) damage, making sure that if we are deflecting we are doing so deliberately, and say so. There is of course no one "answer," in "technique": the work under inquiry commands the method of inquiry—which is what "method" means; we need to make that clear too.

Whether it is possible for any one person to achieve what I am talking about I am not sure; but I am confident that, given some vital sense of direction, some sense of the nucleus that will energize whatever we undertake—no matter how minute or even (on the face of it) detached from the nucleus—we can conduct our work at all levels with success, leaving deposits of the solid verbal footing from which a person cannot easily be dislodged. I often wish that there had never been "the New Criticism", splendid, rich, and penetrating though its best results have been; I wish it were issued with instructions, not on *how*, but on *when* and how much; it offers possibilities, it does not provide answers, and it can lead to barren ends. Indeed, in tracing this thread—or even if we are prepared to go no further than to hang on—our concern must be for fruitful questions, not for answers. When literary studies propose only formulated answers, routine "techniques", and judgments that are expected to be repeated by those who have not discovered and shaped them for themselves, the thread has indeed been lost and the study of letters has come to a dead end.

NOTES

1 Since writing this essay I have noticed in the writing of educationists a sudden eruption of the word "numeracy"—which, I suppose, by loose

analogy means the ability to add and subtract (a mystery that even navigators by tradition seldom master). In such grand vestments now creep the three R's, under a new name, with added bleach.

2   Cf. *The Letters of Mercurius* (London, 1970), p. 46: "Dr Chadwick is held by all to be a man of sense and learning . . . as also an excellent preacher, able to put together an English sentence, with subject, verb and syntax, which is rare enough in these illiterate days, and would doubtless do much good to the young, were they not artfully discouraged from hearing him."

3   In my family, my mother was fond of reading aloud to us when we were children. In the summer, on an island on Devil Lake, a favourite place to read was a little glade by the water. Sometimes an old groundhog who lived at the edge of the glade would clamber out of his burrow and listen "motionless and still" as though, even in a world haunted by the white-throated sparrow, the whisky-jack, and the loon, the sound of my mother's voice reading was a marvel not to be missed.

4   A pianist can learn agility at the keyboard by practising scales and arpeggios with increasing precision and velocity; he can work at "*études*", preferably those of Chopin, Brahms, and Bartok, which combine musical interest with concentrated technical difficulty; he can work at compositions of high musical quality and sort out the technical difficulties as they turn up. In writing (except in some kinds of verse) we cannot "practise" in so direct a way, and it is very difficult to contrive technical exercises that will develop competence in writing. Probably the nearest we can get is in a patient study of the dynamics of any writing we admire, and an attempt to match the quality of it. But writing will come to life only if the writer cares about what he is writing; and parody is too subtle a matter for weak heads.

Is Your English Destroying Your Image?
MICHAEL HORNYANSKY

When I let it slip among ordinary company that I'm a professor of English, you can guess what the reaction is: "Oh-oh," they say with nervous smiles, "I'd better watch my language." No use explaining that I don't teach composition. If English professors hit the front page, or confront public awareness at all, it's not when they have had profound or brilliant ideas about literature, but when they are testily muttering that their latest crop of freshmen can neither read nor write. And the truth is, of course, that we are—we must be—concerned with language. It is the medium both of the works we study, and of our attempts to teach it. If language should decay far enough, the study of literature becomes difficult or impossible. I won't play for headlines by pretending this is the condition we have reached; but such a condition is at least imaginable, as things are going. So I worry a good deal about language, myself. And I think the most useful way to put my worries before you is to pursue that automatic reaction: "Oh-oh, I'd better watch my language."

It's a touchy area. People are as anxious about the impression their words make as they are about their clothes or their faces or their waistlines. If you catch someone in an error, he is mortified. If you suggest he doesn't speak well, you wound his vanity as sharply as if you claim he has no sense of humour. Sniping at other people's mistakes is a favourite sport of those who write letters to the *Globe and Mail*; and there are always other correspondents to jeer at the snipers. And even when there are no English teachers (official or amateur) within earshot, private citizens go on fretting over what words to use, and whether they're using them properly. I know of a group which spent hours wrangling over whether a certain person should be described as *responsible* for the task assigned to him, or whether that didn't seem to wag the finger at him needlessly. They finally settled on *accountable* instead—a word in fashion these days, but one which to my mind conveys a good deal less personal dignity and freedom than *responsible* does. That's how it often goes: the questions we're least certain about are the ones that arouse our stronger feelings. And when it comes to language, most of us are uncertain. The frequency of little check-up phrases in our normal speech—"you know? eh? like? see what I mean?"—is a symptom not so much of sloppiness, but of concern about whether we're getting through.

This is why I thought of offering some helpful hints. I don't aim to give you a lesson in grammar. Think of this chapter as an essay in linguistic psychology, not in rules. Remember my title: "Is your English destroying your image?" I put it that way not to be cute or disarming, but because that's the form our anxiety takes. I shall be asking not just what errors we make, but why we make them, and how they affect our view of each other; and after that, how to set about improving matters. To tell you that this is Right and that is Wrong (even if I had the confidence to do so) wouldn't be much help, anyway. Far better in the long run to try to understand why some things work and others don't—so we can judge for ourselves instead of carrying around a list of lapses. I say "we" because I talk for a living, and I am reminded daily of how my words can undermine rapport, or on good days virtually magic people into understanding me. I dare to advise you not because I'm a professor, but because I've been there, and I have some practical knowledge of what can go wrong and how to cure it.

If I am to write about mistakes in our use of language, I had best begin by establishing what makes a mistake—what standards to measure by. There are two possible misconceptions here. At one extreme is the idea of Correctness. Some people still hold to the notion that there is such a thing as Correct English: the King's English, possibly the Queen's, existing as a heavenly paradigm to which only educated people and professors have access. (Francophones are even more prone to think of Correct French, because they have an official Academy to act as its guardian and legislator; but as they are beginning to discover, their hopes are misplaced.) There are several reasons why this mystical notion won't do. One is that educated people—even teachers; even, heaven knows, Her Majesty—do not always speak well. How can we be certain when to follow them? Worse still, the belief that a correct pattern exists can become, in a curious way, a cause of errors: for the people who most firmly believe in the King's English are usually hazy about *what precisely it is*, and in their anxiety to be proper they lean over backwards, into slips that would not befall a more natural stance. No, the idea of Correct English has at best a social validity. By speaking like the Queen you may prove your loyalty and your place in society, but you do not exempt yourself from error. In fact there is no enduring pattern of correctness. As most people have come to realize, language changes, constantly and irresistibly—and correctness, if it's a workable idea at all, must change too. The purists are remembered as quaint defenders of the last ditch: like Jonathan Swift, rejecting the uncouth expression "mob", because all right-speaking people knew it should be *mobile vulgus*. (Swift also won a few, however. See Dwight Macdonald, *Against the American Grain*, Vintage, 1962, p. 323.) Or like the person who answers the telephone with "Hello: it is I, Clifton Webb."

At the other extreme is the notion that since language constantly changes, then anything goes—there are no rules at all, Usage is king. It will not be so easy to persuade you that this too is a misconception. The barometer of our times is set at Change. A recent letter to the *Globe* condemns the declared policy of Ontario's Minister of Education to return to the 3 Rs: "[he] invites our children to take firm, confident steps backward into the future. Pity." (Ray MacLain, *Globe*, 25 Feb. 1975.) The CBC's news-readers, once modestly reliable (meaning they could be counted on to apologize for errors), have lost their supervisor of broadcast language, and now commit cheerfully such barbarisms as "It sounds like he's going to reform." This is the age of Humpty Dumpty, who claimed that words meant what he wanted them to mean; it was simply a question of who was to be master. You will recall what happened to Humpty Dumpty. But his fragmented soul is still with us: it lives on in the third edition of Webster's *New International Dictionary* (1961), which makes no attempt to distinguish acceptable usage from colloquial, slang, or illiterate. "If it is used, it is usage": that is Webster's principle in a nutshell—and a nutshell is where it belongs. To see the enterprise mercilessly analysed, read Dwight Macdonald's patient and savage review called "The String Untuned". (Reprinted in *Against the American Grain*, p. 289.)

Those who appeal to usage as the final arbiter seem to march under the banners of Life and Progress. In fact they are making a mystique of change, supposing that since it is normal it must also be good. Happily, the letter columns of the newspaper do feature other correspondents, who realize that change may be not growth but decay, and that mere growth is not always welcome, in language as in life.

> It is fatuous (publicists please note: this word does not yet mean stout or plump) to argue that the language is undergoing positive and dynamic change in the hands of our public figures. Only fools would unreservedly maintain so.
>
> (C. C. J. Bond, *Globe*, 17 Feb. 1975)

(I expect a later correspondent observed that it wasn't their *hands* but their mouths that did the damage.) Not all change is progress. Some of it has to be resisted, and when possible reversed. If the last ditch needs defending, I'll take my place alongside Sam Johnson:

> If the changes we fear be thus irresistible, what remains but to acquiesce with silence, as in the other insurmountable distresses of humanity? It remains that we retard what we cannot repel, that we palliate what we cannot cure.
>
> (Preface to the *Dictionary*)

That final sentence, by the way, is a grand example of how to project the image of Doctor Johnson.

But I don't think the situation's quite so desperate. One can take account of a flood without drowning in it or becoming flotsam. Call me Noah. I think that even for a language in flux, certain firm criteria can be proposed. They are based on this assumption: *that language is a means of giving a precise pattern to thought and feeling, and a means of conveying that pattern to other people*. I do not claim this is the only assumption possible. Language is commonly used for several other purposes. It is used to make up for, or disguise, the absence of thought, and to mask one's feelings; and it may communicate nothing more than a soothing assurance of togetherness. But for this purpose, as politicians (and some married couples) know, almost any noise will do: there is no question of Good Usage, or Correctness. Language can also be used deliberately to deceive. Here the question is skill, not usage. An assumption more likely to mislead us is one I've already alluded to: that language is above all a badge of social position. Here usage does matter. But which usage is socially acceptable (and that is the criterion, even though it may be called "proper"; for instance, there was a time not long ago when saying *ain't* and droppin' your final g's were the signals of aristocratic talk)—that is a question that varies rapidly with time and place, so that no general criteria can be proposed. One has to play it by ear, or find a member of the desired club who knows the passwords and is willing to tell, like Nancy Mitford or Henry Higgins.

My concern, however, is language that communicates thought and feeling—the kind I am trying to use now. This is where it makes some sense to apply standards of proper, or good, usage. And the standards I propose are these three: *Clarity, Impact,* and *Idiom.* (Not *correctness*, as you see, but bases upon which we can decide what *is* correct, or at least what is preferable.) *Is it clear? Does it hit home? Is it English?* These are the only reasonable standards I can find; and since they apply, so far as I can see, to a language at any time, they need not be surrendered under the pressure of change.

Clarity is of course what we aim at when we want to express thoughts with cool precision: easy to talk about, hard to achieve. It will govern our choice of words, the design of our sentences and arguments. It is the standard that causes Humpty Dumpty to fall, or at least to remain babbling to himself in a private lingo: for we all should know from experience that if we use words arbitrarily, instead of in their agreed senses, we will not make contact. Clarity also governs the gradual smoothing out of inflections (that is, variations in the form of a word according to its grammatical function, like *who/whose/whom*). Presumably it was in the interest of clarity that primitive tongues established remarkably complex systems of inflection (and of syntax generally); but as the history of our language shows, the complicated patterns that make French or German (or Latin) hard for us to learn have not proved necessary for speakers of English. Indeed, if clarity were our sole guide, we might wind up saying *he loves she*, or *you did hurt I*—in fact we're well on the way to that. But I proposed three standards, not one.

The second of them, *Impact*, is our aim when we want to persuade or impress rather than to inform; when instead of taking our cue from logicians or astronauts, we speak like witch doctors, advertising men, or poets. We know that by choosing certain words over others (not because they're more exact, but because they're fresh, arresting, expressive of likeness not essence) and by combining them in unexpected ways, we can charge our speech, and make it strike home as clarity alone would never do. We say, "John's a tiger." In point of literal fact, John is a featherless biped rather short on hair; but one simple and overused metaphor conveys more about how he *strikes* us than would paragraphs of careful analysis. Again, however, impact by itself is not a sufficient guide. Without clarity squeezing the brakes, impact may run riot and collapse into nonsense or mumbojumbo—as poetry has been known to do, or advertising slogans, or slang. And there is no dull thud to compare with yesterday's impact: I mean, *lamp the frail with the solo cheater, will ya? Bro-ther, she just don't connect*. And neither do you, I imagine—though thirty years ago you would have followed me without trouble.

The mention of slang brings us at once to my third criterion, the tricky one: *Idiom*. I might have defined idiom as "the sense of linguistic fitness possessed by one who has grown up speaking a language"—I might have defined it so, if I hadn't learned better from experience. For I teach third- and fourth-generation Canadians who have spoken English (sort of, you know?) since the crib, yet who have no more sense of English idiom than a recent arrival from the Old Country.

You might suspect that under the mask of idiom I am actually dragging correctness in through the back door. Not so. By asking "Is it English?" I do not mean to ask, is it *proper* English—but whether it is English rather than Transylvanian or Tagalog. Thus, we accept as idiomatic "That's all right by me", but do not (yet) accept "By me you are lovely" (which is fine in German). This also demonstrates that idiom is not equivalent to usage: for there are some usages which although clear, and even fashionable for a while, are ultimately rejected as unidiomatic. By idiom in general, then, we mean the ground rules or *customs* of a particular language, developed over the centuries—no matter whether all its speakers know them or not. These rules (like those that distinguish Canadian football from the American and the British games) set limits to the ways in which a given language works, the kinds of "play" that are legitimate—limits that may have little connection with clarity or force; indeed, they almost set up an independent standard for clarity and force. I would suppose that idiom arises from the same motive as slang: a sense of clubbiness, of "the way we do things" (as against the way outsiders—aliens and foreigners—handle them). The difference is that in slang the club is narrower, the motive keener and more restless, so that fashions in slang change very swiftly—as I shall be noting later on. Idioms do change, but not too far and not too fast, for the club they signify is the main coherent body of speakers of language; and the changes are not mindless accidents (as the proponents of Usage seem at times to suggest) but organic and adaptive. We may be able to explain why particular idioms arise; but they are unlikely to be logical or even grammatical, even in French. In short, idiom is the human side of language, balancing between the poles of emotion and reason (as we ourselves do). The idiomatic speaker recognizes that his language has a living identity. He will be so intimately acquainted with its every nerve and fibre that he knows instinctively how it prefers to behave, and will not force it into unnatural postures.

You see that these three standards of good usage are flexible, not absolute. I trust you will find them reasonable, not arbitrary. And you will realize that they work together in odd and unpredictable ways, so that we cannot apply them unimaginatively or with stickling accuracy. It should also be even clearer why I have chosen to discuss not "the mistakes we make in grammar," but (using the adman's idiom) the linguistic images we project: there are territories where grammar has little relevance. I shall assume that for the most part we *hope* to project the image of educated people—an image of clear thought, charged only with the emotion we consciously intend, and conveying by the way a perfect familiarity with the structure and temperament of our language. In short, the picture of people in control of themselves. But the fact is that we very easily go wrong, in the sense of transmitting unexpected and damaging pictures of ourselves, because our language is not wholly under our control. My main concern, therefore, will be the images we actually do project without intending them.

I'll start with a group of images that convey—well, I was going to say Ignorance, which has a nice honest ring to it; but it's not quite adequate, because in a way all the faulty images involve some ignorance. Let's try a few, and see what they have in common. First, the image of the Illiterate (the uneducated, the rube, the rough diamond). It is the most obvious, and should be the simplest to avoid; yet even in the guarded speech of Academe you may catch such expressions as *irregardless, equally as good as, a little ways further on, with regards to, anyways, most everyone*. I do not include in this category expressions which are linguistically O.K. but socially taboo, like *ain't*. I am pointing only at those which violate one or more of my three criteria, principally the test of clarity. For instance, *with regards to* is unclear because it's ambiguous; it belongs at the end of a letter—with regards to Auntie May, Uncle Harry, and Roger the dog—whereas *with regard to* is rather pompous but clear enough. A complaint about *how bad prisoners are treated* (on CBC Viewpoint, 17 March 1975) leaves us confused between bad prisoners and bad treatment. Or take the formula beloved of the newspaper reader: "Hey, I see where René Lévesque's been elected." *Where*? Well, in his constituency; where else?

These are the obvious errors, the ones that schoolteachers have hammered away at for years. Then why are they as common as ever? Partly carelessness, no doubt, and partly, yes, ignorance, for education of any kind is the perpetual caulking of a leaky boat. But I think there is another reason, much stronger than these: inverted snobbery, the wish not to seem better than anyone else. Illiteracy is an image often assumed for this purpose. When a mechanic reports that "she's runnin' real good," it takes a pretty stuffy professor to reply that "it is indeed running rather well." Instead, with tact and democratic sympathy, he agrees that she sure is running purty smooth, by the sound of her. For he knows that grammar varies inversely as virility; and that if you *continue on* down to the stadium, you'll find that nobody there plays well. He-men play *good*. In that quaint dream of pioneer society to which we North Americans so desperately cling, careful speech is the mark of the sissy or the dude or the schoolmarm (who isn't even a Real Woman until she takes off her glasses and drops her g's). Fluency is suspect, suggesting a flim-flam man at work: which is one reason why our politicians burble, haw, and drone.

As I shall bear witness, I have every sympathy with changing your tune to fit your environment. Boswell's memory of Dr. Johnson, addressing a baffled stable-boy as if he were a meeting of the Royal Society, should be a warning to us all. By all means let us keep up the fiction that we're all simple country folk—if it makes us talk simply, it can't be all bad. But there are times in the real world when talking like Gary Cooper does not meet the necessities of the situation. Another risk: if we don't watch what we're doing, our assumed illiteracies may become chronic, and we'll find ourselves (at a Home and School meeting, say) unable to shift gears. For instance, in the past ten years it has become chic among fairly well-educated British journalists and authors to imitate the laxer kind of Americanism—at first in a campy way, half-sneering, but then trendily, and at last unconsciously. So that now you find columnists in the London *Observer* "spending money like it was going out of style" (as it is, of course; but the locution doesn't harmonize with the rest of their column), and authors, *veddy* conservative and precise by nature, striving for the Chandler image and descending to vilely un-British depths:

> This man had hooked her *helplessly*. Who now talked *like* he did and sometimes more wildly. (My italics)

That's from a thriller by William Haggard (*The Bitter Harvest*, Cassell, 1971, p. 142), whose normal style is literate and careful. By odd contrast, I find two American authors of fast, tough thrillers being surprisingly choosy. Ross Macdonald has his hero (Lew Archer, in *The Moving Target*) announce that he's the "new-type detective", and soften the illiteracy by carefully putting in the hyphen. John D. MacDonald (in the Travis McGee books) is liberal with illiteracies, but uses *horrid* either in the British slang sense or, it may be, in the original Latin sense.

All right: I've oversimplified the North American scene. Pioneer simplicity is not our only dream, or even the dominant one. We have a strong contrary tendency, to inflate and load down our language with impressive sonorities: to talk like judges and senators rather than cowboys. And for this too there is a trap. It's a subspecies of Illiteracy: call it the image of a *narrow education*—specifically, an education short on etymology in Latin, Greek, or even English. I am not saying educated people all ought to know Latin or Greek (though I opine wistfully that if they knew one or the other, preferably a bit of Latin, they would use English in a less wooden way). I am saying that when English words are imported from those tongues, it is useful to know what they've brought with them. The expression *continue on*, for example, occurs even in ivied towers; but it doesn't take a classical education to know that *continue* means to *go on*, not just *go*. The word *major* is generally believed to be a powerful synonym for *big* or *important* or *significant*, so that one hears visiting pundits speak continually of Very Major Problems. At the risk of offending them, let me spell it out: *major* began life as a Latin comparative, and the comparative flavour is still there—it means either *bigger* or *rather big*. And neither a "very bigger problem" nor a "very rather big" one makes much sense. Or take four common words which afford a handy test of a man's breadth of education: *phenomenon, criterion, stratum,* and *medium*. Two are Greek, two are Latin; and they behave accordingly when they become plural. Yet I have heard a respected literary scholar in a national broadcast refer to "an interesting phenomena"; to appreciate the full effect of this, imagine hearing it in the voice of W. C. Fields. *Criteria* and *strata* are likewise frequently used as if they were singular. They were not; they are not. And everyone these days knows (without pausing to think about it) that *a media* is something you communicate to the masses with. In fact there is only one Media: it's where the Medes came from.

Now I grant you there is a line past which this sort of objection becomes precious. But I think we ought to draw that line with care. For instance, the spelling (and pronunciation) *chaise lounge* is a peculiarly insensitive gaffe to allow ourselves in a country with Francophone leanings. And on our own monoglot ground, "between the three of us" should sound wrong (to the idiomatic ear) not because grammarians say so, but because *between* was once *bi tweyen*, or *by two*. "By two the three of us" becomes a study in vulgar fractions. Keep *between* for intimate moments *à deux*; it was made for you and me.

Pretentiousness in our speech is bedevilled by other dangers. Consider the image of Fogginess, shrouding the speaker who would like to make clear distinctions but has forgotten how. He says, "To me this is a semantic problem in that the confusion centres around a verbal misunderstanding." Sounds impressive at first; but there are three dead give-aways. *Semantic* is a favourite word with people who can't convey their meaning and want to shift the blame. *In that*, as my students seem to know by instinct, is a dandy way of implying a subtle connection when you are actually going to repeat the identical idea in different words. And *centres around*, as the critics have pointed out long ago, betrays a confusion in basic geometry. Nothing centres *around* anything. Things may *revolve around*, if they must, but if they centre at all, they centre *on*.

A frequent cause of fog is choosing the wrong word in a pair: *continual* for *continuous, differential* for *different, lie* for *lay*, and so on. (For a charmingly outdated list, see Fowler's *Dictionary of Modern English Usage* under "Pairs and Snares".) The normal result is haziness of outline, but at times it may be something more risky: "Oh, I was just laying around." One of Richard Needham's correspondents cripples his indignation with this kind of error:

> When the Government takes over Bell Canada—as *regretfully* they will one day—does anyone seriously think that either service or costs will improve?
>
> (Needham, *Globe*, 25 Feb. 1975; my italics)

Regretfully imputes an emotion to the government which does it too much honour. And come to think of it, what does a cost do when it improves? *Nutritional*, much in people's mouths lately, is either ambiguous or an unnecessary variant of *nutritious*. And *disinterested* has virtually lost its useful idiomatic meaning of "impartial". I have had people tell me no thanks, they were disinterested in football—the perfect qualification for a referee, but I was looking for someone to use the other ticket. The most common confusion is that of *infer* with *imply*. I am quite aware that even a good dictionary gives *imply* as one meaning of *infer*. That simply proves you cannot always trust dictionaries. The words are so obviously meant for each other as opposites (the speaker *folding in* an extra meaning, the listener *taking it in*) that I mistrust the judgment of a person who mixes them up. Perhaps the most noticeable symptom of the foggy speaker, or woofer, is addiction to *facts* and *factors*. He speaks of a *fact* when he means an opinion, a risk, or a possibility; and he says *factor* when he senses that something is important but doesn't know how or why. Allow me to offer you a brief cautionary tale about factors. Originally, you recall, factors were the men in charge of trading posts for the Hudson's Bay Company; but they proved to be such willing workers that when the Company retrenched, the factors went forth and multiplied—and became factotums.

Remember that I am speaking of inadvertent fogginess. Conscious or deliberate blurring of outlines belongs to propaganda. No doubt we condition ourselves to be its victims if we use, or even listen to without comment, such expressions as "the military *internationalization* of Arab oil" (proposed in a bloodless way by a U.S. commentator not long ago). Others have pointed out that the use of woolly abstractions (*defoliation* being one of the mildest) to disguise ugly particulars is one of the sorry consequences of the war in Vietnam. A senior American journalist (Edwin Newman, in *Strictly Speaking*, Bobbs-Merrill, 1974) has been so appalled by it as to cry out against the murder of the language; once *that* murder is accomplished, it makes others easier to excuse or condone. I think it is fair to describe this as the Nazification of English. It is the process that caused George Steiner virtually to give up on language altogether (see *Language and Silence*, Atheneum, 1967). I shall content myself with this brief reminder that the seemingly trivial effects which I am discussing do border on sombre realities; and that if I choose to play it light, that's because lightness makes for more clarity than does indignation.

Close kin to fogginess is the image of what appears to be the absent mind—which cannot remember how it started, three words ago. It goes to pieces over what the grammarian calls Agreement, because it forgets both the person and the number of what it was talking about. Try this: "Bell Canada refunds your money without question if you tell *them* you reached a wrong number." How many Bells are ringing here, and for whom? Or this advice from a TV golfer: "*a person* of short stature should take care in grasping *their* club. *He (or she)* should grasp *their* club firmly . . ." Who grasps whose club, exactly? Does the owner know? But I'm being unfair. The difficulty in both cases has to do with pronouns which won't do precisely the job we intend. For one thing, speakers of English feel the lack of a genuinely impersonal pronoun like *on* in French: the nearest we can come to *on dit* is "they say", or "it is said". Actually *on* derives from *homo*, the Latin word for *man*—just as the impersonal *man* in German is connected with the masculine *Mann*—but in French the derivation is so masked by time that I doubt if most French speakers recognize it. Our convention in English is that *he* does duty for both *he* and *she*, and can be used impersonally. Evidently this was felt to be awkward or misleading even before the voice of women was heard, and so it has been replaced by something even more awkward, the explicit *he or she*, or in some places *s/he*. English does have the alternative *one*: "one should grasp one's club . . ." But one hesitates to do much of this, largely because the British are prone to use *one* as a coy or playful self-effacement for *I* and *me*. Perhaps you recall the courtship of Princess Anne, when in interviews with the press Captain Phillips proved far too well-bred to draw attention to himself, and therefore became *oneself*: one belonged, one gathered, to the nation. . . . When the princess replied in kind, the two dear things practically faded from sight.

In such a cleft stick, what is the average speaker to do? I'd advise him to rely on *they*, and to avoid awkwardness by carrying the plural through: for instance "When you tell *them*, Bell

Canada *refund* your money.'' Besides, it's good psychology to treat corporate entities like Bell or the government as plurals rather than monoliths; it helps remind us they're made of people, and can be reached. Another device is to stop being so impersonal, and use *you* instead: "If you're short, grasp your club." And try to stay out of ambiguous situations like "Everybody thinks they're in charge."

There are clearer test cases for this image (the absent or sieve-like mind). One is the formula so many people find irresistible, especially politicians talking to us on television: *as far as [X] is concerned* . . . By beginning the formula, one stands pledged to follow through, eventually, with the rest of it. But usually the windbag who starts out with a really big X, "*as far as* low-rental housing developments and their location within the metropolitan area within the foreseeable future, by which I mean until the next election, ah . . ."—well, such a man is lost. He's forgotten his launch platform, and we could wait for weeks without hearing a whisper of *concern*. Strip it down, and he's left with a silly dangle—"as far as housing." (If this is your problem, let me recommend some safe and easy alternatives, like *as for*, *as to*, *concerning*, or even *with regard to*. You might play it Edward G. Robinson style: "You wanna know about housing? Okay, I'll tell ya.") The other telltale habit is the mixed metaphor, as in "We promise to *harness* those *bottlenecks*," or (to quote an Ontario cabinet minister) "One bad apple can give the whole thing a black eye." Perhaps it is too kind to blame these unconscious jokes on forgetfulness. A truer explanation may be that such speakers are totally deaf to metaphor, and largely deaf to wit as well. A *bad apple* no longer carries for them any memory of fruit, it's just a phrase filed under Crook or Rascal (in the same fashion, I suspect, as jokes are filed under subject headings and "injected" into their speeches at apt moments).

More seductive (and for the discriminating judge, more damaging) is the image of would-be elegance, which produces Genteelisms, like *between you and I*. A little grammar is a dangerous thing. The cause of trouble is something I've already mentioned: a misplaced faith in the King's English, a striving to be correct at any cost. The effect is the same as lifting one's pinkie at a formal teacup—exaggerated propriety, more ludicrous than honest ignorance. (The British used to have a word for such behaviour: *refained*. The Refained Speaker is so anxious not to sound like a Cockney—"the rine in Spine styes minely in the pline"—that he converts *all* his i's to a's; so he cannot even say *refined*.) The psychology of such errors is plain enough. Because one got scolded as a child for saying "Us kids are going to the store" or "Me and Jimmy got whipped," one assumes that *us* and *me* are always wrong. The result is Refained Grammar, like *between you and I*. Educated people, I suppose because they are conscious of having to set an example, are specially prone to this trick. I have heard my own colleagues say, "This report was prepared by Professor Perkins and I." If they reversed the order and said "by I, and Professor Perkins" they might notice the error—but they wouldn't do that, it would be impolite to put themselves first. Or take "you must be tolerant with *we* ordinary mortals": that came from an instructor in English. (No, an English department does not have faultless speakers; what makes it unusual is that the mistakes are more likely to be noticed.) A brilliant philosopher of my acquaintance will construct noble sentences rotten at the core: "Distinctions of this order are of major importance to he who cares about logic." *Him who cares about his image, I bid take note.* And then there is the *whom* problem, which the *New Yorker* used to love so well. "The lady in question, whom our informants advise us is known as Lou . . ." Whom is? Well, in my view *whom* is a booby trap. My advice is to drop it. It's on the way out, and the tactful speaker may avoid it even when it's technically correct. A question like "Whom do you mean?" really deserves the answer it gets from Pogo: "*Youm*, that's whom."

Now for a cluster of images which offend chiefly against Idiom. In doing so they also becloud clarity and muffle impact, for my three criteria intertwine so subtly that to hurt one is to hurt all. This fact strikes me as good presumptive evidence of having hit upon the right criteria.

The image which I confess most quickly riles me is that of the Pseudo-Immigrant—the speaker who blurs or disfigures the native idiom. The irony here, as I've already suggested, is that this speaker has known no other idiom since birth. *Genuine* foreigners who learn our language from the ground up can, of course, put him to shame—as Conrad and Nabokov have demonstrated for the written word. It is not always easy to decide what is idiomatically wrong, and what is merely illiterate or malaprop. What to do with this sentence, spoken by an old friend of mine: "We are enough individuals that we could never expect unanimity"? *Hein*? Does he mean, "There are so many of us that somebody is bound to vote No", or does he mean, "We're so different we'll never agree completely"? I suspect, but I can't be sure. What I do feel sure of is that he's not at home in the language. And that's what he has in common with the speaker who gets his meaning across but sounds all wrong: "If you would have broken that tackle, you may have gone all the way." A clear case of the conditional so *imperfect* as to be totally loused up; and a very common blooper among sports announcers and "colour commentators".

The most treacherous ground of all may be the use of prepositions, for it is here that English idiom hits a peak of unreason. Small wonder that they drive foreigners to despair; but a daily wonder that they also baffle a great many native high-school graduates, who speak of having *a preference to blondes* (or sometimes *an attraction for blondes*, lucky them), *an interest for snowmobiles* (let the finance company handle that one), or *an insight of the problem* (part of the problem being that they will spell "insight" with a C). And the chances are strong that they will compound the crime by leaning significantly on the faulty preposition: "an insight OF the problem." That's a habit they learn from their elders, who may choose the right prepositions but then try to project an image of profound deliberation by weighing them down: "I don't have detailed data ON that, Chief, but my office can get the figures FOR you." A clear and simple case of lead-swinging.

The pseudo-foreign flavour comes back strong with the unidiomatic choice of tenses, as in "Did you have dinner yet?" Did I have dinner yet: let a man ask me that but once, and his image by me is irreparably flawed. A host who understood English idiom (and human feelings) would ask, "Have you had dinner?"—by which he would delicately but unmistakably convey that there was (yet) more in the kitchen. By replying, "No, I haven't," I would likewise convey implicitly that although I had not dined up to that moment, I lived in hopes. That is what is so perfectly splendid about the Present Perfect. But our Alien wouldn't understand; in his world, I eat or I ate. And if I reply in the only language he knows, "No I didn't," it's all over and done with—dinner has fled, there is nothing but bleakness and starvation. I've *had it*.

This did-you-have-dinner-yet is the thin end of a great clumsy wedge. Pretty soon we'll be saying things like "Are you in this country since long?" and "Yes, my god, I was here since I am a child." It's full of rich ethnic flavour, no doubt, the stuff of which warm situation comedies are made, but it sticks in my craw. Why should I have these uncouth alien notions of time and sequence thrust upon me, when English idiom allows me to specify time within time, before time, and after time with infinite subtlety and satisfaction? Take for example this snatch of song from *Camelot*:

If ever you would leave me,
It wouldn't be in springtime.

I object to Mr. Lerner's lyrics because they warp idiom, and therefore wreak confusion. What he means, in his schmaltzy Transylvanian heart, is, "If ever you *should* leave me"—that is, it hasn't happened so far, and with luck it may not happen at all. But he says instead, "If ever you *would*", which conveys something precise but quite different. To the idiomatic ear, it suggests a pitiable stretch of Time Past (*not* time to come), during which You were accustomed in a habitual and rather heartless way to leave Me—though not (one infers) for very long at a time, and never (one knows) between March and June. Given that opening clause, the verse ought really to unfold like this:

If ever you would leave me
I knew you had a reason—
Like wishing to deceive me,
Or wild duck's being in season.

Another form of idiom-smashing that attracts educated people is what I call Literalism. This is the habit of using a word for what it looks as if it should mean, rather than what idiom has brought it to mean. You already know my views about *presently*. A man who asks me for a job, and says he is *presently completing* his thesis, already has one strike against him. Sure, to a foreign eye it appears to mean "at present". But as speakers of English we inherit the English genius for delay (as Samuel Johnson observes, "languages are the pedigree of nations"), and when we say "any moment now" we mean tomorrow. Once upon a time there was a good old four-letter word, *anon*, which meant *in one*, *at once*; but it soon became clear that you couldn't trust a tapster who said "anon, anon, sir," so somebody introduced the precise Latin word *presently* to mean *now*, and all was plain for a while. But the barman dragged his heels again, and *presently* became *some other time*. Now, if you want prompt action, you must specify *immediately*, or *on the double*. And if you mean *at present*, why not say it? It takes not one millisecond longer.

A slightly different case is presented by *momentarily* and *hopefully*. The idiomatic meaning—the only meaning given in a reliable Scottish dictionary, *Chambers's*—of *momentarily* is "for a moment, briefly", as in the poignant phrase, "momentarily she was mine; then, alas, she slipped through my fingers and was gone." (Feminist readers will substitute *he*.) So the fellow who says, with eyes aglow, "She will be mine momentarily," may be in for a big disappointment—and anyone who talks that way deserves it. He means *in a moment*. Other people abuse the word to mean *at the moment*. Thorton Wilder has even used it to mean *by the moment*, or *moment by moment*—and he does it in a stage direction, so there's no way out:

The children lean forward and all watch the funeral in silence growing *momentarily* more *solemnized*.
(*The Long Christmas Dinner*, Harper and Row, 1963, p. 95)

He wrote that in 1931. *Solemnized* is a bonus boner, which happily hasn't caught on. It will do fine as a reminder that if we wish to keep our language undefiled, we cannot always trust reputable authors.

As for *hopefully*, it appears to be a more recent immigrant from Germany by way of New York. But in German it was *hoffentlich*, and meant "hopingly": a detached, impersonal adverb that English hasn't invented yet—because English has other ways of being impersonal. If we want to say "hopingly" we can use *I hope, one hopes*, or even *it is to be hoped*, which ought to be impersonal enough for anybody. When we say *hopefully*, we mean in our idiomatic way that whoever is speaking or acting is *full of hope*. A famous example: "it is better to travel hopefully than to arrive." The man who tells us "She will be mine, hopefully, within the week (*ja*)" may thus be a decent modest fellow by German standards; but in English he's taking an awful lot for granted, for he implies that it's *she* who is so keen. And when the Hon. John Turner advertises in a British newspaper that his four children "require a kind and loving nannie [*sic*], *hopefully* with previous experience," any nanny worth her salt will perceive that it isn't only the children who need her help.

Momentarily, then, is misused through literalness and una-wareness of idiom, as is *presently* (examples of what *Chambers's Dictionary* calls folk-etymology, or "popular unscientific attempts at etymology"). But the case of *hopefully* suggests an additional dimension, at least to my sensibilities. I connect it first with other personal adverbs misapplied in a general, impersonal way—*regretfully* instead of *regrettably*, maybe *pitifully* a while ago. What's happening here is the transfer of a private emotion to "the public sector", so that its source can no longer be traced. No wonder these usages prevail among businessmen and politicians. *Who* is full of hope, or regret, or pity? Not me, not you, not anyone: it has been shifted into a quality of the objective environment, as if there were a something, a process out there which had taken on sentience. Is it fanciful to connect this with other hints of personal abdication, such as is implied by *a decision-making process*? If a process can feel hope or regret, it can surely make decisions. And when decisions are made by a process, no single person can be held responsible; it *happens*, objectively and inexorably, like the march of history. No doubt, the original motive for the phrase was to imply (without promising) the breaking down of tyranny, the sharing of decisions by a number of persons (as in *participatory democracy*). In practice, however, both phrases are cop-outs, and in neither case does anything get decided or done. These are the phrases of people who have no policies, no self-reliance, no confidence—and who deserve none. The only way to bring about decisions and actions is to find some *person* who can *decide*, and *act*.

What disturbs me more than the standard lies and distortions of such propaganda language is this curious appearance of an inexorable process *out there*, because in common parlance we do not merely take part in a *decision-making process*, we are *plugged into it*. Immediately I am reminded of other locutions with the same metallic flavour: "This really turns me on, you know?", and, "Man, she turns me off" (which isn't an action by "her", exactly, nor yet a response by "me"). Who, or what, is speaking? *Where is the switch?* The image I detect here is Mechanism—half surrender to, half propitiation of the great, half-glimpsed machine which we half adore, half fear. By using the language of machines to describe our hopes, actions, reactions, by transferring to a humming external process what was once our private domain of striving, do we placate the Computer Politic, the World Machine, or do we program ourselves for sacrifice? Machines, as I understand them, have languages but no idioms. What I am expressing is not the modern fear that the robots are coming, but the fear that we are *robotizing, dehumanizing, depersonalizing* ourselves through words as ugly as the process they describe.

Another troublesome question under the general head of idiom has to do with the set of sub-idioms we call Slang. There are two opposite causes of concern: whether is it proper to use slang at all, or more commonly the question of *which* slang is fashionable or "in". The motive in both cases is *togetherness* (a piece of manufactured slang which never quite made it), the wish to confirm one's belonging to a group: in the first case the large group, the great club of all those who Speak Properly (and whose slang is called idiom); in the second case the small exclusive group, the tribe of the elite who share a secret attitude (and whose exclusiveness must be assured by continual changes in the password), like adolescents or pop musicians or anglers or astronomers. To those who ask the first question I reply cheerfully, "Yes, by all means use slang—if you know the risks." Those who worry about the second are not likely to ask me, because I am obviously no swinger; all the same, one or two of my random reflections may prove edifying.

Those who ask whether slang is permissible in polite society are really preoccupied with correctness, on which I've already offered my view. Applying my kind of standards, I would repeat that in our democratic, colloquial society you are more likely to be censured for using no slang at all. But of course there are risks in using it too. Some sober groups may find your flip ways unacceptable; argot that suits one milieu may draw sneers in another. My own preference for the simple and colloquial as salt to my discourse leads many of my colleagues to dismiss me as frivolous, unscholarly, simple-minded—a reflection to which I shall return. And slang of all kinds is in constant danger of not being clear, because impact, not clarity, presides at its birth. A current fad leans heavily but ambiguously on the simple word *to*. "To me, he's a wonderful person." (Great, but how does he behave to others?) "To the majority of immigrants, their perception of education is quite different from our own" (a spokesman for the Toronto Board of Education, quoted by Canadian Press, 17 Feb. 1975). Here *to* implies a perception *of a perception*. He means "most immigrants look on education in a way native Canadians don't", but he says, "most immigrants don't look at their perceptions as we would look at *their perceptions*"—which is true, perhaps, but not useful. A short way off is the modish use of *into*: "Yeah, I'm into the hard stuff," "I'm into medieval studies," "I'm into people." The obvious risk is that the literal meaning may overturn the slang one, as with the earnest boy who confides that he's really getting into girls now. Or take the curious American insistence on *human beings* as if they were a species of achievement. "Bruce is a superb human being," they affirm glowingly. (The hell you say; and here I was, expecting a stoat.)

This approaches the image of the Hopeless Square, who keeps treading on verbal land-mines because he is unaware of slang meanings. Scientific colleagues have complained to me of inexplicable merriment in their classes when they speak of a *crude model*; and we all recall the visiting Britisher who apologizes for *knocking up* his hostess at 2 a.m. Words like *cool* and *hot* have a perpetual but fluctuating slang sense: so that Marshall McLuhan's attempt to give them specific content with regard to the media runs into difficulties. The other way to look hopelessly square is to use argot that is out of date (or *old hat*, if you get me). For instance, a few years back *no way* was the all-purpose surfboard of the young, until like so many other passwords it sank from sight. But it did not quite disappear, for adults (in those days when youth could do no wrong) snatched at it eagerly, and have never let go—with the result that instead of being in the swim as they hoped, they are now quaintly stranded on an antique beach.

On the other hand, I observe with an agreeable sense of irony how the whirligig of time brings back the exile. *Groovy*, which I helped to bury 30 years ago, is suddenly alive and well. *Chap*, which in those early days was laughably British and probably a bit effeminate, is now a perfectly normal fella, even in New York. And although *gay* is at the moment unfit for any but its slang use, a fact I deplore, it seems possible that at last *queer* can be reinstated—and perhaps *fruit* as well.

One particular area which I would hesitate to call trendy in itself has undeniably provoked trendy convulsions in language: I mean of course the movement to liberate women. It took me a long time to realize that *consciousness raising* was not a phase of transcendental meditation but a specific manoeuvre in the feminist campaign. And I doubt that *chauvinism* will be fit for its original duty in my lifetime. But the silly edge of this argot shows when the new consciousness starts in on the unsexing of *métiers*. The *Globe* for Valentine's Day carried advertisements for "a Bodyman-woman, a Foreperson and, the most intriguing of all, a Parts man-woman." (Quoted in Letters, 18 Feb. 1975.) Richard Needham notes other transformations: cowboy into cattleperson, bus boy into dining-room attendant, governess into child mentor. Everyone keeps his own list. And because this kind of neurotic fiddling quickly invites a backlash, as we say, everyone keeps a list of put-downs. I have already demonstrated my impartiality, I hope, in various ways. So let me register my objection to the plague of *persons* where hateful sexist English reads *-man*. In

spokesman, chairman, barman, and so on we don't even pronounce it "man", but "mun". I am reminded of a special British
expression in which *person* is not neutral but insulting: "She's
more of a *person*, really . . ." I am also reminded of the ultimate
achievement in desexing language, the invention of a columnist
that would replace *human* with the triumphant neuter *hu-person*.
(And *Mädchen* is neuter, I recall. Do liberated Ger-persons object?)

Trendiness annoys me above all not merely because it is seductive and always has been, but because it seduces us back into the
screwloose religion of change. The man who deplores a return to
the 3 R's as a step back toward the cave is suffering from delirium
trendens. He belongs to the McLuhanite fringe who scream that
print is dead, the book is buried, and citizens of the global village
must be expert in the new mysteries of film and tape and incanta-
tion. I never know how much to blame on the ancient sage
himself, because I'm never sure what he means or how serious he
is. But risking naiveté, let me suggest, to his disciples at least,
that if the universe around the corner is electronic all the way,
then we've got to find someone who can write the *script*, and
someone who can read it, and someone else who can use the
camera properly (the emptiness of handheld scriptless impromptu
inaudible film happenings having at last registered on the most
glazed watcher).

Are we lapsing into barbarism? Will we soon be unable to
communicate except by coos and grunts and formulas? I don't
really think so—though there are portents, dammit: such as my
wife's hitchhiker, a braw school-leaver of nineteen, personable
and polite. When she asked him to find out what was causing the
noisy rattle he checked, diagnosed, and reported, "The uh thing
. . . is, like . . . Uhhh . . ." Aghast, she conferred: did he mean
the back door on the wagon was not properly shut? He heaved a
great smiling sigh of relief. "Yuh," he said, having got through.
No, what I fear is that well before that, we shall have lost touch
with the past. That is the other purpose and glory of language,
which the usage-mongers and the progress-peddlers and the
flux-worshippers forget. The gift of my tongue does not merely

enable me to "interrelate" with my contemporaries; it makes me a citizen of the entire human commonwealth, of an empire across time. I will not exchange that for a wilderness of global villages.

I remember that when I sang "We Three Kings" as a child I repeated the line, "Star with royal beauty *dight*", as generations of children had done before me. Later I learned with pleasure the ancient words to "This Endris Night". But I am hard put to excavate them now. Within one generation *dight* has vanished, replaced by "royal beauty *bright*". And in "Jingle Bells"—now sanctified as a *carol*, together with "Silver Bells"—who sings now of a one-horse open *shay*? (But it's still listed, glory be, in the *Dictionary of Canadian English* as a by-form of *chaise*.) How much longer before the only readers capable of grasping ancient documents (like *Sunshine Sketches of a Little Town* or *The Great Gatsby*) are eccentric antiquarians? You zealots of the flood, explain to me how it is that words can be preserved intact through the centuries, down the ringing grooves of change, and crumble only within our own half-life? I can guess. It is because, through the efforts of traditionalists and tories and purists who refused, God bless them, to believe that all our yesterdays were irrelevant, the barbarous babble current at any one time in the past was not allowed to prevail or prescribe. *Barbarous*: a good honest word. In Greek it meant "stammering", and they used it of foreigners' talk. We should know better. We know that stammering begins at home; and that barbarism begins inside the citadel.

To return, more calmly, from sermon to images. Let me round off my survey by asking what we should project, instead of all these inadvertent and regrettable images. I wonder how many readers will agree with my suggestion that there is no single answer, no proper image for all seasons. There is a whole range of good, desirable, effective impressions we can make with our words. It is our business to choose among them, and the one we choose should depend on the job we want to do and the audience we address. You can see the truth of this when it comes to accent. Only a very narrow-minded speaker would claim that the proper way to pronounce your English is the way they do it in Aburrdeen, or Suhhbiton, or Long Guyland, or Arnpryre. I propose quite seriously that the same is true for grammar, within limits, and above all for style. The style, or *register*, which you use to a bridge partner is not appropriate when you address a tax consultant or a bus driver—though each style may be free of errors. I remember a lady who taught grade nine, and told me of a boy who told her: "Look, I talk the way my father talks. What does my father *do*? He drinks. If I talked the way *you* talk, I'd get beat to a pulp." That boy was *right*. I suspect he was also clever enough to be leading a double or triple life by now, with a perfectly idiomatic language for each (as butlers used to do in England).

But let's take an example closer to hand. I wouldn't mind a small bet that some of you think there is such a thing as a Professorial Style—correct, dignified, formal, impressive, like a god talking. There is, of course; I've put in some examples of it myself, just to prove I can. But what I'd bet on is that you have a sneaky feeling that it's *the* proper style—that we should all aim to talk or write that way, and that when I depart from it (as I do) my image suffers. This is where people go wrong—professors most of all. That formal, god-like style is only too easy to reach; and if reached too often it becomes no style at all, but a disease. This is where Humpty Dumpty's remark does make sense. The question is who is to be master—you, or the style. A man at the mercy of his own style is as comic, and as much to be pitied, as a man at the mercy of drink. Your style ought to express *what you are*, and you are not the same person on all occasions, in every company. If you seem to be, you are a bore.

I see where I am heading. The image which I have really been deploring all along, an image which embraces all the unhappy ones I've described, is the image not of the Poor Boob, but of the Zombie. What I mourn over is not the mistakes, but the *numbness*, to every aspect of language, which they imply. I regret the sort of mind that measures sense by the syllable, and accepts as oratory flannel a yard wide. To such a mind, ideas expressed in a simple, playful way are (necessarily) simple and obvious ideas, not worth having. I regret likewise the mind that must cloak metaphors in prose, apparently believing that naked metaphor is indecent—the progeny of Knowlton Nash, those newsmouths that say "climb off his *legislative* high horse", or "this promises to become a *political* hot potato". I regret above all the mind insensitive to humour and word-play of all kinds —not just the reflex groan at a bad pun, but the total inability to grasp a good one. I regret the mind which wears a superior smile when you play with a deliberate error (for instance, a friend of mine habitually says, "Oh, it was a congenital evening," and people exchange secret smiles because they think he's slipped). I regret, in sum, the mind to which all languages are dead languages, including its own.

The New Barbarians
GEOFFREY DURRANT

*Therefore if I know not the meaning of the voice, I
shall be unto him that speaketh a barbarian, and he
that speaketh shall be a barbarian unto me.*

I *Corinthians* xiv.11.

In the jargon of "educationists", the old emphasis on *English* as
the basis of humane culture has been displaced by the notion of
"communication". The appeal is usually to modernity. "In this
day and age", to use one of the stock phrases of the innovator,
we are supposed to provide an education which takes account of
the "media". This in turn requires an emphasis on visual education. One picture is worth a thousand words; so it is, of course, to
the child or to the illiterate adult. Before they can read, children
need picture books, and the silent film was no doubt invaluable to
the Russian revolution in the instructing of illiterate peasants.
The advocates of visual education, however, overlook our un-
shaken reliance on words. Radio and the telephone greatly increase the range of the spoken word, divorcing it from such
visual aids as gesture and facial expression. Television has
somewhat redressed the balance, but not nearly to the extent that
is often supposed, since in most television programmes the image
is used as illustration of the words. The news may show us a tank
battle, but our understanding of what is represented depends on
the verbal commentary. (This can be tested by the simple method
of turning off the sound.) Commercials use a flowing river, children dancing, or an attractive girl to fix our attention, while the
words do the actual work. The silent film died many years ago,
and the visual art of Chaplin was long ago superseded by the
verbal wit of the Marx brothers, though of course there are still,

in sound films, some elements of visual thought. It is necessary to point to these elementary truths because the advocates of visual education often speak as if language were going out of style, and as if we were entering an age of communication through sign language, film strips, and visual expression. This mystical notion of communication has been encouraged by Marshall McLuhan's works, whether or not he intended it; McLuhan, however, like the rest of us, communicates in language, and indeed in printed books.

The notion that "the medium is the message" has had considerable success both in the popular mind and in the profession of teaching. This slogan has been of great use to the television industry, since it distracts attention from the rubbishy content of commercialized programmes. The doctrine associated with it also suggests that by watching television we are being new made, and are taking part in a significant revolution in modes of consciousness. Who, without the help of McLuhan, would have suspected that there was so profound a meaning to *The Waltons*, deodorants, and sleeping pills? Without the mysticism of the electronic consciousness, we might perhaps have had a more energetic attempt to provide English-speaking Canada with a civilized and civilizing television service.

Inspired by the doctrine of the medium's message, and by the prevailing anti-humanism, a journalist seriously informs his readers that he communicates with killer-whales and dolphins; the grunts and squeaks in the aquarium are, so it seems, untranslatable, even crudely, into human language, so that the medium is the whole of the message. In schools and universities, sensitivity sessions, the linking of hands and other physical organs, mutual strokings, deep breathing, obscenities used in the past only by the illiterate, and the communion of pot, have all been experimented with and in their turn abandoned in the search for some more immediate, less difficult, and more deeply unifying a medium than mere human speech. All these experiments show at least a deeply felt need to communicate, and a general refusal by young people to accept the role assigned to them in what McLuhan has called "the global village" of the television age —that of village idiots.

There is, however, a sense in which the medium is indeed the message. Every method of recording or of communicating carries with it implications for the maker of the communication and its recipient. In the priestly and mandarin societies of ancient Egypt and ancient China the message was basically pictorial and visual; consequently it was manageable only by a priesthood or a mandarin caste who could give a life-time to the mastery of the ideographic system. The common man found a gap between his habitual mode of communication—the spoken language—and the medium in which thoughts were officially expressed and recorded. The invention of the phonetic alphabet made possible a cheap, permanent, and accessible medium of thought and communication based on the language used by ordinary men. We take this stupendous invention far too much for granted, and are even bored or irritated with it. It seems attractive to consider a return to visual and pictorial methods because these are more immediate and vivid and promise a mode of instant communication. However, the complications of electronic visual communication are at least as great in their way as were the complications of an ideographic script, and when linked with modern methods of dissemination they are even further from the reach of the common man. McLuhan's global village (in fact two global villages, one American and one Russian), in so far as it uses film and television and other visual modes, is in practice as much in the hands of its technical and financial controllers as Egypt and China were in the age of priests and mandarins. (University mandarins, especially those with priestly tendencies, are of course attracted by this prospect.) For every person who finds expression in the electronic visual system there are thousands who are condemned to passive looking and passive reception. The message of the visual media is that you cannot answer back. Ancient Egyptian ideographic writing excluded the common man from communication; the modern visual media include him only as a recipient. Not only have most men no technical means of answering back, but since most men are relatively skilled in verbal language, perfected over generations, and unskilled in visual modes of expression, they find it difficult to criticize effectively even the crude ideas presented to them electronically in visual form. The verbal electronic media—telephone and radio—do of course allow for answering back, as we see for example in open-line radio programmes. To answer back in visual terms would, however, require either a sign-language like the deaf-and-dumb alphabet, or a television camera in every home, together with the technical and intellectual control, by the individual, of pictorial logic. The prospect of any such change belongs to science fiction; and even if it were possible, why should we wish to give up the subtlety, the flexibility, and the greater accuracy of verbal language for deaf-and-dumb signalling, even in technicolour? Fortunately, the threat is limited by the tediousness of the visual medium, in which it takes—as for example in the ''art film''—more or less an hour to express the intellectual equivalent of five minutes of verbal language. There is no great actual threat, and no great promise. Film and television generally remain visually illustrated *linguistic* modes of communication. We do not even bother to invest in television-aided telephones, knowing that the visual addition to speech is scarcely worth the expense. In education, the visual is a useful supplement to the verbal mode; what it cannot supply is the structure of interpretation, which only language can adequately provide. For good or for ill, man is a verbal animal, and his whole intellectual, moral, and social life is rooted in language. This is not to belittle the importance of the visual arts, or of music. These are, however, not ideographic systems, and the cult of ''communications'' is not concerned with them.

Behind the merely fashionable undervaluing of language there lies a more permanent distrust, not only on the part of practical men, who observe how language can be misused to substitute fantasy or untruth for a firm grasp of reality, but also on the part of those philosophers in the nominalist tradition who object to what Berkeley called ''the embarrass and delusion of words'', and seek for some purer and more exact mode of thought than human speech. The thorough-going critique of language undertaken by modern positivists not only corrects or limits the misuse of words; it also leads to a wide-spread distrust of words. In addition, language is often thought of as separate from and even hostile to experience, and in an Anglo-Saxon world dominated by the philosophies of experience and of doing, by empiricism and pragmatism, the separation of words and deeds leads naturally to an undervaluing of language. Since human language cannot be perfectly exact, since it may be used to deceive oneself and one's neighbours, since it may be used as a substitute for experience and for action, it is easy to forget that all our experience as human beings is penetrated and modified by linguistic consciousness, and that language is not merely a means of communication, but the mode in which we apprehend our world. As I. A. Richards writes:

> So far from verbal language being a "compromise for a language of intuition"—a thin, but better-than-nothing, substitute for real experience—language, well used, is a *completion* and does what the intuitions of sensation by themselves cannot do. Words are the meeting points at which regions of experience which can never combine in sensation or intuitions, come together. They are the occasion and means of that growth which is the mind's endless endeavour to order itself. That is why we have language. It is no mere signalling system. It is the instrument of all our distinctively human development, of everything in which we go beyond the animals.[1]

What Richards asserts in scholarly prose was more succinctly stated by Wordsworth, when he wrote of the poetic endeavours of a young lady:

> She will probably write less in proportion as she subjects her feelings to logical forms, but the range of her sensibilities, so far from being narrowed, will extend as she improves in the habit of looking at things through the steady light of words, and, to speak a little metaphysically, words are not a mere *vehicle*, but they are *powers* either to kill or to animate.[2]

The "common man" understands this well enough, and expects the school to give his children a command of language. His means of measuring this command may be uncertain, and in letters to the newspapers and outbursts on open-line radio programmes it is spelling he complains of, because bad spelling can be pointed to as a definite symptom. It will not do to suppose that these complaints about spelling and "bad grammar" are to be dismissed as the prejudices of unenlightened parents or greedy businessmen; more often than not the complaints are an indirect way of saying what the critics of our schools and universities generally understand, but cannot vigorously argue—that the education their children are getting is not giving to them the power of *articulation*. Without a steady growth in the power of language, the individual is left confused and helpless. He is surrounded by persuaders, hidden and open, in the classroom, on television and radio, in the press, and in every public place where advertisements can be displayed, but he himself is given no comparable power of persuasion, still less of self-knowledge. Hence the dominant mood of today's students, who as a group are either placidly or cynically conformist, recognizing that they have no choice but to go along with "the system", or, at times, to behave irrationally and violently. They feel helpless, and, inasmuch as they are inarticulate, they *are* helpless. What is more, the many educational reforms suggested to revitalize the school and the university, to remove this helplessness, to encourage "participation", to make learning a "creative experience", must always fail so long as students lack the verbal skills that are the very condition of mental liberty.

A care for the English language is sometimes regarded as an aesthetic luxury, of no great importance in the conduct of business. This Philistine view has in recent years infected the university. The cult of "action" and "commitment" leads university radicals to use language with deliberate looseness, so that one cannot even say that they tell lies; a lie is usually a controlled misuse of language, not a mere linguistic blur. When the RCMP was accused of sending an armed force to remove demonstrators from a building at Simon Fraser University (though they were unarmed) the authors of the accusation, when challenged, replied that the police were indeed armed, since they *had arms at the police station*. A faculty member at the University of British Columbia, having accused the President of speaking like a Nazi *Rektor*, was unabashed by a demonstration that the President's expressed views were the exact opposite of those of National-Socialist university administrators; he answered that such views made Nazism possible. One cannot say that these intellectuals were lying; they were simply indifferent to the need to maintain any connection between words and facts. Such brutish indifference to language has become a characteristic of our society; since words are misused by advertisers and politicians, it is rightly thought that society is corrupt; the conclusion drawn is that corrupt language is an appropriate weapon to use against it. This seems to me an error. The corruption of language in contemporary society is the weakness of this society, not its strength, and any genuine revolution will have to clarify its own language if it is to succeed. The French revolution was made possible by the prose of Voltaire, Montesquieu, Diderot, and Rousseau, not by the guillotine. However, those who are incompetent in the use of language are forever condemned to believe that language is ineffectual, since they never experience its effective use. The schools and universities have a heavy responsibility for student helplessness, and for their occasional irrationality and violence; not because the student slogans are accurate, but because the linguistic education of students has been so neglected that parrotted slogans are the only language their leaders can command. There is evidently something radically wrong with a system of education that leaves many of its more adventurous, idealistic, and intelligent products with no better control of invective than they demonstrate in calling a university bureaucrat a "fascist" or a policeman a "pig".

The most serious of all the results of inarticulateness in students is what it contributes to the intolerance shown by their leaders. Disturbed and affronted by ideas which they dislike but cannot persuasively refute, student idealists have no other recourse than to deny the right of free speech to their opponents. Physical disruption of lectures is followed by attempts to justify such behaviour on the grounds that the experience of Nazi Germany must not be repeated, and that students have a special right and duty to silence "fascists" and "racists". Ignorance of history plays some part in this; students are generally unaware that in the Europe of the Thirties, and particularly in Germany, students as a class were the standard-bearers of fascist and racist ideas, and that the German student organization was the first national body to become national-socialist. However, ignorance alone cannot explain the claim that fascism can be prevented if students behave like fascists; physical disruption is the natural resort of those who lack the capacity to argue and persuade. Student activists have just cause to complain of the educational system; their own arguments and their own language are the best testimony to its failures. But although we need to oppose all disturbers of free speech, the cure cannot be found in discipline. It must come from greater efforts to teach students history and science, to encourage their powers of criticism, and to give them the skills that are necessary to answer in speech and writing the ideas they believe to be wrong and wicked. *The only answer to barbarism is the arduous mastery of the skills of a civilized existence.*

Of course teachers of English in the universities have for many years complained about falling standards, and we may be tempted to believe that it is all an illusion and that little has really changed. Since public examinations conducted by impartial committees of examiners have been generally abolished, there is no reliable means of proving whether or not there has been a decline. Fortified by a neutral science of linguistics, which makes any usage legitimate simply because it exists, some insist that all there is to complain of is a greater freedom and flexibility in the use of English, in which an increase in spelling mistakes and a few breaches of the rules of formal grammar are more than compensated for by increased spontaneity and "creativity". Unfortunately, neither spontaneity nor genuine creativity can flourish without competence, and without the confidence that only competence can give. Where there are no agreed rules, or where the rules are not clearly understood, a general uneasiness infects both speech and writing. The emancipation from grammar has produced, not ease and confidence, but a great increase in linguistic nervousness. The age of grammatical liberty has turned out to be an age of anxiety, an anxiety masked by a pretension to ineffable and mysterious modes of communication.

The anxiety can be so extreme as to lead, with some assistance from currently fashionable notions, to a formal abdication of professional responsibility. At a conference held a few years ago in Vancouver, a speaker who had been asked to address his professional colleagues called on the assembly to rise. They did so, somewhat surprised. He then invited them to close their eyes. Many politely obeyed him. A long and uneasy silence followed, lasting for several minutes. There was some shuffling and coughing, but the invited "speaker" maintained his resolute silence.

After what seemed like an eternity of embarrassment, one member of the audience finally summoned the courage to blurt out: "What is this in aid of?" "I want you," said the speaker, "to confront yourselves." This was his total contribution to the debate. The theatrical stroke, of course, fell flat; but the significance of the incident is that this was not a meeting of educational psychologists, or of the prophets of the latest Californian religion, but of high school teachers of English. When those whose task is to safeguard and encourage the art of speech are subjected to so extreme a statement of disbelief in their profession and in its aims, and accept that statement with so little protest, one must suppose that the current depreciation of language, and the lack of confidence in the ability to use it effectively, have led to some demoralizing of the profession itself. Teachers of English may perhaps be forgiven if the steady stream of propaganda for visual education—encouraged of course by powerful vested interests in the electronics industry—has made them unsure of their aims and confused about their methods.

In the classroom the emancipated view of language plays its own part in the spreading of confusion. The eager young liberal addresses his students in a free-and-easy "with-it" language in order to reduce the barrier between himself and them, and to "communicate" more fully. He is however of a different generation, and his attempts at the current language of the young will always be slightly foreign to them. To the student, however, the professor, whether he realizes this or not, speaks with the authority of the university; what he says is taken to be "good English", and is introduced by the students into their essays. The professor is anxious to "communicate", and the students are anxious to use appropriate language in literary discussion. The result is that students write that "Othello is upset when he believes Desdemona has been unfaithful," and that "Pope is poking fun at Lord Hervey"; and instead of asserting that they "think" or "believe" something, they will often write that they "feel" a proposition to be valid. (One sign of an all-pervading fear of committing oneself to any definite thought or value is the almost automatic substituting of "I feel" for "I think" or "I believe".

If action is to be effective, if the individual is to realize himself, if society is to be reformed and life made human, we must learn again an art that seems almost to have been lost—that of exact, confident, and vigorous speech and writing. There is of course a cult of false simplicity that would deny the richness, variety, and poetic mysteriousness of the English language. It is not this I have in mind; there is no one model for English speech and writing. I mean that we must use responsible language —language for which each takes full personal responsibility. Most of the feeble and pretentious speech and writing today is the result of moral cowardice. The speaker who says: "Hopefully the government will recognize the need for a change of policy" is evading the direct statement that *he himself* hopes for this. We have long been accustomed to impersonal constructions as a means of avoiding open responsibility for acts and decisions. ("It has been decided to reduce the cost-of-living allowance.") With the vogue of the unattributed "hopefully" we have now made it possible even for personal feelings to be detached from the particular persons who feel them, and left floating where nobody can be embarrassed and nobody has to admit that they are his own hopes he is speaking of. To say "I hope the government will recognize the need for a change of policy" is uncomfortably direct and open. Academics above all distrust the personal pronoun, preferring, like Norman Mailer (who oddly enough himself remarks on lack of courage as the dominant evil of the age), to refer to themselves in the third person—"this reviewer", "this reader", etc.

A further sign of linguistic anxiety is the nervous avoiding of value-judgments. In all the humanities, in the study of the arts above all, the making of value-judgments is primary and inescapable. A scholar like Housman, who sternly rejected in his academic work anything so unscientific as criticism, nevertheless based a large part of his life on the judgment that the poetry of Manilius was important enough to justify the spending of many years and endless pains on the establishment of a correct text. Yet the proposition that Manilius is worthy of such devotion is itself a value-judgment, if it is not a mere parrotting of received opinion—a passive value-judgment, in other words. The academic fear of value-judgments and "loaded language" is of course one result of a proper care for rationality, and for the pursuit of disinterestedness—both indispensable virtues in an academic. Still, when we choose to study Shakespeare or Keats or Dickens or Faulkner, and invite our students to do so, we acknowledge that these are good and important authors—valuable authors. It is, however, very rare today to read of a "good book", except as a jest; nor do we hear of valuable literature, or important works; the characteristic jargon of educational discussion does not include the notion of learning something *good* or *valuable*, but instead refers to "a worth-while learning experience". A book is said to be *relevant*, or *insightful*; a poem is found to be *meaningful*; and only the most naive will nowadays risk describing a poem as *good*. Such imprecise terms are preferred, I think, because they appear to be merely descriptive, though they are no more descriptive or factual than the value-judgments they replace. When we describe a book as "worth-while" we suggest that we have a measure of its value—it is worth the time, the "while" we give to reading it. If one could attach any accurate meaning to the expression it would represent a very limited approval, since most readers no doubt hope for a profitable expenditure of their time in reading, and not simply to break even. However, it is probably wrong to look for any exactitude in the expression; its appeal to educated writers and speakers today seems to lie in its pretension to exactitude, its avoidance of any frank *valuing*, and its inherent vagueness. Much the same may be said of *meaningful* and *relevant* as used today. Behind these feeble usages lies a great confusion about the nature of human activity, and in particular about human activity in education and the arts. The success and the prestige of the physical sciences have led some humanists to believe that it is possible to achieve the impartiality of physics by avoiding the value-judgments that lie at the heart of all the humanities. Of course it is impossible to avoid value-judgments; but it is easy to use language that evades the acknowledgment of their use. As with verbal "impersonality", the use of bastard terms that are neither clearly descriptive nor frankly evaluative seems to arise from a general pusillanimity, a desire not to stick one's neck out, and above all a desire not to appear naive. The sophistication of the modern academic is often merely the outward form of his timidity.

Another sign that schools and universities are not giving their students the confidence that comes from mastery of their own language is the readiness of educated people to adopt modes of speech and writing out of conformity with the latest fad, or from a fear of offending against some new shibboleth. Such expressions as "Chair-person" and "ombudsperson" testify to social sensitivity, but not to respect for language; and the literally unspeakable *he/she* and *his/her* have been widely adopted as an advertisement of the writer's progressive attitude to sexual equality. The university and its students have also shown themselves surprisingly vulnerable to political cant; terms like "relevant", "commitment", "participation", are freely used in contexts which rob them of exact significance. At the same time, a strange linguistic snobbery persists; graduate students in particular interlard their English with misunderstood and often misspelt expressions from Latin and German; a story begins not in the middle, but *in medias res*; a writer cannot have a philosophy, but must have a *Weltanschauung* (almost invariably misspelt, as *in medias res* is almost always syntactically misplaced). The novel of education is referred to as the *Bildungsroman*, and a theme is a *motif*. In speech, a similar pretentiousness shows itself, in the use of *vis à vis* for the simple English *towards*; in the display of grand words like *charismatic* (for *popular*) and *macrocosmic* (for *large*). The stalest leavings of the advertising industry (for example the indiscriminate use of *colourful*) are permitted to corrupt the speech and writing of educated persons. There is something pathetic in the attempts of students and others to give their language some kind of dignity by such shabby means; it would be better to give them no education, and leave them with the honest language used by the plumber or the carpenter, than to educate them to be nervous and worried about their language, and yet incapable of using it accurately. Our system of education leaves lawyers, national leaders, journalists, and university professors linguistically nervous, yet unable to deal confidently with common forms like "I" and "me", "he" and "him", "who" and "whom". The errors are not important; what should dismay us is that they so often come from a desire to be correct.

The general anxiety about language is caused partly by a confusion between the role of the grammarian and that of the teacher. Since modern linguists rightly see their task as descriptive, and not as legislative, it is concluded that teachers must not say that one mode of speech or writing is better than another. What this ignores is the necessity, for any civilized existence, of the learning and using of arbitrary rules. If one is not to eat like a pig, one must have some rules for eating. Whether one uses knife and fork, chopsticks, or the fingers of the left hand, is decided by arbitrary rules accepted and applied by a particular society. The table manners are necessary, though the rules are arbitrary. In the same way, the rule that we drive on the right-hand side of the road is arbitrary, but a teacher of driving in North America must make sure that it is known and obeyed. A teacher of driving in Australia must make sure that his pupils keep to the left of the road. In the same way the arbitrary rules of the English language must be known and followed if we are not to have endless linguistic accidents and the general anxiety about language that at present permeates our society. The rules of the English language, like English common law, are flexible, complex, subtle, and changeable. We have no *Code Napoléon*, no Academy, to clarify and fix them, yet the speech and writing of educated persons are guided by an intimate knowledge of these rules. To list "ain't" in a dictionary as an acceptable equivalent to "is not" or "isn't" presents no dangers to the speaker well educated enough to know when he may use this locution as a joke. It ain't so funny for the student from an illiterate home who is seeking to master an acceptable educated English.

Undergraduates who have been exposed to undisciplined and loose discussion commonly express themselves in feeble conversational terms rather than in the authoritative tone and impartial manner of the specialist. The writing of most undergraduates, though often loose and feeble, usually has some direct link with the characteristic speech of the writer; it is at least to that extent authentic. What the student learns to write in the graduate school often lacks even that virtue. In a few months of graduate work, students who have in the past written out of personal understanding, however confused and unformed, learn how to write the jargon of scholarship. Here is an example of this jargon, taken from the journal of the Modern Language Association, which instructs its contributors that "articles should be written in a clear, concise, and attractive style, with documentation held to a necessary minimum." To get an article published in this journal is the ambition of many young Canadian academics, and its practices strongly influence the study of language and literature in Canada:

> Despite its appearance as a miscellaneous collection of lyrics, Dylan Thomas' poetry is a closely united body of work. Poetic unity customarily reveals itself in cohesive imagery . . . and in the repetition and development of related themes. Thomas' *Collected Poems* possesses such imagistic and thematic coherence, and these images and themes, furthermore, have as their subsuming source the Bible.

In plain English this seems to mean something of this kind:

> Although Dylan Thomas' poems appear to be individual separate works, they are all alike in relying on the Bible for images and themes; and this gives to his poetry a kind of poetic unity.

Though not characteristic of its author, this passage illustrates a general tendency. Writers of dissertation-English are required to add to the sum of human knowledge, and this is sometimes hard to do. Any Welsh farmer can read Dylan Thomas and respond to the many echoes of the Bible in his poems. What a Welsh farmer cannot do is write dissertation-English. He lacks the necessary panoply of abstractions, bogus entities, and tautological notions. It would not occur to him to say of a flock of mountain sheep:

> Despite its appearance as a miscellaneous collection of quadrupeds, Dylan Thomas' flock is a closely united body of animals. Genetic unity customarily shows itself in the repetition and development of related features. Thomas' flock possesses such genetic coherence, and these features, furthermore, have as their subsuming source one ram.

The farmer would say that the flock came from a common stock, and that would be that. Nobody would give him tenure for that, or a research grant in genetics. It is only in the academic world that men and women are rewarded for disguising the simplest of notions in obscure and pretentious language. This is not merely a question of style; style and thought are inseparable, and both reveal the degree of responsibility to his subject that the writer is prepared to assume. What should appal us about dissertation-English is the frivolity, the irresponsibility, of this dignified and solemn lingo. The critic's first responsibility to the poet, the novelist, or the playwright is not to muddy the language with which the literary artist has to work. It was Mallarmé, I think, who said that the poet was like a painter into whose palette the public was always sticking its dirty brushes. With ever more scholarly and critical activity in the universities, academic jargon spreads into common speech, through university-educated journalists, broadcasters, and "communicators" of all kinds. Natural harmony has become "ecological balance", shyness is "inhibition", anger is "aggression", greed is "acquisitiveness", litter is "pollution", chastity is "repression". It is impossible nowadays simply to learn something; one is "engaged in a learning process", or one is "in a learning situation". Modern man lives in a world haunted by bogus entities, by processes, by essences, and by tendencies that underlie all natural appearances. Everything becomes a symptom of something hidden, and possibly sinister. It is no coincidence that the university is the home of paranoia, since it is in the university that the search for the hidden process, the unifying explanation, and the illuminating abstraction is pressed most continuously. The result of all this "scientific" activity, in fields which do not lend themselves to genuine scientific rigour, is the continual invention of bogus entities, the nurturing of projects worthy of Swift's Laputa, and the weakening of common sense. Only in a modern university, for example, could large sums be spent on television equipment to make a lecture course available in many rooms; and only a modern academic would be surprised to find the television sets performing to empty seats. The abstract idea of "visual education", however, has a magical appeal, reinforced by the general love of innovation.

Recently academics have allowed themselves to suppose that there is an abstract quality or hidden essence of "good teaching" which exists in varying degrees in professors, and can be measured like the sugar content of the blood. To this end they set up batteries of tests, sometimes quantitatively graded, in the hope of determining the amount of "good teaching" that enters into the activities of each professor in the classroom. In order to do this they divide ''good teaching'' into its constituent parts —enthusiasm, degree of preparation, encouragement of discussion, legibility of handwriting, audibility, and so on—which they try to put together again to give a reliable measure of the whole activity. Of course good teachers have no identifiable common characteristics except vitality, articulateness, and intelligence; and the hallmark of the good teacher is that his teaching is his own inimitable style. The modern academic in this too is the victim of his love of abstract notions. ''Good teaching'' is thought of not as Smith or Jones teaching physics or French well in his own individual way, but as a common entity which exists independently, and can be tracked down, measured, and taught to other persons. Many hours are wasted in committees and in classrooms, and much paper is used up, in an activity that every serious teacher knows to be bogus, but in which the academic community has been trapped through its incapacity for managing its own language.

In questionnaires that investigate ''good teaching'', and in the general discussion of what makes a good teacher, the command of language, itself an expression of the teacher's whole personality, is commonly neglected, in favour of such questions as whether he attends his classes regularly. The general nervousness on the subject of language no doubt tends to limit frank discussion of this question, though anybody who listens to public lectures knows what students have to suffer from mumbling and inarticulate teachers. An obsession with the abstract notion of ''good teaching'' helps to divert attention from the simple necessity of having well-educated and eloquent teachers, not merely specialists equipped with educational techniques. William Walsh, Professor of Education at Leeds University, writes as follows:

> Language is the one indispensable means of education, both in the stricter sense of formal education, in which stress falls on the communicative aspect of language, and in the lesser sense of incidental education, in which the expressive function of language is emphasized. No matter how practical or empirical an education may be, language must serve as the agency by which the teacher is related to the taught, and each to the subject of instruction; no

matter how individual an education, how independent of the fluid
and intricate relations constantly forming and wavering among the
members of a group and expressed in the modulations of speech,
language must act as the fine tool of analysis, the instrument of
intellectual construction, and the medium, plastic and responsive,
of emotional expression. . . . The quality of an education depends
most on the quality of the teacher, and the quality of the teacher is
best indicated by his use of language.[3]

Such views are, unfortunately, rarely expressed by professors of
education; and they are seldom taken into account in "evalua-
tions" of teachers. No visual education, no use of film strips,
tactile experiences, or sensitivity sessions can remove the need
for skill in language as the first necessity in a teacher. The attacks
on "verbalism" that are so common today are usually attacks on
the active principle of intelligence, on the mode by which we
make sense of any set of facts, and by which we experience any
subject. For some years now, for example, there has been a
tendency to encourage student discussion, and to slight the formal lecture, the systematic use of language by the teacher. Student discussion, if carefully prepared and based on genuine
thought and knowledge, is an indispensable exercise. It does not
follow that the formal lecture ought to be discounted. On the
contrary, a lecture should be an occasion of pleasurable discovery
for those attending it. The lecture has fallen into disrepute, not
only because of ideological objections to its "authoritarian"
nature—objections which are too absurd to merit serious
discussion—but because so many university teachers do not trouble to master this difficult art. Those who have learned to express
themselves well, and lecture with energy and conviction, have no
shortage of students. As for the schools, it is evident that those
few that still maintain the activity of public speaking and debate
send to the universities students well equipped to take advantage
of discussion.

Lecturing is not important only as a means of conveying a
critical view of knowledge and involving a number of students
in the active thinking of the teacher, but also as an occasion for
articulate and controlled speech, directed to an actual audience; it
is from this activity, I believe, that the liveliest and most humane
academic writing proceeds. It is true, of course, that the

academic who *reads* a paper is usually dull because his writing is dull; on the other hand if he were capable of discussing his subject without the necessity of a prepared script he would be a better writer as well as a better speaker. The present disconnection between speech and the printed word is one of the chief reasons for student discontent, and for the boredom suffered at meetings of learned societies. It is also one of the reasons why so many academic books, even on literature, are less than delightful to read.

One of the university's tasks should be to look for and welcome vigorous and lively academic writing. This, in the study of literature, most often appears when the critic pays attention to particular works, and shows at least some sense of a particular audience. The following passage comes from the journal from which I took my example of academic jargon:

> What, more precisely, are the sources of our satisfaction with *Pearl*? The language, of course; but language expressing what? A ratiocinative argument? A witty manipulation of esoteric symbols? A homily wrapped in a vision? We might say with more justification that the vision satisfies by providing the doctrine and solace of an elegy; that we learn many lessons along the way, and are consoled to see the state of the blessed which we may be destined to share. Yet we leave *Pearl* instructed and consoled not so much by its doctrines, which are as commonplace as they are wittily expressed, as by the experience represented through character and event in a certain pattern, culminating in a strongly satisfactory resolution of the protagonist's debilitating problems.[4]

This is evidently learned language; but the professional habit of writing abstractly and impersonally is here under the pressure of the need to say something about the poem, to rescue an actual literary experience from the history of ideas and from limiting classifications. The scientific manner—almost always a sham in the discussion of literature—is not allowed to dominate a discussion which, because it is the record of a personal reading, must address the reader as a person, in the rhetoric of question and answer, but in the rhythms of speech. The appeal is not to rules of evidence, but to the only competent court in the judgment of literature—the actual experience of the work by the individual serious reader.

The passage, which I think is fairly representative of the better kind of academic prose, shows distinct elements of life—life struggling to escape from the characteristic jargon of the profession. I have, however, no doubt that there is more and more of the feeble kind of writing, and less and less of the lively. One must suppose, from the quality of writing by graduate students—not from one university only but from many—that the elements of life in the passage I have just cited would be objected to by many instructors. A graduate student who wrote "The language, of course; but language expressing what?" would probably be instructed in the need for a more impersonal and abstract style, and above all for a style that does not jolt the reader, or expect of him an immediate and crucial response.

We ought not to be surprised or pleased to find that professors of English do not always write badly. They are, or ought to be, continually absorbed in the language of the best writers; their subject matter is, after all, literature—"news that stays news"—and therefore they should have no great difficulty in writing about it in a lively way. The wonder is not that some write well, but that so many write so badly. It is perhaps not surprising that philosophy, history, or sociology can be made to seem boring; but only a profession organized for that very purpose could succeed in making poems, plays, and stories boring. This has been achieved by treating criticism as a science, with literature as the collection of "phenomena" to be listed, classified, and reduced to rule; in the process the very nature of a work of literature is denied, since literature is designed in the first place to give delight, and any study of it that loses sight of this must falsify the object it claims to examine. How far our universities have allowed a misplaced respect for systematic science to lead them away from a respect for literature as a mode of intellectual delight we can see by testing the activities of any graduate school of literature by the words of Sidney, writing on the value of poetry in education:

> Now therein of all sciences (I speak still of human, and according
> to the humane conceit) is our poet the monarch. For he doth not

only show the way, but giveth so sweet a prospect into the way, as will entice any man to enter into it. Nay, he doth, as if your journey should lie through a fair vineyard, at the first give you a cluster of grapes, that, full of that taste, you may long to pass further. He beginneth not with obscure definitions, which must blur the margent with interpretations, and load the memory with doubtfulness; but he cometh to you with words set in delightful proportion, either accompanied with, or prepared for, the well enchanting skill of music; and with a tale forsooth he cometh to you, with a tale which holdeth children from play, and old men from the chimney corner.

(The Defence of Poesy)

If we cannot say that the study of literature today offers the delight that Sidney speaks of, if students do not see the graduate school as a fair vineyard, it is because we have assimilated the study of literature to that of history, psychology, philosophy, and sociology, and have lost sight of its uniqueness; and also because, as the readiness of many to study poetry in translation indicates, we place too little value on skill in language and on sensitivity to the finer meanings of words. While conservative academics find the direct study of literature too little scientific, the apostles of self-expression have no zest for the strenuous exercise that is necessary if there is to be any delight in the arts of language.

Each poem, novel, or play is a unique act of mind, a complex and yet single thought, an experience in its own right. The scientific method—triumphant in so many fields of thought—is hostile to literature, because it must by its very nature concentrate on the properties that literary works have in common, on what may help to produce a general theory, a classification, an account, in short, of works of literature in alien terms. In so far as the language of criticism pretends to the impersonal, abstract, and generalizing force of science it necessarily reduces any work of literature to pointlessness. To say of Wordsworth that he is a ''Romantic'' poet is the first step to a misreading of each of his poems; by the very fact of so classifying his poems we have placed them in a falsifying context. Of course we cannot know too much about the past; and scholarship ought to illuminate the great works that exist in the present but were produced in the past. Literary scholarship, however, consists first of all in that "long-continued intercourse with the best models of composition" that Wordsworth lays down as the condition for reading and understanding his lyrical ballads; it ought not to be confused, as it has been under the influence of scientific method, with the discovery of general laws and the making of classifications. What is of interest in a work of literature is that in which it is distinctive, not what links it with members of a class. Consequently, the language of criticism should be designed to make exact and fine distinctions, rather than to roll the works of Wordsworth, Coleridge, Shelley, Byron, and Keats into a ball and call it "Romanticism". The educative and human value of the study of literature consists precisely in the practice it gives, or ought to give, in the making of necessary distinctions. Writing of the value of poetry in education, Coleridge makes this observation:

> When we reflect, that the cultivation of the judgement is a positive command of the moral law, since the reason can give the *principle* alone, and the conscience bears witness only to the *motive*, while the application and effects must depend upon the judgement: when we consider, that the greater part of our success and comfort in life depends on distinguishing the similar from the same, that which is peculiar in each thing from that which it has in common with others, so as still to select the most probable, instead of the merely possible or positively unfit, we shall learn to value earnestly and with a practical seriousness a mean, already prepared for us by nature and society, of teaching the young mind to think well and wisely by the same unremembered process and with the same never forgotten results, as those by which it is taught to speak and converse.[5]

If this is true, as I believe it is, the language of criticism and of literary scholarship ought to be adapted to this task, and we should resolutely reject the abstracting and generalizing methods appropriate to the physical sciences and aspired to by the social sciences.

This is not to assert that the study of literature concerns itself only with the making of distinctions. On the contrary, great works of literature—and even minor works—present us with unified accounts of human experience. The mind is always engaged, when reading Shakespeare, Dickens, Faulkner, or Milton, in the making of connections between experiences which are usually separate, in seeing the many complex details of the work as a whole, and then in seeing the details as they are sharpened and made significant by their relationship to the whole. There is an active unifying intelligence in works of literature, and it is the task of the reader to recreate this unifying act of mind, the task of the critic to help him to do so. What we too commonly see, however, especially in academic criticism, is the substitution of the ideas and intelligence of the critic—including at times his skills as an amateur psychologist—for the much more powerful intelligence of the writer. For wholeness of vision and unifying intelligence it is better to go to poets than to professors. What professors can do is to help our students to attain a full and exact perception of the writer's intelligence, by increasing their under-standing of his language and by helping them to see the unique-ness of what is achieved in any great work. Too many of us—to judge from the tone commonly taken in dealing with the work of imaginative writers—regard literature as raw material for the more serious intellectual activities of the academic—as *phenomena* which can be given significance only within an academic classification, preferably "scientific".

The habit of speaking of scholarly activity as a mode of "re-search" tends to blur the necessary distinction between literary scholarship and the activity of the natural scientist, and it tends also to discourage attention to the quality of the language used. We are interested in the "findings" of the researcher, not in the language in which he thinks; and we are ready to tolerate obscure language in the humanities because a specialized language is necessary in the sciences. The traditional view, from which uni-versities have recently departed, is expressed well by Pater:

> That living authority which language needs lies, in truth, in its scholars, who, recognizing always that every language possesses a genius, a very fastidious genius, of its own, expand at once and purify its very elements, which must needs change along with the changing thoughts of living people.[6]

The objection to a specialized jargon is not that it is ugly, but that it is dead; it can neither reflect the living thoughts of the writer, nor address itself to the imagination.

Much of the dull and boring language comes from writing books too early. Some compulsion is of course needed, if students are to learn to write, but a sensible teacher arranges the writing so that it has some chance of being grounded in a genuine need to say something. To ask students to write on *King Lear* after they have read and studied the play is reasonable enough; under the immediate impression of a work of imagination they often bring to their own accounts of it a heightened intelligence, a sharper perception, than they are normally capable of. Such writing is often marked by those flashes of intuition which no system can guarantee, but which are kindled by great imaginative works. Under the pressure of such thoughts, students otherwise inarticulate or half-articulate suddenly become eloquent. By contrast, the M.A. thesis or Ph.D. dissertation is often a dreary tract, a series of observations tacked together in accordance with some pre-arranged scheme, in weary and lifeless language. A student may perhaps, in theory, have learned in two years or in four years some new insight into literature or some new significant facts about a "period" or "genre" that are worth recording at book length; but in practice this so rarely happens that the requirement of a dissertation as the key to the academic profession merely deters the more adventurous minds, and encourages pedantry. I have been told by assistant professors that, having written a dissertation on Smollett or Peacock, they hoped never to open his works again. The agony of producing, under pressure, a book that nobody wants to read, and that its author did not want to write, is enough to turn most independent minds from the profession of letters. If he is prudent, the young assistant professor will carve out of his dissertation one or two articles for learned journals, an activity required by tenure committees, but—for all the polishing and "up-dating"—from the young teacher's point of view a retrograde and boring activity, a return to his intellectual past, not a march into the future. For promotion, a book is required; so the dissertation, written deliberately to be an unreadable book, must be re-written in readable form. The graduate school has taught its students to write barbarous books; they must then try to learn to write in a civilized style in the hope of having the work printed. We leave it to publishers to maintain standards that have been abandoned by the university.

Some of the best minds from William James to Edmund Wilson and Jacques Barzun have attacked the Ph.D. octopus, but in these matters it is not the best minds that prevail. Since the Ph.D. programme has to provide a more or less standardized product for the North American academic common market, it will not easily be reformed. Those who have suffered from it often persuade themselves that, much as they disliked it, it was a kind of baptism by fire, an initiation which turned boys into men, and they do not see why new entrants to the profession should fare any better than they. Yet it is as well to recognize that a Ph.D., even from the best of universities, may mean only that its possessor showed patience and fortitude.[7] In the meantime it is one of the chief reasons for the poor quality of the English used in the academy. The style it encourages is scientific, objective, and abstract; a style for recording the results of experiments in chemistry, not a style appropriate to the discussion of literature, or likely to make the student into an eloquent teacher in the classroom. We require of students that they should be scholars before they have been adequately educated, that they should master the European background and the major classical authors with no Greek or Latin and only a smattering of French, that they should pronounce critically on works they cannot in any exact sense be said to have thoroughly read. *Beowulf* remains on lists of works for study, even though most graduate students know no Old English. Students busy themselves with defining Romanticism while they are still struggling to understand Shelley's "Mont Blanc" and are making their first acquaintance with "Don Juan"; and the history of criticism is discussed by young men and women who cannot confidently make sense of a tightly written passage of good critical prose. Those who have read the attempts of graduate students at practical criticism know that the need at the graduate, as at the undergraduate, level is to help students to improve their writing and reading. The edifice of scholarship is built on shaky foundations when students are required to criticize works they cannot properly read, and when theses and dissertations have to be corrected or re-written by a supervisor. The first requirement is an honest recognition of the fact that, in the contemporary world, the attainment of an adequate degree of literacy is an arduous and lengthy process and must take preference over more ambitious forms of scholarship.

The eagerness of Canadian universities to achieve, if not international excellence, at least a continental esteem, has led them to require their teachers to publish as much as possible. Most of this publication, in English studies, is not in Canadian journals; it is designed for the continental specialist audience, and is therefore framed in terms acceptable to the American tradition of scholarship, a tradition deeply influenced by the older German idea of philology and literature as objective sciences. This tradition, admirable though it is in many ways, and great though its accomplishments are in all those areas of knowledge in which systematic research is appropriate, is by no means so respectful as is the French, British, or Canadian tradition of the need for lucid, lively, and civilized language. The notion that learning in the humanities should always be *humane*, should address itself as much as possible to the common reader, has consequently been undervalued in Canada in recent years. It was not always so; and the memory of the great teachers of the past, like Sedgewick in British Columbia, still remains in the minds of their former students and colleagues.

If what one has to say about a writer is addressed not to an immediate audience, to one's students, colleagues, and fellow citizens, but is instead addressed to a small and distant group of specialists, a change comes over the language of discussion. The need for vividness, lucidity, and freshness gives way to the need to make some new observation, however slight, and to make it without risk of error, controversy, or offence to established opinion. This is a recipe for deadness and dullness; and deadness and dullness are what we get when we require of university teachers a steady stream of publication in "reputable journals". We should therefore encourage university teachers to try to make Shakespeare, Milton, and Dickens intelligible and delightful to their fellow citizens, in public lectures, on radio and television, and in adult-education classes. Once the university teacher gets in the habit of addressing not only bewildered young students and the specialists who delight in specialist jargon, but mature non-specialists, the need for direct and lively language will become evident, and the ability to use it will increase.

Since the language used by many teachers of English is often dead, over-abstract, and imprecise, it is not surprising that the language in which educational problems are discussed is in even worse shape. Reviewing a recent educational work, *The Failure of Educational Reform in Canada*, Professor Russell Hunt quotes the following passage:

> Reform is the activity which links the past and the future, it is the ratio between the past and the future, and, in that sense, it is synonymous with intelligence. Reform is intelligence, the human mediation between various elements in the social and physical environment, the process of interaction in an insistent present. Reform, like intelligence, is not relevant, it is relevance, and it signifies whatever continuity our lives may have.

Of the abstract and confused language in this and other contributions, Professor Hunt says:

> When it comes to prose, professional educationists are, by and large, fluff merchants. The skill of premature or even entirely unjustified abstraction, the ability to wield disguised logical fallacies, the strength to flail a subject with mixed and inappropriate metaphor as though it were the jawbone of an ass against the Philistines—all these are weapons with which the citadel of bureaucracy can be made secure against even the most modest changes. What's particularly distressing is that the people who employ these weapons are very often precisely the people who think they're assailing the citadel, and who don't know that the weapons can only be used in its defense. For the lifeblood of paralytic bureaucracy is abstraction.[8]

This is well said. The only way of bringing life to a dead system is to speak and write in vigorous language. Unfortunately those who claim to speak for "life", instead of trying to use language as it was used in the discussion of education by Swift, by Samuel Butler, by D. H. Lawrence, or by Ezra Pound, have fallen into an evasive cant in which such indistinct watch-words as "relevance", "creativity", "communication", and "self-expression" are used not as a mode of thought, but as a substitute for thought. At the same time certain crucial terms are shunned. No skill of any value can be achieved except by effort, practice, discipline, and application, but in contemporary educational discussion these terms are *taboo*; I recently experimented with their use in a panel discussion on the teaching of English, and was told for my pains that I was "like one of the aristocrats, waiting to have their heads cut off". Even the word "teacher" causes some distress to progressive educationists, so that the barbarous term "resource person" is now fashionable, and appears even in the official publications of universities. There can be little hope of any useful discussion when "concerned persons" shy away from the elementary terms of a discussion like Victorian maiden ladies affronted by talk of legs. The educational philosopher Kingsley Price wrote in 1956:

> There are many words, ideas, or concepts in the discipline of education, both in its factual and recommending parts, which are obscure beyond all management. Consider, for example, such terms as "integrated", "child-centred", "the whole person", "core curriculum", "on-going process", "experience", "shared experience", "citizenship", "loyalty", "disloyalty", "enrichment", "growth", "meaningful", "value". It is doubtful that many have a very clear notion as to the use of these terms, and certain that some employ them rather to signal an attack or justify a defense than to make clear statements of fact or intelligible recommendations. Yet it is in such terms that entire programmes are praised or condemned, and personnel evaluated.[9]

Unfortunately this linguistic confusion has spread even into our Faculties of Arts, among whose tasks is the safeguarding of the language. Anybody who has taken part during recent years in discussions of new programmes in the humanities will recognize the jargon described by Kingsley Price. It is the new working language of the humanist.

Many people must by now be weary of the calls for "innovative methods" in education. The cult of innovation is in itself a sign of cultural disintegration. A society which cannot acquire and transmit the experience necessary for the management of its affairs constantly seeks something new that will make, not a modest improvement on existing methods, but a radical and transforming change. Contemporary prophets offer everything, from the abolition of all schooling to the extension of schooling from the cradle to the grave, from teaching by machine to teaching by mutual palpation. Society as a whole has, however, not yet reached the total isolation from the past, the total disregard for acquired experience and common sense, that are needed for the acceptance of many nostrums now proferred. Teaching goes on not only in schools and universities, but in the swimming pool, the skating rink, the chess club, the driving school, and the dancing class; and here, where the educationist cannot penetrate, traditional methods quietly persist. Here it is well understood that only those who can do ought to be allowed to teach, that results are important, and that theories and "innovative methods" have a limited usefulness. Many Canadian children learn to master skills, and to do this they submit to the authority of a teacher and to the discipline of practice. From competence in these physical arts they learn self-confidence and grace. Unfortunately the experience of learning and genuinely mastering a skill is almost unknown to them in their academic pursuits. They study French, but cannot use it in Montreal or Paris; they study literature, but seldom enjoy it; they study English, but cannot read accurately; they study "human relations", and cannot talk to their parents; they study mathematics, and cannot make change; they take courses in "communications", and tell you that they sort of, like, man, you know, dig their teacher. I suggest that we ought to begin to take the skills entrusted to the schools as seriously as we take, for example, driver education. Here we insist on competence and on knowledge, and we set a minimum standard, which we test by formal examination. We make sure that young drivers know the rules, and we encourage them to be proud of their skill. We impose sanctions to prevent any damage to society from the mishandling of motor vehicles. Language is even more important to society than the management of physical traffic, and the dangers of its misuse, though less obvious than those caused by misuse of the roads, are no less serious in the long run. In the past, society accepted the need for competence in the mental arts, and insisted on a knowledge of the rules, on the authority of the teacher, and on an impartial test of competence before it permitted the student to assume professional responsibility as a journalist, a teacher, a lawyer, or an administrator. Most of these sanctions have been weakened or abolished in the name of democracy, though nothing can be more destructive to a democracy than to permit its citizens to remain incompetent in the use of the instruments of thought and discussion. The schools, of course, hardly have much time for the old-fashioned teaching of skills; they have to undertake their tours of world art, world literature, their psycho-sociological adventures into personal counselling, their study sessions and research projects, their courses in film-making and amateur carpentry. They are also troubled by vandalism, drug-taking, shop-lifting, and other activities of the liberated young. It does not strike many educationists that the root of much of this trouble is boredom, and that the best cure for boredom is work; nor does it strike them that learning, if properly directed, need not be all spontaneous play, but can generate its own more rigorous pleasures.

There is a good deal of support among academics for "progressive" education, by which is usually meant that formal teaching and systematic study are discouraged, and that great stress is laid on creativity and spontaneous learning. This presents no great difficulties for the children of academics. With books and intelligent conversation at home, they are well placed to learn informally both in school and out of school. If they fail to learn French in school, they will be given a year in France or Switzerland. If they are backward in English, the university provides remedial English to help them into a professional career. Even so, the number of children from "good homes" who drop out or take drugs ought to alarm us; they usually do so because they are bored, because the school provides insufficient intellectual stimulus and no serious moral challenge. What should most concern our educational progressives, however, is the fate of children from illiterate or semi-literate homes. They, above all, need systematic formal teaching if they are to gain admission to the university and the professions. I do not suggest that educational "progressives" are indifferent to the interests of children from poor homes; but the policies they advocate, by their very design, perpetuate the present domination of our universities by the sons and daughters of professional middle-class families.

What is needed above all is that the central importance of

language in the education of all our children shall be fully recognized. When it is widely understood that a mastery of language is vital to every human being, the resources of the schools and the universities will be given, not to the invention of new methods for bringing about an educational Utopia, but to the daily task of struggling with words and their meanings, the slow and sometimes painful acquisition of mastery from which, in the end, will flow delight. We understand well enough that the pleasure of mountain-climbing, ballet-dancing, skating, golf, and football depend on exercise, practice, and discipline; that without sore muscles there can be no accomplished skill, and that without skill there can be no delight. I do not think it fanciful to see teachers of the humanities—and especially of English—as largely divided into two hostile and mutually uncomprehending camps—that of the believers in "discipline" and that of the believers in "creativity". This unhappy and unnecessary division must be overcome if English studies are to fulfill the hopes that in the past were placed in them. D. H. Lawrence, a great artist who was also a teacher, describes as "the best of school" a period during which the small boys in the classroom are writing an essay; their delight in the task to which only the presence and authority of the teacher holds them on a sunny morning is seen as an indispensable condition of achievement:

> This morning, sweet it is
> To feel the lads' looks light on me
> Then back in a swift bright flutter to work;
> Each one darting away with his
> Discovery, like birds that steal and flee.
> Touch after touch I feel on me
> As their eyes glance at me for the grain
> Of rigour they taste delightedly.[10]

"The grain of rigour", as every serious student and teacher knows, is the very source of mastery and of delight. There is no inevitable opposition between authority and freedom, structure and growth, work and play, effort and spontaneity. It is the task of a teacher to provide the *rigour*, the framework of order and attentiveness, within which intellectual skills can be mastered.

Lawrence, like every teacher, knew how often one fails in this task, and records the price that is paid in a poem of unusual honesty:

> No more can I endure to bear the brunt
> Of the books that lie out on the desks; a full three score
> Of several insults of blotted pages and scrawl
> Of slovenly work that they have offered me.
> I am sick, and tired more than any thrall
> Upon the woodstacks working weariedly.[11]

One cannot imagine Lawrence falling back on one-word-answer tests, or the gimmickry of electronic devices to escape this distress. Nor can one imagine him pretending to himself that the "slovenly work" of his pupils was a kind of child-art, redeemed by a mysterious creativity. That he regards such work as "insults" shows a personal commitment to excellence, and a profound respect for the capabilities of his pupils when he has succeeded in committing them to the *rigour* which they require for their growth. In this, Lawrence is a representative of the great humane tradition which ought to provide teachers with common ground for their endeavour.

Perhaps I may usefully illustrate the practical implications of what I have been asserting by considering the study of Shakespeare. Shakespeare's plays are above all an appeal to the intellect and imagination of the audience through the medium which is universally "human"—that of language. His actors say to us: "Piece out our imperfections with your thoughts"; and in doing so they offer us the rich and subtle words with which a great poet defines the action. When the dawn comes in *Hamlet* we are shown this in words:

> But look, the morn, in russet mantle clad,
> Walks o'er the dew of yon high eastward hill.

This can of course, in a way, be represented in a colour film. We can have a pink light reflected in the sky. But what then becomes of the suggestions of health and sanctity, of the freshness of the dew, and the holiness of the East? And if we have the colour-film effect together with Shakespeare's words, what is the colour-effect but a distraction from the poetry? It is true that students find it easier to respond to a film of Shakespeare than to a production in the theatre, or to their own reading of the play. *This is a result of deficient education*. In the same way, young children find picture books more appealing than *Robinson Crusoe* or *Treasure Island*, and we provide illustrated editions to help them with their reading. The aim of an education in literacy, however, is to release them from a childish and passive dependence on pictures, and give them the freedom of the great realm of language, the natural domain of the human mind. In teaching students to respond to Shakespeare, the use of films has a similar and strictly limited value; the pictures are a concession to verbal weakness, and the teacher's aim must be to wean the student from this childish dependency, not to suggest that a modern art-form has made Shakespeare's words less crucial, or made them into decorative additions to a more direct and universal medium. I have the impression that some teachers are proud of the continual use of film in the teaching of literature. As a result of the cult of audio-visual aids, propagated by faculties of education, young teachers especially think it virtuous to give class time to films, though this is almost always a waste of time. The use of recordings of the voices of good actors is, of course, a very different question, though it might be said that a competent teacher ought to be able to speak the lines of a Shakespeare play well enough to bring them to life for his class without the fuss and complication and distraction that are always caused by the bringing of mechanical devices into the classroom. The use of recordings is often justified; but too often it is resorted to by teachers who do not wish to master those elementary skills of declamation that are needed for all teaching of poetry, and above all of drama, in the classroom. Shakespeare's art is a verbal art; and it is for this reason that it is of value in the education of students. The visual equivalents into which it is translated are necessarily crude and falsified; what is worse, the preference for visual communication in the study of Shakespeare is in itself a surrender to the forces of barbarism, since it admits the principle that human language is obsolete, and that the machine has triumphed. I have known a number of inspiring and illuminating teachers, and I have never known one of them to use a mechanical device in

Where Are English Studies Going?
GEORGE WHALLEY

There is real danger that English studies are going to pieces—not in the production of learned treatises (which goes forward like a wound healing itself in the body of a condemned man), but as a central discipline in the universities and the schools. In the last four or five years the universities in general, and English studies in particular, have suffered some shrewd blows, administered inexpertly and out of ignorant goodwill, as is the way of experts and of our elected representatives. The schools have suffered even more lamentably than the universities. Lack of money is a condition always to be counted on; in a materialist society it provides an incontrovertible argument for brief discussion, abrupt decision, and rough handling. I wonder how long it will take the universities to recover—because recover they certainly will—from the combined afflictions of elephantiasis, inept bureaucratic intrusion, and clumsy tinkering with delicate structures. But I say nothing of these things because I am sure they are not the source of our troubles in English studies. The enemy is within.

Overgrowth has no doubt introduced into our ranks some persons that we could well do without; and we could never have seriously expected that outsiders would ever understand anything quite as odd as a healthy university or the value of studying language and literature. But we could have been expected to have understood ourselves—if we hold with Jung that the unexamined life is not worth living. We have failed to recognize the doubleness of our work as professionals and the doubleness of our task as instructors, the two not being coincident. We have also allowed ourselves to accept—and even to endorse—certain plausible sophisms that disguise our true purpose and progressively undermine it.

Some years ago, the people who conduct the study of English Language and Literature in Canadian universities and colleges formed a professional association in order to provide occasions of fruitful meeting and to foster the good health of our art. The title chosen for this loosely articulated group was the "Association of University Teachers of English" (ACUTE). Like many things Canadian, the title was not indigenous: in modelling the title on one already established in another country we were prepared to identify ourselves officially as "teachers"—"university teachers". One of the oddities of my upbringing was that it instilled in me a half-mystical veneration for what happened in universities and for the sort of people who devote their lives to a university. I am still surprised and flattered to be included in (what I take to be) the company of Erasmus and other learned doctors; and I had always supposed that, in a university, "teaching" was what we—as humanists—never admitted we ever did. Our business was more recondite, oblique, and fertile than that. To my ear the word "teach" is not much less aggressive than a pair of dentist's forceps or a stomach-pump. At school, perhaps, there is teaching. There you teach children—or used to—to add and subtract and multiply, to fog out words from printed characters and to shape characters into the semblance of spoken sounds; you teach spelling and the rudiments of grammar and the dates of kings and the size of the annual crop of copra in Malaya and of coffee in Venezuela, the names of early explorers and rebels and of a few prime ministers; you teach children to colour maps correctly, and to draw diagrams of the steam-actuated, self-propelled, rail-guarded traction engine, because that is a little easier than the Industrial Revolution or the Diet of Worms (and for children probably more suitable). But at a university, I had innocently supposed, professors don't *teach* people, unless it be as a desperate expedient marginal to our true calling.

In the "professions"—medicine, law, engineering—a student *must* be taught a good deal by rote, otherwise his case will be dismissed, his patient will die, his bridge will fall down, his still might blow up. Occasionally, it is true, we may agree (very reluctantly) to *teach* "remedial English"; I'm sure "teach" is the right word for our attempts to effect a transformation that we had hoped would have happened a little closer to the cradle. There is,

I must admit, something a little importunate about some of the things we try to insist upon our students getting right—spelling, grammar, dates, conventions for citing references, the correct ascription of authors to works, generally doing things in what looks like an orderly manner: that is, it isn't all improvised games and free uninformed discussion. Importunity and a hunger for the correct answer are the earmarks of "teaching".

'Yet the most eloquent lecturer I have ever listened to was a naval commander who instructed us in astronomical navigation. He unfolded the mysteries of the celestial sphere and of spherical trigonometry with the rapt lyricism of a star-gazer and with the shameless delight of a cellist playing a sequence of harmonics in the fifth position. What he told us certainly helped us to keep ships off rocks and out of mine-fields, and to that extent he "taught" us; but his performance was also what is called "an education". Even after more than thirty years the sight of a sextant or a set of navigational tables will recall the expression of his face as he spoke and the movement of his arm (with the three gold rings on the sleeve of his superb Gieves monkey-jacket) as, with fluent incisiveness, he would draw a diagram and sketch in a succession of modifications that kept pace with his discourse.

When we think of the memorable things we have seen our instructors doing over a literary text, or reflectively over some subtle point of articulation, or across some great sweep of time and space, it has been as though we were privileged to overhear an interior monologue; we might intervene occasionally to touch upon the reverberant strings of it; it did not seem to be spoken *to* us; certainly it was not spoken *at* us. I don't know what is the right word for that exalted humming, that transfigured chewing of the mental cud; but "teaching" doesn't seem the right word at all. Not being the right word, it may be a bad word for us to get used to using unthoughtfully when we think or talk about our work. If we are not careful, that is precisely what—through the subversive efficacy of sheer reiteration—we shall find ourselves doing: *teaching*. And that, unhappily, is what, as university instructors, we spend far too much time doing.

One of the commonplaces of our academic system of credit-rating is that we are expected to "perform well" as "teachers" and as "scholars". It is also a commonplace in arguments presented to fund-granting committees that the two functions are so closely related as to be virtually indistinguishable, and that therefore there should always be more funds for "research". I am not against "research funds", but the argument seems to me a specious one, especially when it goes on (as it usually does) to assert that "research" is indiscriminately a good thing and that other academic responsibilities that might interfere with it should to some extent give way.

To have persuaded somebody somewhere to put one's scholarly lucubrations into print is no doubt a sign of life of some sort; the failure to do so, however, or the failure to want to do so, is not necessarily a sign of death. A university being a place of learning, surely there must be learned people about; and to be learned is presumably not a terminal state. In the humane studies it is an advantage if an instructor ferrets away at some reading or studying in his spare time—not that that gives him "more knowledge" but that he is then able to move with greater ease. Good university instruction, like careful writing, is always icebergish; only journalists are so hard-pressed that they have to put all their wares in the shop window at once. Perhaps a university instructor should normally be talking over his students' heads—otherwise no effort is involved, and they might get the impression that there were no heads more exalted than their own, which could have negative educational results. What matters is not to "know more" (which isn't difficult if a person sets his mind to it) but to achieve in discourse the disciplined fluency of a dancer. What is being declared is not simply the subject of the discourse but also the fact that a certain movement of mind is possible. To be a little learned secures the possibility of such a movement. Since good university instruction in English is an imaginative activity, we should not assume that we can always tell the dancer from the dance.

We need to fulfil both roles, as instructor and as scholar (though not necessarily to the extreme of cold print), but securing as far as possible a seamless relation between the two. Too often the split between them occurs not through neglect but through misplaced zeal: the unassimilated detail of the work-in-progress comes to the forefront to disrupt the reflection proper to the work in hand. It is so easy to become "expert beyond experience" that perhaps most of us do our best work as instructors when we are not working in our "special field".

To "*teach* a course", I take it, is to assume that the subject matter defined by the title of the course is what must somehow be impressed upon the minds of those students who "take the course"; to treat the time available as a vacuum to be filled with discussion and interpretation of that subject-matter to the general exclusion of everything else so that students will be able to answer pointed questions about the subject; to establish for the subject-matter an orthodox method of inquiry and a received interpretation; to urge students to use their own judgment and to seek their own conclusions, but at the same time insisting that they know "the right answers"; to exhibit a strong proprietary interest in the subject, being if need be a little pugnacious in defence of it; and if the subject falls within the compass of one's "research specialization" to give a notable performance on the hobbyhorse.

If we try to construct, from the biographical notes on contributors to the learned journals "in our field" and from the articles themselves, a portrait of a University Teacher of English, we get the impression that his prime function is to "make a contribution to knowledge". He seems to emerge, not as a commanding Abelard or a boisterous Giordano Bruno, but rather as a small, almost anonymous, creature who adds to the coral-reef of scholarship. Turning to my one-volume encyclopaedia (which sits on the shelf next to a copy of *Old Moore's Almanac*) I found the following:

> *Coral*—a small invertebrate characterized by its outer skeleton and by its sedentary habit of life. Most corals live in colonies although there are some solitary forms. Each polyp is mainly a hollow digestive tract with a single opening at the free or unattached end of the body. Reproduction results in the production of an individual which moves about freely in the water before attaching itself and secreting its skeleton. As the colonial forms produce more polyps, the lower members die, and new layers are built up on the old skeletons.

It would be a pity if our "teaching" became no more than secretions from so sedulous a process.

The attitude towards "English" has changed a good deal in the thirty years since I first had the temerity to stand at a lectern (we wore academic gowns in those days) and tried to engage students in what was called "English Language and Literature". By that time, "English" had already taken up from the Classics the role of the central civilizing discipline. We were the transplanted heart of the humanities, and nobody had yet studied the immunology of such a case. We were a little startled so to assume that responsibility. We accepted it as the Damocles sword of a noble enterprise rather than the sceptre of divine authority. We had (as I said at the first formal meeting of ACUTE gathered in Edmonton in 1958) the air of elderly gentlemen who unexpectedly find themselves running in an egg-and-spoon race. But we had no doubt what the race was for, and were in no doubt that —despite the enormous hazard and despite certain physical disabilities—we could carry the egg triumphantly. That confidence has now largely evaporated. If we could find a wall we would have our backs to it.

On the whole, the universities—like the schools—have abrogated their prime responsibility to give coherent purpose to the grand subversive work of education; not only of passing on our literate heritage, but also of liberating the minds of the young and helping them to find a disciplined order for their inner lives. This has come about through a sequence of academic propositions, all of them allegedly egalitarian, none of them apparently of much importance at the time, yet all of them anti-educational.

First the equivocation, established long before the first student activist sloped towards a Senate chamber, whereby it was established that the word "required" as applied to a course meant "compulsory" and therefore socially "unacceptable": at one stroke this removes the responsibility of giving educational direction according to experience, tradition, and judgment. Again, Snow's journalistic fantasy of "the two cultures" has been effectively used—as no doubt it was intended to be used—as a ploy in the silly game of one-upmanship; even in faculty boards of some judgment and stability it has provided the means of denying that the humanities *have* a central civilizing function and of asserting that English is "just another subject-area". This glosses over the fact that a university, even a small one, has to fulfil a number of different functions, many of which involve straightforward, high-pressure, technical training. The sophism in this case consists of maintaining that all instruction that goes on in a university is accurately described as "education": therefore there is no educative difference between one kind of study and another—the only difference is in the "subject-area". Yet the engineer's training, or the chemist's, or the medical doctor's is not an "education" in the sense that an honours programme in philosophy or literature is expected to be an "education". That is not to say that no engineer or chemist or doctor can ever become an "educated person", but that his special university training will not be able to do much to make him so. Nobody has any hesitation in rating programmes according to their alleged "social relevance", but our sensibilities seem to be too exquisite to allow us to say that one faculty or programme or department is *educationally* more influential than another. And what are we to say to faculties of education in which the word "education" seems often to assume a meaning bizarre and inscrutable?

In the name of "freedom" the view has prevailed that every "subject" is equal in educational virtue to every other "subject"; that every "subject" is a "discipline" (jealously guarded by the home-made mystique of its practitioners); and that every "discipline" (that is, "subject") must be given equal time, space, and lighting in the academic midway so that students can pick out from a bewildering profusion of wares "the subject of their choice". According to this curious figure of the free market, business opportunities must be equally spread; the consumer's choice must be guided entirely by his own digestive tract; we must never seem to discriminate against Linear B or the microbiology of the lesser lepidoptera. It is tacitly agreed—as bibliophiles tacitly agree not to embarrass each other by asking questions about what is written in the books they collect—that no question should ever be raised about the educational quality of a programme or the paedagogic virtue of a course. The same complicity applies within English departments: nobody dare hint that Sean O'Casey is inferior to Ben Jonson or that there may be more value in studying Milton than Edgar Allan Poe: that might imply that "our O'Casey man" or "our Poe man" is of less stature than "our Ben Jonson man" or "our Milton man".

So "English" now sets up its stall submissively in the fly-

blown academic midway, doing a pathetic shuffle-dance to attract attention to the Bearded Lady because good manners prevent us from hiring a barker. Surely in these circumstances
every university should now have a Fair Practices Committee and
an array of anti-combine regulations. I have heard the preposter-
ous suggestion, uttered with no sense of the barbarous implications of it, that English should now be considered a branch of
"communications" or a wing of that fashionable high-flyer,
Sociology. But that is hardly surprising when we remark that no
university seems to have any educational philosophy beyond
some soothing principles of socio-economic accommodation and
the divine right of students. And after the midway where the
recruits are unwittingly beguiled into their chosen corrals, there is
the academic self-service supermarket of courses, where packag-
ing and promotion are paramount, and the prices—in intellectual
and emotional terms—are cunningly concealed. In such a setting
it would be impertinent to ask: "What educative result is my
course (programme, department, faculty) supposed to have? And
what subject-matter and what processes of mind would be most
powerful to induce it?"

Beyond this cluster of damaging assumptions, two others need
to be noticed, possibly more insidious than the others. One is the
uncritical acceptance of the behavioural figure of a man as a
not-very-efficient, problem-solving animal, whose actions and
choices are represented as mechanical responses to a complex of
forces from within and without, all of which are definable and to
a large extent programmable. According to this scheme, instructors produce the "stimuli" (the loaded questions?); students provide the "responses" (the expected answers?); the "results" can
be "quantified". The other damaging assumption is the canoni-
zation of "research" in the humanities, claiming for it a status
and function similar to research in the sciences, the case being
supported, and the issue confused, by applying the scientist's
word "research" to all kinds of independent and methodical
inquiry in the humanities. I have said elsewhere that the word
"research" can be made to refer—and should be made to
refer—to a definable concept, and that that concept, scrupulously
applied, refers properly to some activities that are essential to
English studies, but as ancillary rather than central. We need

reliable texts and glosses; we need to set down, at various levels of minuteness, veridical facts as far as they are available and relevant. Our work of inquiry demands the utmost discrimination and precision within lattices of fact; but the "facts" that are central to us are judgments upon events, and most of the crucial events are interior to ourselves, accessible only to direct qualitative apprehension.

The marks of a good literary scholar are a highly developed sense of fact and of relevance, and an acute feeling for distinctions and differences and the precise scope of them. I am not sure that we foster those qualities much by trying to make students of literature into "researchers"; yet if we place a skew value on "research" our self-justification may produce monsters in our own image. As instructors we are transmitters. Much of our care is to help people tune their circuits, partly to what we are saying, but mostly to the literature we invite them to study. Some of the equipment looks pretty ramshackle at first—not much beyond the cat's-whisker stage; but we have to make a start somewhere, and the choice of a starting point requires tact, and sometimes charity.

The practice of marketeering has put some strange goods on the shelves—symptoms of feeble educational purpose or infirm confidence, echoes of the entertainment industry, evidence of the easy slide into comfortable zones on the fringes of literature: histories and backgrounds; themes, trends, and genres; "history of ideas", "critical approaches", "research techniques"—all of them interesting enough but having in themselves surprisingly little to do with the substance of literature. For certain other delicacies and sweetmeats there is less to be said—children's literature, the folklore of the Alleghenies, witchcraft and utopianism, orientalism in the nineteenth-century essay, alienation as a major theme in emigrant novels, etc., etc., etc.: these are clearly digressions from the strenuous business of coming to terms with great works of literature.

Only great works of literature and great writers make heavy enough demands to induce the activities of intellect, and the exact emotional definitions, that can make the study of literature an educational instrument of unique power. When time is short and distractions manifold it is idiotic to squander time and attention on peripheral activities and third-rate materials—third-rate, that is, in paedagogic efficacy, which usually also means third-rate in literary quality. Survey courses, for example, commonly have no purpose beyond presenting a microtome slice of a large number of "representative works" interlarded with brief dogmatic judgments easy to remember and handy to repeat. What is worse, first-year courses are often tarted up with fashionable and sensational trifles that students can be expected to applaud for their salacious topicality but which can do little enough to induce worth-while reflection.

Our business is to do with seafaring, not basking in the warm shallows. If, as instructors, we succeed, we shall have added another ancient mariner to our company—a wary and skilful navigator capable of making accurate landfalls in deceitful weather. The fact that some will jump ship and that others will suffer cruelly from sea-sickness is not reason enough to stay tied up at the marina within comfortable reach of the gin-shops and the bikinied sunbathers. The marina-courses usually justify themselves on the grounds that we have to make ourselves accessible to "modern taste". The accessibility of literature, however, is to be found elsewhere—in our inheritance of language and in our need to clarify our selves and to escape from the disease of self-indulgence. We all tend to dislike danger, to prefer a safe berth. Only the frontal assault of fully realized literature is likely to startle us into one of those acts of recognition and commitment that mark the end of foolery and the beginning of serious inquiry.

It is so difficult to sustain our attention upon a complex poem that our attention naturally drifts outward and the heart of the matter slips away from us. Since there is probably no such thing as an elementary poem, it is difficult to persuade students that it is possible to sustain critical attention; difficult to show that we are not inevitably forced to talk about something we hadn't set out to talk about. Nevertheless, out of misguided compassion, we are tempted to offer panaceas, short cuts, formulary devices, interpretative charms, so that the burden of critical initiative will not have to be taken up; and all these have a sickening way of dissolving the realities of literature and breeding dreary tautologies.

If we are not *using* literature with some educative purpose we are unlikely to make much educational headway. Teaching something *about* literature—by glossing, digesting, explaining—is not the same as using literature for an educative purpose; for there is as much difference between knowing something and knowing *about* something as there is between observing and seeing, between hearing and listening, between dream and vision, opinion and judgment. Certainly we want to study literature for its own sake; but we also want to study it for *our* sake. Since our work is, like the working of art itself, an art of indirection, it is quite possible to combine a clear sense of purpose with a disinterested means of fulfilling it.

We can usefully think of our work as falling into two phases—"acquaintance" and "inquiry"—the phases being conceptually distinguishable but concentric and proceeding together by interaction. Both phases begin, as Plato said philosophy begins, in a sense of wonder, and both lead to an extension of awareness; and both need to be overarched by a quality of attention that Owen Barfield ascribes to Coleridge: reverence and its twin sister reticence.

Whether or not a student comes to university fairly widely read, it is unlikely that he will have more than a smattering, even of some acknowledged giants of English literature. As instructors we may not have much more than a deeper smattering, with some special areas where we have done some quiet browsing or earnest excavation; and all of us will have to live with the fact that few will ever get much beyond that, and that those who do may, in extending their scope, have to rely for much of it upon their own generalizations from fragmentary impressions. Our first task with students is to initiate the process of acquaintance, or if it has already begun, to accelerate it.

Nothing much can happen in English studies until a person has established, with some works of literature, an active personal relationship that goes beyond general interest or technical curiosity: the guiding impulse is delight. Poets are magpies; students should be encouraged to be magpies—becoming in this at least a little poetical. What we want to encourage students to recognize is that they have a capacity for complex response much wider and more sensitive than they had supposed, and that that capacity can be extended, refined, and disciplined; that their response can be more or less appropriate, advancing beyond the mere triggering of an emotional "mood" towards a supple state of mind that is shaped in detail by the poem itself; that as we become increasingly deft at attuning our awareness to poems there will come a growing sense of the otherness of a poem, its substance, autonomy, and strangeness—that the poem can become genuinely "knowable" and not simply "knowable-about".

To begin with we should not be too busy in correcting choices, though we might at some time hint that there may be more intellectual and emotional reward in John Donne than in Thomas Hood or Robert Burns, or that the *Grosse Fuge* may prove more durable than the *Nutcracker Suite*. (All of us who lay claim to an informed taste would cringe to see paraded in public the history of the development of that taste—through what shallows, by what paths of blind ignorance, through what shameless indulgence.) We need to be careful not to insist too urgently upon what they *should* enjoy or admire; they will find soon enough what things are pure gold and which are as thin as gold-leaf without being gold at all, and that there are a great many poems this side of "greatness" that charm and delight us and can be a possession for all time. And we must be especially careful—this is where the reticence comes in—not to remove or impair that most precious possibility, of their discovering something really first-rate for themselves. (I am grateful to have discovered for myself, along the path of ignorance, John Donne, W. B. Yeats, and David Jones, and I treasure all three of them the more for that.)

At the beginning we can advance emphatically the injunction: "Connect—enjoy—listen—don't fuss." What looks like the line of easiest access, through the topical and the familiar, engaging the echoes of our (so dreary) social milieu and our (so pathetic) personal preoccupations, will almost certainly prove a nauseating dead-end. Somehow a personal and not very sceptical relation must be discovered. Here the instructor's business is not selling goods but disclosing and unfolding marvels; establishing for literature the simultaneity of everything that lives and deserves to live, cultivating a sense of wonder for the physical substance and intricate specificity of works of imagination. I am sure that sensibility develops little, if at all, by disliking and rejecting; it develops most rapidly towards accurate apprehension when confronted with work increasingly powerful and strange. In art, as in life, there are no classes for beginners.

The progress will not be either uniform or linear—a pattern of rabbit tracks over a rough landscape, with a little bloodshed at the places where we detached ourselves from straw gods and the mirror of Narcissus. In this phase there is no place much for argument or exposition; rather the lightest of frameworks is required so that an occasional fix can be taken, and every temptation to catholicity placed in the path of the unwary. Above all, a deepening sense of language and of the sounds and rhythms of it; the sense of the inventiveness and autonomy of language heightened by asking, not simply "What does this *mean*?", but "What is this *doing*?", and "What exactly is this doing *now*?"

If this seems too haphazard a way of staking out a country of affection, a centre of reference can be found in a unitary view of poetry, on the assumption that "poetry" is a very comprehensive term, and that although poems are many and various, poetry is one and has its specific *frisson*. This is done, not by generalizing from the whole body of literature, but by shaping a figure from the best evidence we individually have available—that is, the things we know best and care most about. A fashionable counsel of despair says that there are too many kinds of literature, too many single works of literature, for anybody to attempt such a view. That is really a consolatory evasion: there has always been too much to learn and know; the capacity of the mind is prodigious but not infinite. Yet we are ill-advised not to make the attempt.

One of the beautiful features of the mind is its power to select, and the tendency to select and stow away what we care most about—even though the caring may sometimes be from fear or revulsion. The mind remains agile by forgetting as well as remembering, by emptying as well as filling. The healthy mind is ringed round by unknowing as a poem is ringed about with silence; unknowing is the matrix of knowing. Perhaps the best beginning for a unitary view of poetry is to find out what poets themselves say makes them do what they do, how they work, and what axioms guide their work. That may not provide a definition of poetry, but it will certainly remove some absurdities. For those who have never seriously engaged the poetic way of mind this may be strange country; but we can at least learn the axioms, if necessary by rote, so that we do not entertain inappropriate assumptions or disseminate corrupt analogies.

If we are constructing an illustrative analogy for the way poems get made and how they "work"—a figure that will be used not to classify poems but to bring to our attention distinctive peculiarities of individual poems—we should be ill-advised to go to a psychologist, a sociologist, a historian, a linguist, or a computer expert—least of all an expert in "communications". None of these will have made any careful study of the facts and axioms of poetic making, or if they have they will have selected their evidence according to their own working assumptions and will have phrased their findings in an analogical vocabulary (almost certainly causal-mechanistic) constructed for a purpose so different from the purpose of poetry as to exclude most of the distinctive characteristics of poetic making. Each "outsider" will in his own way—looking at poetry through his own methodological spectacles—describe poetry as a projection of his own guiding analogies.

I turn aside for a moment to examine an analogy that has come from "outside" to gain some currency among our people: the analogy of "communication" as promulgated by those experts in auditory and visual presentation who are convinced that coherent speech and the printed word are obsolete. Departments of "Communications" have already been set up in some universities. It is fair enough that somebody should study the various technical means of "getting things across", but it is difficult to see any connection between that and the assumption that "Communications" possesses, or can provide, the central theory by which all modes of intelligible interaction among human beings are to be interpreted.

Whether or not, as an economic or administrative convenience, English is threatened with being swallowed up by "Communications", we could hardly deny that the jargon of the subject has already invaded our classrooms with the terms "information", "medium", "message", and "audience-appeal", and has called to its support certain relics of a pre-parascientific age—"meaning", "intention", and "the poet's philosophy". "Communications theory", properly so-called, is to do with mathematics, cybernetics (computer theory), and the design of certain kinds of electronic equipment, and has a history that can be traced back more than a hundred years. The theoretical under-pinning of academic departments of Communications however has a different origin and a much shorter history; since much of it is arcane, assertive, and incoherent, it might be considered speculative rather than theoretical; and since these speculations grew up largely as a self-justifying offshoot of the advertising and propaganda industries, the purity of its theoretical position may be thought to be in some way a little contaminated. But there are other objections both logical and linguistic, and it would be salutary to notice some of the ambiguities and distortions that the unexamined analogy of "communication" can bring to the study of literary matters.

The radical sense of the word "communicate" lies in the area "to bring together into one, to hold communion with, to share closely with, to hold intercourse with". The sense of an intimate coming together into a condition of union is intrinsic to the word—a meaning that could well carry with it some hint of the reason why language is more refined than grunts, squeaks, and whistles, and how, in that development, language has been able to secure and delineate the most subtle relations between one person and another. These implications survive in the semi-technical jargon of "communications", but only as an escape hatch in argument or as an emotive aura.

The ancillary terms "information", "medium", and "message", however, show that "communication" is being used in the military or telegraphic sense: a line of connection (a wire or a suitably directed radio wave) is established in order to pass messages from one person to another. If there can be shown to be a "communicating" link, it follows that it could be there only to "communicate"—i.e., to pass messages. If messages are to be passed there must be somebody who initiates the message, and there will be somebody to receive it and read it intelligibly (because there's not much point in sending a message that the recipient cannot understand). The line by which the message gets from one person to another is the "medium of communication". This is all quite elementary and perfectly clear.

The trouble begins when the analogy is applied to persons

standing close enough to each other that no wire or equipment is needed, or to the circumstance of writing something (as is the case with most works of literature) that is addressed to nobody in particular. By a process that for convenience we could call "nominalism", each item in the elementary figure is given the status of a "thing", something that exists, and each item must then be accounted for in any situation that is alleged to be analogous to the illustrative figure.[1] The sender of the message is identified as the poet; the recipient is the "audience" (conceived of as an indolent or resentful TV audience that has to be persuaded to pay attention); the "medium" is "language". (Here the terms of the figure have slipped a little: by rights the "medium" corresponding to the wire that carries the electrical impulses would have to be the air carrying sound waves or a piece of paper carrying written characters on it.)[2] By definition, a "message" is anything that can be sent; it does not follow, however, that anything that can be sent is a "message". When we apply this to poetry we are in trouble: there is usually no evidence that for the poet there was in fact any sending or intent to send, and although a poem *can* have a "message" we usually suspect a poem of having an impure intention if it does have a "message". By trying to make "message" mean too much it means almost nothing. Correspondingly the apparently forthright term "information" dissolves when on the one hand advertisers plead that everything they publish is "information", and on the other hand computing people define "information" as anything that their technical system can accept for processing.

Once the analogy of "communication" is accepted for poetry we *must* look for a "message"; but what we find is either nothing, or else something grotesquely at odds with the poem itself. Yet because the figure insists that *something* has to be sent, the "message" gets desperately transformed into "meaning" or "intention": the "message", even if in soldierly terms it is obscure or indecipherable, is still what the poet "meant" or what he "intended to say". If the poet's "meaning" or "intention" eludes the grasp, we then regress to "the poet's philosophy" in search of a key to interpretation—forgetting that "philosophy" is a shifty term, and that to work from the general to the particular is at best a hazardous procedure.

It is obvious that a "medium" is a vehicle for transmitting. A telephone circuit with a narrow range of audio-frequencies is an unfaithful medium for the human voice; a radio circuit of unstable frequency response is an unfaithful medium for any kind of sound. A medium (in this sense) has definable characteristics and limitations, but no character; it initiates nothing, and it does not partake of the nature of what it transmits. By asserting that language is a "medium", the "communication" analogy insists that language is either a neutral conveyor of messages (meanings, intentions?), or else a conventional code in which messages can be conveyed.

It is true that we can indeed utter and write messages; but that is far from all we know we can do in language and far from what we commonly use language for. We know, for example, that we manage intelligible speech with primitive simplicity and directness: it is a gesture, an act, and typically an inventive act; we do not first conceive a "meaning", then translate it into language as a "message", then "send" it by speaking or writing it. We know that, because it is a person, not language, that means, the saying of anything is typically a delineation of what the speaker guessed he might find himself saying. To put it another way, *what* is said in speech—if it is of more than the most rudimentary indicativeness or abstraction—cannot be separated from *how* it is said. We know, for example, that language is often used as a way of *preventing* disclosure of feeling, thought, intention, meaning. We know that it is possible—and not very exceptional between people who are "close to each other"—to speak in such a way that what is actually said becomes a carrier-wave for matters quite different from what the words seem to be about, and that this is so because what is put on the carrier-wave could not be said in any other way. It is true that language can (in the loosest sense) "communicate" and it is true that poetry can "communicate"—that is, can transfer something more or less intelligible from one person to another. But it is a very slack kind of logic that would find those two statements equivalent to the statement that "Language is communication" or that "Poetry is communication". For a beginning we should have to do something about that slippery verb "is".

The "communication" analogy as applied to literature seems

to commend itself for its cheerful plausibility, perhaps most of all to those who may have hoped that there would be some easy and straightforward way of dealing with poetry. But in spite of its lively vogue it isn't very useful in literary studies. Its assumptions about language and the functions of language preclude much more than they illuminate, and what they illuminate is of little importance in the field of literature. The most serious objection to the analogy is that it misrepresents the prototypal nature and functions of language as we know them. Another serious objection is that virtually every term in its battery of special words is either ambiguous or circular: the analogy readily produces a sequential equivocation that may be useful in case-making, or even in a court of law, but it does not help us in our inquiry into poetry, inasmuch as poetry is a continuous affirmation of our nature as articulate, discriminating, and inventive.

While we are thinking of analogies and their appropriateness it is perhaps just worth pointing out to students that—contrary to the working premises of anthropology and psychology—some people sometimes do things simply for the fun of it; that perhaps not all symptomatic indications are "deeply significant"; that perhaps not all human actions are adequately explained in terms of "drives" and "motives", any more than a theory of ballistics will tell us what it feels like to shoot at somebody with a pistol with deadly intent; that when we "see", it doesn't *feel* as though we were experiencing a "neuro-visual reaction"; and that when we speak, it doesn't *feel* as though we were "constructing a verbal-semantic string of indeterminate length".

Coming back to "acquaintance", there is no need for separate "courses" in it. Indeed much heavy-handed damage can be done to a student's grasp of literature by spending too much time over works that do not reward the effort, writings not strong enough to arouse delight and not profound or intricate enough to shape response into sustained scrutiny. The trouble with marina-courses is that they provide themselves with a vacuum so spacious that it has to be filled out with factitious entertainment and special pleading. Also they tend to isolate themselves from other staple courses because direct comparison would show them to be peripheral.

This is my objection to "a full range of courses" in (say)

Canadian Literature. There are many reasons why we should be acquainted with our own best writing; but you don't have to "take a course in the subject" to do that. Our primary purpose is educative; the accident that certain works were written by our fellow countrymen is no guarantee that they are strong enough or intricate enough to induce—in the very limited time at our disposal—the activities of mind that alone make the study of English Literature a powerful educative discipline. To use up time and energy on "acquaintance" with works that will not sustain worth-while inquiry is time ill-spent; our main educative task is subtle and slow-burning, and needs all the time-for-gestation we can possibly find for it. If we are really working *sub specie aeternitatis*—as I think we should be—declarations of national pride and ambition, though pardonable, are beside the point. If we are not playing for keeps, English is indeed "just another subject". As educators we should be much more concerned than we are with the *function* of what we study, and much less with the subject-matter of it. It is even arguable that, unless we do our work with serious intent, we shall be making less contribution than we could to the climate that brings great works of literature into being.

The process of acquaintance need not be isolated, and is probably better if it isn't: it goes forward at every stage in the development of taste, advancing—and retreating too—by quantum steps, responding to inquiry and nourished by reflection. A person can read Pope or Milton or Dante or Aristotle one day; two weeks earlier it would have been impossible; a year later (for a variety of reasons) it may be wormwood and gall; yet later again it may return as a new thing. Because the process of acquaintance is continuous and proceeds (not without effort) by unpredictable stages, the ordonnance of possibilities in any single mind is as mysterious as the way a poem comes into being—yet familiar enough (one would have thought) because it is the way our minds order themselves, preparing a spider's web for a fly that we do not yet know exists, and which we may not like when we come to eat it. If "criticism" is understood to be a process of getting-to-know, it can be seen to be as firmly rooted in "acquaintance" as it is nourished by "inquiry".

In the study of literature we rightly place strong emphasis upon the poem as the centre of attention. That precept cannot be allowed to cut the poem off from its context; yet part of the difficulty is how to prevent the context from swamping the poem. Very little can be systematically excluded from the field of literature: students need to acquaint themselves with the non-literary matters that works of literature are often embedded in and that often give them both energy and direction. It is not well that students be totally unaware that something has happened to physics since Newton, or to labour relations since the Peasants' Revolt, or to psychiatry since Freud; nor should they be ignorant that some things had happened to English poetry before Pound.

If "background material" is merely accumulated as "information" it will tend to deposit itself in the mind at a level of uniform emphasis, either refusing to combine with literary elements or reducing the poem to the same uniform level of evidence. The selective and heuristic activities associated with "acquaintance" can provide a contour of relevance, a sense of a centre and a periphery, a sense of what in any instance is to the point and what isn't, and with what degree of emphasis. As recognitions of quality become reliable we are better able to judge whether we are studying a work of literature as an imaginative construction in its own right, or whether we are using it as evidential material for a quite different purpose—psychology, philosophy, history, sociology. It is in the continuous process of acquaintance that agility of mind and subtlety of perception are fostered. We need to be careful that what should be a continuing process is not arrested by activities dominantly analytical or merely cumulative.

The other phase—"inquiry" or "reflective inquiry"—is what we *do* with the knowing we have gathered up in acquaintance. Inquiry does not wait for acquaintance to be completed, but is rather the means by which acquaintance advances beyond mere accumulation to a progressive exploration of new modes of imaginative activity.

Reflective inquiry is the crowning intellectual and emotional achievement of our art; but I want to consider it here only in its paedagogic aspects, for it is in this that the Aristotelian principle especially applies: we become what we do. As instructors, our first and crucial consideration is the choice of works that students are to inquire into and reflect upon. Ideally we should like them in the end to be able to inquire into any literature whatsoever; but at first—and probably throughout an undergraduate programme, because time is very short—a careful selection needs to be made according to the paedagogic *function* each work is to serve. The selection has to begin "at the top", with works of unquestionable toughness and achievement, works that force us to recognize the poetic way of mind that they declare, because that is actually the way of mind we, as individuals, are trying to discover—with the whole person, intellect, emotion, and imagination, in due consort. Some works need to be intricate and difficult in order to force students out of prosaic assumptions into the specific verbal world of poetry; but not too many of these, otherwise students (like many of their instructors) might think that there's nothing to the study of literature but ingenious puzzle-solving. We also need to choose works that combine great power with unmannered simplicity and translucence, poems that at one stroke bring into coincidence the qualities of the extremely simple and the extremely complex—the indelible mark of all imaginative work. Works need to be chosen also that will demonstrate beyond reasonable doubt that the poetic mode is not a modification of the conceptual mode, but distinct from it, even though it uses "the same language" and embraces many of the same logical and syntactical principles.

Here the imperative to "respond *to*", which is paramount in the phase of acquaintance, turns into a family of questions: How can I respond less accidentally, in a more sustained, more informed, less private way? How can I get to know the *poem* rather than merely my response to the poem? How can I sustain inquiry and reflection without getting stuck in some analytical backwater, the poem disembowelled and no way onward?

As instructors we want not only to show *how* to inquire, or that it is possible to inquire and to sustain inquiry; we also want to show what to inquire *from*, what to respond *from*. In the gradual development of critical maturity, the centre of attention shifts from the responding self to the poem as an entity in its own right, to the poem as reshaping our response in detail and guiding our reflection, to the poem as something that we can genuinely *know*. The foundation for this change is the secretion of critical experience that transforms "response" from a more or less accidental personal reaction, neural and emotional, to a distinct cognitive act: from "I feel" to "*I* feel *this*; *I* value *this*; I *know* this poem."

The gathering together in memory of our experience of poems becomes a foundation for both our responsive activity and our reflective activity; it becomes the personal counterpart to the poem, the experiential complex that each of us, being what he is, can hospitably present to a poem. The accretion of critical experience, when fully assimilated at each stage and taken up into ourselves, becomes a subliminal part of our selves, being the selected impressions, known-and-forgotten-but-never-lost, that we now bring to our recognitions and judgments. We are then no longer merely a responsive mechanism triggered by what we read, nor a brain that can do nothing but think *about* what we read. We have acquired, and continue to nourish, an imaginative darkness *from* which we go out toward poems, recognizing them not as projections of ourselves, nor as gratifying emotions that we may wish to have aroused, but as having their own life and integrity, and as having in a real sense a nature resonant with our own. What we respond *from* is not simply our cumulative acquaintance with substantial works of literature, but also our sense of the nature of poetry itself, how it lives and functions; and also our sense of our selves. Gradually, through recognition and discovery, we gain confidence in our responsive selves, and in those crazy bird-cages we call our "minds".

When a concept of poetry and a concept of mind come into conjunction, a crucial assault occurs, because the two concepts are mutually constructive. Except for a few conceptual purposes the terms "subject/object", "subjective/objective" dissolve. We are suddenly denied what we thought was a common-sense foundation for our analyses. The realities of imaginative works defy the "realist's" assumption that all events must be analysed—can only be analysed—into subject/object, cause/effect, conscious-purpose/intended-result. For we find that our inquiry—like the making of poetry itself—cannot proceed except through a sequence of recognitions and judgments of value; that our knowing, thinking, perceiving is incorrigibly subjective in the sense that it is always anchored in the experiencing self, I-knowing, I-thinking, I-perceiving; that the relation between reader and poem, and between poet and poem, is not a subject/object relation but an intersubjective relation—two I's going out to meet each other. For the poet's chief preoccupation is, not to write something that will have a certain effect, but simply to make a poem.

In matters of this sort I think that our training (as instructors) does us some disservice: we pay far too little attention to the pervasive presence and activity of *mind*, and we think too little about the metaphysical status of a poem—how it can be said to exist, how it can be said to be knowable. Yet literature itself, with poetry as its prototypal function, provides all the evidence we could possibly ask for if we are to inquire into the mind and its functions and relations—not least in what it can tell us of the way poems come into being and of the ways they can become the embodiment of mental events. We are remarkably insensitive to speculative possibilities if we do not see that the order of language we call "poetic" or "symbolic" forces us to inquire into judging, perceiving, knowing, recognizing, discriminating; and that any serious attempt so to inquire into the poetic way of mind (the peculiar inheritance of man) forces us to define activities, relations, and orders of mental certitude that lie outside the compass of experimental psychology as we now have it, and of positivist philosophy, and of the behavioural-mechanistic account of man.

It is our responsibility to make the range of mental activity as comprehensive as possible. Yet the trend of literary studies since the Second War has narrowed rather than extended the field of our work, by tacitly excluding much that is fertile—and even essential—in an attempt to "define the discipline". That circumscription has been further endorsed by the specialization that has accumulated quantities of microscopic and unrelated detail —that seems to argue that the field of literature is too multitudinous to be embraced, and that therefore either the boundaries should be drawn in or else that the country should be subdivided in order to keep control of it.

A "discipline" is characterized, not by its subject-matter, but by the ways of mind it typically and necessarily evokes. Yet in desperation, and afflicted by a "technical" climate of opinion over which we have little control, we have turned too much, and too uncritically, to semi-technical manipulations, analytic procedures, patchwork rather than synthesis. Our tendency to rely on formulary procedures in the classroom is as much a symptom of this as it is a symptom of laziness and timidity. We forget that the mind is both a perceptive and a selective instrument. To match the imaginative source of literature, the dominant process of inquiry needs to be synthesis—or more properly, a synthesizing rhythmic movement from synthesis to analysis and back to synthesis, forgetting as well as remembering, so that we can discover the true patterns of literature and not impose upon it preconceived patterns that we insist (for other reasons) that literature must exhibit.

Literary studies now seem to have fallen into three strains: the principle of "close reading", the "history of ideas", and the grand conspective scheme. All these, when they become ends in themselves rather than instruments of inquiry, become deflective rather than constructive: "close reading" often fails to show us what we can *do* with the elucidatory detail it brings to the surface; the history of ideas has difficulty staying in the field of imagination at all because of the working assumptions it has to make about the nature and identity of "ideas"; the grand scheme —except perhaps in the hands of a master—collapses into plausible classification or proliferates into allegorical ingenuity. Even the dictum "Consider the poem and nothing else" can become a preclusive principle, a fixative procedure that prevents the poem from growing in the mind because it shuts out much of the nourishment we could conceivably bring to it.

All procedural devices have a limited function; they are at best instruments of inquiry, not metaphysical principles. A good part of our discrimination needs to go into discerning—in any particular critical activity—the precise limits of any procedure or analogy we decide to use. Our schools and universities are dominated by the assumption that "to know" can only mean to acquire and possess some*thing*(s) called "knowledge" or "information". We have to make an effort to remember that there is another kind of knowing that we recognize whenever we say "I *know* that person"—a kind of knowing that is paramount in our study of poems. The way we "get to know" a poem, and find it growing in stages of fullness and vivacity in a process that has no end, is through a sequence of risky losings of it in analysis and restorations of it in synthesis; then, in fact, we are moving back and forth between two kinds of knowing, each distinct, each with its own peculiar function. Analysis is characterized by a regressive movement toward increasing multiplicity and a uniform emphasis among the things-known. Synthesis—an elegant selective process—is characterized by clarity, wholeness, simplicity, shapeliness; it liberates us from the confusion of multiplicity and allows us to see what is the "right thing" to do with our knowledge. In our studies we must evoke and clarify both these processes.

Because the things we study are at once physical and elusive, we need to be tactful as well as skilful; we need to recognize that no analogy can be better than a *suggestive* analogy. Many analytical procedures can be directed upon the body of literature for various purposes, and many different ones are needed. The trouble with analytical procedures is that they are very easy to teach: hence the besetting temptation to teach formulary procedures. But no analytical procedure can of itself engender the synthesizing grasp that is our only direct way of sensing the substance and life of a poem. To come upon a poem as a living thing takes a simplicity of mind that few of us, out of sophistication, can muster at will. To hold a poem as a living thing in the centre of attention takes—as calligraphers say—a light hand and a light heart. The more earnest we become—the more importunate, analytic, and "teachy"—the more heavy-handed we become, the more violence we do to literature, to our students, and to ourselves.

The deflective drift away from the reality of literature and the fertility it offers us occurs through excessive cerebration and misplaced conceptuality. The way of dealing with what may seem an inevitable digression would probably occur to us more often if we were less uncertain of our own capacities. We need to concentrate firmly on the centre—the poems, the works of literature—resolutely following the threads of inquiry wherever they may lead; *but*—and it is a very large *but*—continuously cycling the inquiry back through the poem so that the poems can select and shape the inquiry. Literature being what it is, the distinctive method of literary inquiry is truly a *method*, not a technique; it is established and commanded by the peculiar identity of what in any instance is under inquiry; it discovers the minute specificity of the particulars when most of the particulars are impalpable. It requires some conscious effort because it runs counter to the habitual movement of our minds: instead of moving from the less to the greater, from the particular to the general, we must move from the greater to the less, from the general to the particular, because poetry deals with universals. Universals are discerned, not embodied in generalizations: they are only found symbolized in particulars.

As for the larger question of how we may regain confidence in the wider ambience that the classics moved in, I should say that it is not to be found in what is fashionably called "interdisciplinary studies", unless we recognize that there are in fact very few disciplines, and that they do not coincide with the traditional boundaries by which scholarly activity has been delimited. A definition of "discipline" is very much needed. For a start we should notice how far the habit of thinking in terms of "problems" and "solutions" produces method-oriented problems rather than problem-oriented method; that the problem is adjusted to fit the expected solution or made to conform to the investigative technique. There is a further objection. The "solution" of anomalies is, in any kind of inquiry, the most fruitful thing we can attempt. But explaining is almost invariably explaining-away; a "solution" is a destruction; the ultimate solution is the ultimate destruction. The last thing we want to do is to dismiss or destroy the very things we want to get to know.

If we ever lose sight of the poem as a thing-made, out there, with its own identity and existence, infuriatingly impervious to anything we may say or do about it, we shall probably find ourselves "teaching literature"—that is, providing students with *our* learned acquaintance with some literature and our conclusions upon it, showing students how to give the impression that they too have a learned acquaintance with literature when, in fact, they may as yet have no vivid sense of the work they are writing their "research papers" on. We are even in danger of trying to manufacture intellectuals out of people who are not particularly intelligent. By absent-mindedly propagating our professional kind, we may find ourselves testing our students for "results"—that is, seeing whether they know the drill, whether they can handle the "tools" and "techniques" well enough to produce the expected "answers".

It is one thing to be acquainted with literature; it is another thing to be able to talk intelligibly about the subject-matter contained in literature. But our *central* concern is neither of these if we are to fulfil our task as a seminal humane discipline. I suggest that our purpose is to encourage our students to discover, exercise, refine, and extend their own mental and emotional capacities, and to do that in the study of literature because it is there that such a purpose can be most concentratedly brought into focus; and in doing so, to leave the wonder and integrity of literature intact so that, either drawing upon that or the memory of it, they will thereafter bring those qualities to everything they see and touch in their lives.

In a task so delicate, and even intrusive, we should never find ourselves pleading that we didn't know that our task was at once momentous and almost impossible. If we hum, we hum for keeps; if we doodle, it is a form of wisdom; if we sigh, it is because our lives are short. We must be eager to abandon prepared positions and stand in the open; as professors, bold to profess; as masters, not magisterial; our commerce not with commodities or options but with discoveries and marvels; not with opinions and varieties of opinion but with judgments of value; not with explanations but with knowings and resurrections. We need to try to know something about knowing; we need to be quizzical about confident statements about how we know and what we can know. We need to know a good deal about our "inner goings-on"—how we respond, hear, see, listen, attend, discern, recognize, choose, judge, not begging the question with preformulated theoretical answers. We need to see how we "think"—in starbursts and constellations, forgetting and losing as much as remembering and finding, in no linear mode, groping towards what we know we are looking for though we cannot possibly know yet what we shall find. We need to be aware how our minds are not computers; how feeling is psychic energy, the formative initiative of knowing, recognizing, remembering, dreaming; how language is not simply a medium in which we record our feeling and thinking, but an articulative process in which feeling and thinking can unite, with great subtlety and precision, to discover and realize themselves; how language is our most inventive characteristic and our specific endowment; how imagination is our capacity for transfiguration, inalienable.

Paul Valéry, in his early twenties, wrote a brilliant essay on "The Method of Leonardo da Vinci". As a poet and as a trained scientific observer he was fascinated with the way of mind that brought poems into existence. In a later imaginary dialogue entitled *Idée Fixe* he coined the word "Implex" to refer to "our *capacity* for feeling, reacting, doing, and understanding —individual, inconstant, more or less known to us—but always imperfectly and indirectly—and very often misconstrued by us—and also our capacity for resistance." From that dialogue I have pieced together his account of how, through this capacity to implicate, a "thought" or an "idea"—or a "poem", it may be—comes into being: it is very much to the point in this discussion.

The sense of fitness—rightness—is the intelligence of the Implex. Which amounts to saying that, in a given circumstance, what is most needed is summoned up, attracted by the circumstance itself. There is a state of mental effort completely removed from the mind's ordinary kind of freedom and haphazardness, a state equally opposed to distraction or fixation, and which can only satisfy itself (unless forced to a standstill by fatigue) with the possession of a sort of mental object, which the mind can recognize as the thing it was searching for. And yet it *did not know* what the object was which it now recognizes—but there is no mistaking it. . . .

A certain pattern takes form—a pattern which no longer has anything to do with your volition. What is required is submission to a certain constraint: the ability to keep this up, endure it fixedly, so as to give those elements of thought which are present, or in operation, the *liberty* to find their affinities, the *time* to combine together constructively and to assert themselves in the conscious mind—to impose some indefinable *conviction* upon it.

If, as instructors, our idea of poetry is based on recognitions much less subtle than Valéry has set down here, or on patterns of much less exact introspective depth, we shall probably sooner or later go astray; the work will go coarse in our hands and cease to be seminal.

In face of the difficulties and subtleties intrinsic to our work, what matters is that students be instructed—that they discover in themselves a clear structure; it may not matter that the theory of that instruction be disclosed to them. A surgeon treating a patient does not begin by teaching his patient surgery: he operates. An instructor inspired by a clear understanding of the materials and of the purpose to be served will tend to work with the radical simplicity of a gesture. But we should not let our students suppose that the central issues in literary studies are less complex and subtle than they are, or that they are less accessible or important than we take them to be. Whatever can be taught can be tested; whatever is teachable can be taught rigorously and with delight. And as for ourselves, in handling whatever cannot be taught but can be transmitted, evoked, induced, each of us can have a fine sense of his own peculiar capabilities and the operative limits of them. The rest is a matter of clear purpose, a light touch, a sense of wonder.

NOTES

1 That is (in this context), the assumption that every name used for a distinguishable detail in conceptual analysis stands for, or refers to, a "real thing". The fact that we can meaningfully speak of "a work of imagination" does not necessarily mean that some *thing* called "imagination" really exists, or that that "thing" has caused the "work" to come into being. The "thingi-ness" of abstract nouns makes it difficult for us to handle such pairs of terms as "science" and "poetry", "imagination" and "fancy", "actual" and "real", because in each pair the terms seem to be mutually exclusive, whereas in fact the concepts to which the terms refer in each pair are either concentric or overlapping. The objection to "nominalism" in the analysis of acts and judgments is that it ascribes "real existence" to abstractions that are applicable only within the limits of a particular analytical procedure.

2 Sometimes exponents of "communications" refer to "the printed word" and to performances of radio and television as "media", but the outcome is the same: aspects of the "effective" (or promotional) use of language, gesture, and "effects" have been surreptitiously transferred to the "medium". A medium is by definition a neutral vehicle: the user de-

cides what use he will make of it. But a speaking voice is not a medium. A similar sleight-of-hand is attempted in the argument that all printed matter should be rejected because it makes language "linear". The fact that printed language is traditionally disposed "in lines" to represent the unidirectional flow of the speaking voice does not make language "linear": it is visual-semantic *reading* that makes language linear by shutting out the "upper partials" of implication and by destroying the rhythmic ambience of sound and implication that continuously acts as a reminiscence as well as an anticipation. To transfer the visual linearity of print to the language as printed is surreptitiously to alter the statement "It is *language* printed" into "It is language *printed*" (and therefore "linear" and therefore not language at all). It is curious how the obsession with the "visual" has led "communications" doctrine to reject coherent language on the ground that it is not visual. Since language is our prime means of communicating with each other we might do better, instead of rejecting printed forms of presentation, to get people to listen carefully and to read well. But there is no solution there either, because both listening and reading are bad words in the vocabulary of "communications".

Respecting Our Organs
MAURICE S. ELLIOTT

I

"English composition is beyond the grasp of almost 40 per cent of this year's freshman class at the University of British Columbia." With this sentence a reporter in a Toronto newspaper recently began an article under the headline: LITERARY STANDARD OF UBC STUDENTS FOUND TO BE LOW. Perhaps this is not a very good example of the legendary superiority of Upper Canada, but the conjunction of literacy with literature is fortuitous and will serve to introduce my theme: Reading cannot be overrated, or, Some legends are better than others.

I begin with some generalizations. There is a great deal of loose talk about the illiteracy of students nowadays. We are told that it is not simply their inability to read or write which seems so evident, but they are not motivated to read or write. They don't speak too good neither. Yet students are not involved in a malignant conspiracy against their fellow humans; their illiteracy is not ill-willed. A student of my own acquaintance, who has probably never heard of the 1870 Education Act which proclaimed instant literacy, recently wrote with poignant optimism: "If one removes illeratcy [sic] and introduces education then famine and disease naturally disappear."

There is also a sense that departments of English in schools and in universities are private worlds divorced from the real needs of students' lives. Universities are supposedly full of academics whining about the inability of the schools to provide them with young men and women who can be turned into copies of themselves, irrelevant and cantankerous. In some schools and community colleges the teachers of a subject which they feel is unpopular in so far as it is challenging are demoralized by administrative pressures to attract students. They may either try to disguise literature as something else, or phase it out entirely in the name of the accelerating change of the "electronic age", substituting "Communication Arts". Teachers in technical schools (the polytechnics in England) who feel that their students are somehow closer to the "real world" or (unhappy phrase) "life outside" will perhaps buttress a hostility to English departments by emphasizing the isolated and purely literary nature of English studies. The hunting gentleman who said in 1517 that "the study of literature should be left to rustics" would probably find considerable popular support today. After all, it is written (or was it said?) by Marshall McLuhan: "the new media are the 'real' world." It would be no surprise to find that there were classes once known as "English" but now called "Today" or "Daybeat".

It is not original to contend that the reality of our individual worlds is represented by language, or that our very individuality and human community is enriched and vitalized by our common tongue. Without it, to adapt the poet John Montague, the whole landscape becomes a manuscript we lose the skill to read. The reality which is represented by the new media of the electronic age is appropriately represented by the metaphoric properties of the term "network". The net binds us to a mechanized, commercial, suburban world ("global village" sounds pathetically pastoral) and, although it may seem the technological triumph of the industrial revolution, the reality is a threat to all meaning and significance in our lives. Under the pressures of the here and now the past disappears. Literature and sensitivity to language would seem to present a redundancy resembling that of most of the goods mass-produced for "consumers". Literature in the container form of books is a "good" which, if not dispensed, might well be dispensed with. In the Plutonian world of Ray Bradbury's *Fahrenheit 451*, firemen are the custodians of "our peace of mind", and the Captain of the Fire Station lectures on the mental landscape of hell:

> Give the people contests they win by remembering the words to more popular songs or the names of state capitals or how much corn Iowa grew last year. Cram them full of noncombustible data, chock them so damned full of "facts" they feel stuffed, but abso-

lutely "brilliant" with information. Then they'll feel they're thinking, they'll get a *sense* of motion without moving. And they'll be
happy, because facts of that sort don't change. Don't give them
any slippery stuff like philosophy or sociology to tie things up
with. That way lies melancholy.

A professor of English literature could be forgiven for sympathiz-
ing with the fifteenth-century King of Castile who wished he had
been born the son of a mechanic. I pray with Spenser, "God
helpe the man so wrapt in *Errours* endlesse traine."
Of course students are not more illiterate than anyone else.
They are simply under closer scrutiny, but the separation of the
"real" world of the student from that of any other person is, in
respect to illiteracy, artificial. It is, however, sometimes convenient to isolate the illiteracy of the student because it may turn
attention to the fact that someone is not doing his job—probably
the professor, and particularly the professor of English. This
failure helps to reinforce a more serious separation or isolation
which is sometimes shamefacedly expressed by professors themselves, aided by some schoolteachers and encouraged by the
popular press. It is this: in some way professors of literature are
not of the "real" world—particularly in the summer. In so far as
much professional literary work is self-serving and trivial there is
support for a charge of irresponsibility; but not all professors
write books about books without the solidity of their specialized
scholarship affecting the whole language. Lack of conviction and
passionate intensity have no fixed abode, but there seems to be an
encouraged hostility to the professor when he can be isolated
from the community, when he can be seen as "not for real".
To be more particular, I shall suggest how such abstraction
might operate in the language which turns people into things. The
word "faculty" has an accumulation of enriched meaning: ability, a power of mind, aptitude, a department of knowledge, a
dispensation, the members of a learned profession. In recent
years the word has become a convenient means of isolating a part
of what should be seen as an organic community. "Faculty" may
be spoken of in percentages, or there is talk of faculty "growth",
which is the jargon of economics, not an assessment of developing
mental powers. I take a representative example from the Council

of Ontario Universities, titled *Notes of Fourth Meeting of Special Committee to Assess University Policies and Plans* (January 31, 1975):

> *Faculty Numbers.* There was some discussion on the problem of differential growth in various programs. Certain areas (fine arts at York University was given as an example) are in the developmental stage. With a fixed amount of resources, growth of these programs will mean phasing down others, and this means reducing the number of faculty positions. Also, if productivity increases must be shown, and there is a reduction in growth, there is more pressure on the dismissal of faculty. Members felt that it was easy to rationalize in the long term, but in the short term, one is up against the faculty redundancy problem. Normal attrition in the system is likely to average around .7 to .8 percent per annum over the next five years, i.e. 100 faculty members out of 11,000 per year. The Ministry representatives were asked whether the government was aware that drastic steps might need to be taken to reduce faculty numbers.

I shall not enter into an analysis of the "sense" of this ("Notes" may be a way of saying exactly—or inexactly—what one pleases, and they may not have the refinement and polish of an Official Report—the language is inexcusable none the less) beyond noting the jargon and cliché of the industrial plant. Rather, I ask the question, "Is there any conceivable way that this could refer to human beings?" If the answer is "yes", then we all go into the dark

> into the silent funeral,
> Nobody's funeral, for there is no one to bury.

The collective title "faculty" abstracts men and women from their individual professions—law, medicine, letters—and converts them to units, albeit "bargaining" units. A faculty member is then someone who may be seen as having different aims and claims from other departments of the university community. It is now possible to speak of "faculty cut-backs" without squeamishness, and with the production of the catchword there appears a whipping-boy. The procedure is analogous to the way in which it became possible to speak of nineteenth-century factory workers as "operatives" or "hands", or, more recently in the history of people as things, to refer to university students in Ontario as BIUs.

All kinds of cant words are used to encourage the fear of the "academic" or the "highbrow". He who would make a vigorous defence of the study of literature and language as intimately connected with the quality of our lives as human beings, or who has the temerity to speak of a universal illiteracy, could well find himself a so-called intellectual élitist in an ivory-tower establishment.

II

At this point I should like to put a date and place to my observations on the language of some other artificially isolated "realities". I do not live in the world alone and this verbal gesture of identification will perhaps help to explain the process in which my own language, that essential part of my total human world, informs my reality and will introduce the challenge to what Coleridge calls "modern slip-slop".

It is the time of the year that Robert Henryson called "Ane doolie sessoun to ane cairfull dyte", as he began an unhappy poem. I am sitting in an office located on the seventh floor of a very large concrete building. I am in what is known as the South Tower. My telephone is out of order (not disconnected) and I am dislocated from the "outside" world by the fiercest snow storm of this winter. All traffic is at a complete standstill. My connection with the "electronic" age is maintained by heat and light so I am aware of the folly of false primitivism or a stance against progress. Another reminder of the times: yesterday, April 3, 1975, the tallest building in the world, the CN Communications Tower, was topped off with daedal ingenuity—for data, see *The Guinness Book of Records*. The imagined presence of this spike confronts my very real ivory tower. It would be pleasant but sentimental to follow all of Henryson's fifteenth-century comforts:

I mend the fyre and beikit me about,
Than tuik ane drink, my spreitis to comfort,

And armit me weill fra the cauld thairout.
To cut the winter nicht and mak it schort
I tuik ane quair — and left all uther sport —

Before I began to write (not type) I was reading "ane quair", Charles Dickens's *Martin Chuzzlewit*—some parts of it aloud. This is not because, like a medieval monk, I am incapable of reading silently, but for the delight of sounding out the words themselves. The process of transcribing a passage now for its appropriateness to my theme is a further extension of the sensual pleasure. To quote a passage at length will put the reader into a way of discovering, or exploring, the "country" in which I find myself. Martin is talking to the American, General Choke, who displays a Republican's nonchalance towards accuracy concerning the Queen's residence. "Have you been in England?" asks Martin. "In print I have, Sir," says the General. "Not otherwise. We air a reading people here, Sir. You will meet with much information among us that will surprise you, Sir." The Old World and the New then converge in the double meaning of the word "speculation" as Martin contemplates settling in "Eden":

"We have very little to venture," said Martin anxiously "only a few pounds; but it is our all. Now, do you think that for one of my profession, this would be a speculation with any hope or chance in it?" "Well!" observed the General, gravely, "if there wasn't any hope or chance in this speculation, it wouldn't have engaged my dollars, I opinionate."

"I don't mean for the sellers," said Martin. "For the buyers —for the buyers!"

"For the buyers, Sir?" observed the General, in a most impressive manner. "Well! you come from an old country: from a country, Sir, that has piled up golden calves as high as Babel, and worshipped 'em for ages. We are in a new country, Sir; man is in a more primeval state here, Sir; we have not the excuse of having lapsed in the slow course of time into degenerate practices; we have no false gods; man, Sir, here, is man in all his dignity. We fought for that or nothing. Here am I, Sir," said the General, setting up his umbrella to represent himself; and a villainous looking umbrella it was; a very bad counter to stand for the sterling coin of his benevolence: "here am I with gray hairs, Sir, and a moral sense. Would I, with my principles, invest capital in this speculation if I didn't think it full of hopes and chances for my brother man?"

Martin tried to look convinced, but he thought of New York, and found it difficult.

"What are the Great United States for, Sir," pursued the General, "if not for the regeneration of man? But it is nat'ral in you to make such an enquerry, for you come from England, and you do not know my country." (Chapter 21)

I should like to think that all readers would immediately abandon my essay and turn with curiosity and wonder to Dickens's novel. I suggest, however, that my world in this snow-encircled tower is as real at this moment as any presented by the spokesmen of politics, commerce, or journalism, who may claim to speak for me or try to isolate me. I am able to align this moment and General Choke's print/information/speculation world of the nineteenth/twentieth century—the tower of Babel, the ivory tower, the CN tower may merge in the reflective pool of the imagination faster than I could flick a switch and certainly faster than I can move my pen across the paper. Were I here involved in formal criticism of Dickens, the complexity of my experience would still need to be represented by verbal language, and my perception of this present reality is represented by words which must have as much clarity and precision as I can possibly provide. By using words rather than languages of gesture, music, paint, film, or even waves of electricity, I use a totally human medium the special variation of which I share with the whole of the English-speaking world. This is my life itself, for it is a medium which I must keep vital in order to sustain a wholeness which is more than mere taxes, economic growth, votes, educational systems, or choking information. Like Eliot's Sweeney "I gotta use words when I talk to you" anyway, for my access to a transmitting station, a satellite, or a film crew, is not only economically controlled but it could also be politically impossible.

That last sentence contains a note of menace, a suggestion of the nightmare underground I wish to explore. My use of language may shape my reality and, if truly literate, if precise and discriminating, I have the possibility of a community with others which is not entirely dictated to me by the pressures of a commercial society. I also have the subversive possibility of privacy.

The importance of literature in this context is that it presents the reality of an imagined world, or of a past experience which enables the critical reader (which is to say, a reader who does more than exercise his eyes) to question and define the contours, substance, and texture of his life in society. Continuously assaulted by new modes of communication, subject to pressures of and manipulations by the selected and selective images of electronic sight and sound, the individual *needs* the privacy, detachment, and critique of the printed word. He needs to form his "own Countree", and here literature is permanently relevant. Again I hasten to point out that I am saying nothing new (it is even perpetually modish), but in the face of a lack of conviction among the clerks it needs to be stressed over and over again. It was long ago pointed out that in spite of constant re-evaluation and heart-searching, truths can too easily "lie bedridden in the dormitory of the soul".

In the 1880s, Edward Dowden, worried about the dislocation of his students from life, expressed his concern that literature ran "the risk of becoming a mere piece of scholarship and refined culture". Young men and women should be literary, he said, "in order to be something more and better". Louis Kampf's timely statement, "The Scandal of Literary Scholarship", in 1967, indicates that the lessons of responsibility need constant rehearsal. During the first half of this century the steady flow of exhortation and concern for discrimination and clarity in the use of language reached a crest in 1939, a cry to purge the decadence of the educated in a crisis of civilization (see, for example, the works of J. Churton Collins, George Sampson, D. H. Lawrence, I. A. Richards, F. R. Leavis, Denys Thompson, Stephen Potter, Robert Graves, Ezra Pound, and George Orwell). A reflection of the general malaise may be seen in Cyril Connolly's "gravest" warning in his *Enemies of Promise*, a notation of the pressures on the word: "in a short time, the writing of books, especially works of the imagination which last long will be an extinct art. Contemporary works do not keep."

Marshall McLuhan said, in dialogue with Gerald Stearn in 1967, that it is "customary in conventional literary circles to feel uneasy about the status of the book and of literacy in our society'', and certainly the last twenty-five years have made the stance of those who would urge the study of literature seem even more defensive behind the crumbling edifices of humane education. Bleakly and desperately, George Steiner has spoken of ''creation falling upon silence'' in the face of barbarism, and of the ''suicidal rhetoric of silence''. In Europe and North America the campus disturbances of the late sixties were linked directly with ''crisis in the humanities'', and there were new looks at the relationship of literature with ''total'' culture, with the ''popular'' arts, in a desperate try for relevance; and, less constructively, a radical movement which, in at least one case, suggested that language is ''the ultimate weapon in the colonial kit of the English teacher'', and that ''civilizing is a mode of exploitation.''

It would not be very helpful at this moment for a man of clerkly acquirements to point out that a useful distinction may be drawn between cultivation and civilization, or to discuss *Culture and Anarchy* (again). Coleridge and Matthew Arnold must be read. What is interesting are the metaphors in the radical statement I have just quoted (e.g., ''ultimate weapon''): they are those of lethal confrontation. What is at stake (and conflagration is also deadly) is more than mere words or ''high'' culture; it is the meaning and quality of our whole lives. We ignore F. R. Leavis's persistent and dauntless championship of ''significance'' and ''sincerity'' at great risk, and no economic ''growth'' will prevent the stunting of sensitivity and consciousness. Leavis's mental fight is unequivocal: ''the complacent 'understanding' with which the enlightened contemplate these things is not understanding or enlightenment, but merely a manifestation of the disease from which our civilization is suffering'' (*Nor Shall My Sword*). If our vital organs wither, we die.

Any attempt to turn off confrontation, to replace it with genuine exchange, is not going to be furthered by an injection of literary culture, by correct orthography, by studying the newest grammars or the oldest rhetorics, by subjects like ''englit'' or ''canlit'' or ''canned/lit''—by even the subtlest arrangements of curricula. Nor can the written and spoken word be avoided by the latest nostrums about the ''new media''. The teacher as a literary mechanic is perhaps in the position of the Australian member of parliament who received the following communication from a disgruntled elector:

> Deer Sur, You're a dam fraud, and you know it. I don't care a rap for the billet or the muny either, but you could hev got it for me if you wasn't as mean as muk. Two pound a week ain't eny moar to me than 40 shillin's is to you, but I objekt to bein' maid an infurnil fool of. . . . Yure no man. An' i doan't think yure much of a demercrat either. Go to hel. I lowers meself ritin to a skunk, even tho I med him a member of parlerment.

The language of this letter is vitally connected with the political life of the writer. This is language that works. It is a confrontation of a kind, but the conviction of the statement is derived from principles which can still find expression in a mode which has not yet degenerated to the desperate terror of the jungle or the alleyway; the indifferent bullet or casual bomb.

In *Civil Elegies* and in his talk "Cadence, Country, Silence", the poet Dennis Lee movingly urges the necessity of the continuous search for the authentic amidst the helpless feeling of "beleaguered drifting". Not only the artist, but each of us must look for a place to stand with conviction. We must all refuse to be exiles within our own community of language and seek out the kindly light of those "makers" or craftsmen who are the guardians of the word in the encircling gloom of the world. Artists have always known that external blight is but the outward symptom of the diseased human condition. It is no accident that Evelyn Waugh, at the beginning of *The Loved One*, acknowledges those "who corrected my American", and "who corrected my English". He is indicating that his book is not merely a broad joke on American funeral customs but a carefully crafted indictment of a whole civilization which has ceased to "make any sense":

> In that kindly light the stained and blistered paint of the bungalow and the plot of weeds between the veranda and the dry water-hole lost their extreme shabbiness, and the two Englishmen, each in his rocking-chair, each with his whisky and soda and his outdated magazine, the counterparts of numberless fellow-countrymen exiled in the barbarous regions of the world, shared in the brief illusory rehabilitation. (Chapter 1)

The struggles of the writer with the word are efforts to strip illusion and to make "rehabilitation" permanent. There is a choice. It is possible to choose hell because one likes it; to remain unregenerate. In *Under the Volcano*, Malcolm Lowry creates Geoffrey Firmin the Consul as a representative of weak mankind in wandering mazes lost. This doomed "compañero" is unwilling to do anything but escape responsibility. He will not act to save himself. The Consul's own quest and death are inseparable from the decay of civilization and he struggles with a sickness which a vigilant friend suggests is "not only in body but in that part used to be call: soul", and in the mesh of nerves resembling "how do you say it, an eclectic systemë". Throughout the novel we regard his hellish fall.

III

As he left the White House last year, Richard Nixon said: "I kind of like to read books. I'm not educated but I do read books." In the murky gloom of what may be forever but half-known, these words might be set alongside a passage from a work of contemporary literature, Kurt Vonnegut's *Mother Night*:

> I, too, knew Rudolf Hoess, Commandant of Auschwitz. I met him at a New Year's Eve party in Warsaw during the war, the start of 1944. Hoess heard that I was a writer, and he got me to one side at the party and he said he wished he could write.
> "How I envy you creative people—" he said to me. "Creativity is a gift from the gods."
> Hoess said he had some marvellous stories to tell. He said they were all true, but that people wouldn't be able to believe them. Hoess could not tell me the stories, he said, until the war was won. After the war, he said, we might collaborate.
> "I can talk it," he said, "but I can't write it." He looked at me for pity. "When I sit down to write," he said, "I freeze." (Chapter 5)

The chilling link of the concentration camp and the festivities of a party, the connection of gruesome inhumanity with a confessed lack of articulation, the alignment of the anaphoric "he said" (which suggests the dictator who always has the last word: "I can talk you to death") with the laconic distance of the reporter, and finally the cathartic hints of pity and fear after the irony of "collaborate", all make this short piece a suggestive and tragic admonishment on the failure of articulation. The passage continues with the discovery of the potentialities of articulation for manipulative purposes. As the "last full measure", the benighted writer translates the Gettysburg address for Herr Goebbels, "Head of the German Ministry of Popular Enlightenment and Propaganda". It is not merely an exquisite sensibility which must shudder on hearing students say "I can talk it, but I can't write it down."

In 1946, in his classic essay on "Politics and the English Language", George Orwell noted the link between tyranny and the abuse of language. Three years later in the appendix to his novel *Nineteen Eighty-Four*, Orwell's invention of the term "newspeak" showed how it was possible for the subtleties of the language of the Declaration of Independence to become "crimethink". This was a baleful prognostication and might entitle Orwell to rank with those poets whom President Truman preferred to journalists because some of them "write about what is going to happen".

The words of at least three of the most recent leaders of what one of them called the "richest most powerful country which ever occupied the globe" have progressively indicated this connection between the abuse of language and the exercise of power—have delineated a region of chaos containing, as Milton envisioned, "eternal anarchy, amidst the noise of endless wars".

President Eisenhower seems to have lost General Choke's bland confidence in the "regeneration of man". He was certainly in some place other than Eden when he delivered the following "at a time of bewilderment":

But we wonder what is the outcome of every decent, proper gesture we make to those that live in the other camp. They live in a closed society, secrecy of intent—which we try to penetrate, and in my opinion properly, but we are certain of this: Our problem is not only keeping ourselves strong, and by strong I don't mean merely militarily, I mean spiritually, intellectually, scientifically, economically and militarily; and then, we must make certain that all those people who live with us, in the hope that those concepts of human dignity and freedom and liberty are going to prevail in the world, will stand always by our side in the determination that freedom and liberty will eventually triumph over tyranny. . . .''

The following sentence of President Johnson may be his impromptu revenge on what he called ''our sophisticated self-styled intellectuals'' (Adolf Hitler also had no time for ''lemonade-like outpourings of literary aesthetes and drawing room heroes''):

> I hope that we will stress imagination and creativeness, initiative, new ideas, how we can do something quicker, how we can do it better, why we ought to discard the status quo, and proceed to things we know not of, sometimes, in the hope that out of that will come something revolutionary and something worthwhile.

I would call this ''nowspeak'', the language of the technocrat who not only has forgotten yesterday, but is unable to recall the beginning of his sentence. The fact that the language is out of control and that neither of these two Presidents seem to know what they are saying is an indication of what Sean O'Casey's Joxer Daly called ''a state of chassis''. It gets worse.

The next President said of a ''plan'' (he meant a ''crime''): ''I don't give a shit what happens. I want you all to stonewall it.'' To make oneself perfectly clear came to mean exactly the opposite during the last years of the Nixon administration, but perhaps this was not perfectly clear until we could see for ourselves:

> Nixon: No, seriously as I have told both of you, the boil had to be pricked. In a very different sense that's what December 18th was about [i.e., the decision to renew the bombing on North Vietnam]. We have to prick the boil and take the heat. Now that's what we are doing here. We're going to prick this boil and take the heat. I—am I overstating?
> Mr. Ehrlichman: No: I think that's right. The idea is, this will prick the boil. . . . The history of this thing has to be though that you did not tuck this under the rug yesterday or today, and hope it would go away.

Yes, yes. Of course! What the hell is going on ''though''? It is not that these people do not know what they are saying, although they probably do not. What is far more important to them is that they know what they are not saying.

Nixon's understanding of the importance of the broadcasting services, his surrounding himself with ad-men like Haldeman who were concerned with "results—not methods", the continuous attempts to interfere with network managements, correspondents, and producers of news programmes; all this would indicate that we have lived through a very dangerous and frightening time. The thugtalk of the White House—"That's right. The main, main thing is the *Post* is going to have damnable, damnable problems out of this one. They have a television station—"; or, "Well, the game has to be played awfully rough"—was supported by bully boys producing the same anti-intellectual stance evident in the catchwords and jargon which seek to divide professors or students from the "real" world. "Who else but management can or should correct so-called professionals who confuse sensationalism with sense and who dispense élitist gossip in the guise of news analysis." The speaker here is Clay Whitehead, head of the White House Office of Telecommunications Policy, and he is complaining of what he called "ideological plugola", meaning anti-administration news.

I have been speaking of American leaders because I believe that the United States is a powerful and important country which we scorn or ignore only in folly. Diabolic confidence men, however, have no particular country. William Cobbett's nineteenth-century account of proclamations, orders in council, state papers, and reports, has a certain universality. He noted that they were "without parallel in the records of human ignorance", and the accompanying meaninglessness and chaos may be identified in our own ministerial proclamations:

> Uncertainties at the government level induce confusion in the private industry ranks that combine to lead to delays in energy development "that have an extravagant effect on the public interest," in particular in cost escalations "at a time of double digit inflation."

This is a reporter's account of the words of Ontario's Minister of

Energy and Natural Resources. Presumably there is some reference here to the world in which I live, or perhaps I am not
supposed to read the financial pages in which this gobbledygook
appeared—perhaps a "speech-writer" is to blame. The recent
interest in energy problems results, says the Minister, in "the
consumer becoming the instrument of purposes that do not serve
his perceived ends". Does my deception perceive me? Are not
words also my "natural resources"?

"I intuit your hostility, software man," says an engineer to a
reporter in one of Donald Barthelme's short stories (and speaking
of engineers, the word "generate" seems to have undergone
some mutation recently). If language is the living behaviour of
such men as lead us, if it is a determining force in our growth, it
must be continuously regenerated, made muscular and energetic
with conviction. The entropic abstraction of the language of politics propped by the inflated jargon of the market-place must lead
to confusion, corruption, and decay. If there is such a thing as a
punched-card moral sense it has been stapled/folded/and bent.
Such mutilation is the beginning of human dismemberment and
language will become a machine-tool for the production-line of
automatons. Ontario's Minister of University Affairs recently
made the analogy explicit in a discussion of university education:
"It's like building a car. The first one costs a hell of a lot of
money. The second one if it's a copy is a lot less." It should be
added that English professors are sometimes no less sensitive
than Ministers of the Crown and they may even add the spice of
ambiguity. One was reported recently as saying: "English composition is like driving instruction. It improves with practice."
More chassis!

We cannot tell our piteous hearts there's no harm done. One
consequence of dehumanizing men by allowing language to atrophy and decay is to turn the world into a labyrinthine prison
with monstrous or brutish inhabitants. "You taught me language," says Caliban to Miranda, "and my profit on't is, I know
how to curse," and it is the monster who calls for the "burning of
the books", in *The Tempest*. Perhaps the curse is the closest that
articulate language may come to violence and the poet Amiri
Baraka's appeal for "poems that kill" is a re-statement of an
ancient tribal need for the word. The Irish have a long tradition of

satirists, and Edmund Spenser warns of the danger of displeasing
the bards who could inspire terror with their blistering curses. In
the twelfth-century prose epic, *Táin Bó Cuailnge* (The Cattle-
Raid of Cooley), Queen Mebd sends satirists to shame the
champion of Connaught into fighting Cúchulainn, "so there
would be nowhere in the world for him to lay his head in peace".
But even the violence of the curse assumes a common understanding of the living and magical properties of the word. In
1968, Bernadette Devlin was simply sustaining a tradition, but a
tradition losing its vitality. "If this Bill is passed through Parliament and is going to become law, may the hand of the President
who signs it wither as he signs it, and may every one of his dead
comrades who fought and died for this country appear before his
demise and curse his beating heart."

Travelling along the Crumlin Road on the way to Aldergrove
airport outside Belfast, the most casual observer will not fail to
notice armed soldiers standing on the street corners. They joke
and shout across the intersection seeming to protect nothing but
the bleak walls between their posts. These walls are the city's
memorial tablets, filled with graffiti: "Is there a life before
death?" or "Fuck the IRA! Fuck the UVF! Jews get off the
fence!" Here is the ultimate result of "stonewalling", a language
finally turned in upon itself, even a colonial language, with no
prospect of action or potency; the tense aphorisms of confrontation with the word literally "up against the wall". These oracles
of the possessed and the dispossessed are like the assertive names
"spray-gunned" on the New York subway cars, the desperate
signals of those without language enmeshed and exiled forever
within systems of communication.

IV

In the "image" world of the advertising industry, or what
Coleridge would have called the despotic world of the eye, more
attention seems to have been given to Mr. Nixon's five-o'clock
shadow than to the substance of his words. In choosing to make
words mean many things in order to retain the mastery of the
White House he had a great fall into print. The President and his

advisors seem to have failed to estimate the power of the "common reader", perhaps feeling that people are now so conditioned that they are unable to read. Certainly everyone at the White House had been numbed and was unconscious of the shock which the printed version of their tapes would occasion.

For the five years prior to his resignation Mr. Nixon and his professional word-manipulators had applied pressure to the American television networks, both directly through Charles Colson and indirectly through the more conservative affiliated commercial stations, to control the "news"; in other words, to interfere with free speech. It is a bleak irony that Mr. Nixon's exposure and eventual downfall should have been the result of routine but careful investigative reporting by the staff of the *Washington Post*. The disclosures not only had the permanence of print, but the reporters were also able to give more space to the events of the past (or history) than could a nightly television or radio news spot. In 1971, Mr. Ehrlichman noted that Dan Rather of CBS was always being seen "out there on the White House lawn talking as though you know what's going on". Ehrlichman over-estimated the impact of the brief juxtaposition of words and images, and under-valued the lasting and more dangerous permanence of the President's recorded and written words. The gaps on the Presidential tapes, though suspicious, are perhaps less menacing than the silences on paper. Taken together, both contain gestures and hints towards meaning which only serve to underline the danger of half truth and the distance between moral truth and veracity, and clearly demonstrate the use of language to confound the intelligence.

I have been discussing recorded talk—talk that first appeared accompanied by a visual image on television or which has been repeated in newsprint. There is a difference between prose and speech, but this makes it more imperative that the speech of those in power should be responsible, that they should know what they are talking about. It may be argued that a newspaper is concerned with selling the instantaneous and total communication of data—of "bits" of information which do not require that kind of attention and reflection accorded to the more permanent forms of print. Whatever the end, however, the means are the same: words. It is not an indifferent action to commit a word to print and the buyers of newspapers have a right to expect accuracy and reliability.

Such a large portion of the income of a newspaper depends upon advertising that there is a distortion of both ends and means. Advertising emphasizes the "layout" or the visual content and context at the expense of other mental and sensual operations (in a "glossy" supplement or magazine the visual operation may possibly be assisted by tactile sensation). "The Best Looking Newspaper in Canada" was the title of an award given recently by a large advertising firm, but who will say which is the most reliable—anywhere? The cheap satisfactions of the immediate are primarily concerned with the gratifying of the eye, and what is called simultaneity of impact may actually be only another way of decreasing consciousness by emphasizing one sense at the expense of another. Yet even the visual sense may atrophy; as the poet once warned his readers, "you may see and notice not".

WORLD HUNGRY NOT BEING FED BY ROME'S RHETORIC. Newspaper readers are certainly meant to see headlines such as this, and presumably advertisers mean their wares to be noticed. The language of an advertisement which appears on the same page as the leading article on the world's hungry is a simple illustration of the moral triviality and the insensitivity of meaningless advertising which is meant to appeal primarily to the visual sense. The advertising industry may well have adapted the saying that poets must create the taste by which they are read and understood, but to speak of "taste" in the context of hunger emphasizes the inhumanity and complete lack of centre here—although I am aware that the taste is probably sexual in intention. "Distinctive designs inspired by the warmth of exotic rattan. Hand crafted quality in exciting groupings and unique accents. If you love the beautiful . . ." The phraseology has its own banality, but it is intensified by the juxtaposition of "news", the language of the adjoining article on the hungry. If a reader has smiled at the inflation of language used to describe cane furniture and is so numb to the "unique accents" of the advertiser, how may he learn to discriminate and judge the other material on the same page, learn to consider with Coleridge "that the greater part of our success and comfort in life depends on distinguishing the similar from the same, that which is peculiar in each thing from that which it has in common with others''?

WORLD HUNGRY NOT BEING FED BY ROME'S RHETORIC. A bold
title, a banner establishing a crusading tone. ''Rome'' possibly
still retains sufficient impact to create in some readers a certain
sense of theological menace; and the modish use of ''rhetoric'' in
the sense of cant or words without meaning will lead the un-
reflecting to sense the newspaper's concern with the major
human problem of famine—or does ''World Hungry'' mean
Lebensraum?

> It is becoming painfully clear at the end of the first week of the
> World Food Conference that the 123 member nations of the United
> Nations gathered here are not meeting man's greatest challenge.
>
> The World food problem is a two-pronged crisis—one to last
> from the next six to nine months, and the other for the next two
> decades. It is not clear that the world can feed every member of the
> human race in either of these periods. Indeed, the operative ques-
> tion is how many will starve. In both cases, without concerted
> international action the answer is millions. Millions more will have
> their lives blunted from malnutrition. This grim reality is recog-
> nised by every speaker here who goes to the podium. But the poor
> do not eat rhetoric.
>
> The poor eat food. For people to have food to eat, man must
> engage in an age-old process. A seed must be planted, a plant
> nurtured and a crop harvested. If the man who eats it lives in a city,
> then there must be a way of getting the crop from the man who
> harvests it to the man who eats it.
>
> But while the equation thus expressed, is too simple, never in
> human history have the issues been so complicated—and the num-
> bers of people who can be harmed by the failure of the equasion
> [*sic*] to operate so great.

''What is comment?'' asks Myles na Gopaleen in his cate-
chism of cliché: ''Superfluous''. It is a pity to give a passage such
as this more permanent existence than in the files of a newspaper.
The reader will easily recognize the special requirements of journalism, the necessity of conveying information with economy
and in syntactical units which will not impede the haste of the eye
moving down the columns of print. But what information is there
provided for anyone with intelligence? The mere data is infused
with an emotional protest wearing the bravura of authority

(front-page). It is an insincere pose because the whole piece wallows in sentimental sensationalism. It is the very worst kind of simplistic cliché promoting a false consciousness which anaesthetizes any sense of the "real world".

From the opening cliché to the syntactical confusion of the last paragraph with its tired republican rhythm this passage is devoid of any vitality whatsoever. It is "rhetorical" in the sense which the headline proclaims. The sloganizing, the inappropriate metaphors, and the misuse of words, and, above all, the banal impertinence and condescension of the tone, are not only sterilely self-conscious but morally culpable because together they betray that the writer quite LITERALLY does not know what he is talking about. The world he presents has no convincing reality, which is not to deny that hunger is real and painful.

Is "painfully clear" an evasion of the too political "perfectly clear"? Certainly it is an example of the meaningless adverbial sludge which clogs inflated editorial writing: "increasingly, disappointingly, actually, desperately, surprisingly, inevitably, conspicuously, repeatedly, so obviously, surely, leisurely", all of these appeared a few days later in a single editorial on the same subject, headed "While the Hungry Wait" (hungrily?).

The passage quoted above is not isolated carelessness. It continues: "the problem is one of matching the two"; "massive task"; "the major bottleneck is apparently financing"; "rising inexorably"; "the logistics are expanding beyond understanding"; "long journey out of the cave"; "if the process of economic development had been allowed to proceed". Bathos is the art of sinking: "effort must be launched"; "excruciatingly difficult to launch"; "might founder on basics"; "rock-bottom prices"; "the bottom fall out of the market" (once again I find myself in the underworld). Yet this vessel turns out to be "a vehicle that has sputtered on the starting line for more than a year". The language shows that the writer is thinking (*sic*!) of men as units in a reality which consists only of economic function. There is no real knowledge here for the mind is padlocked with words.

Confine the thought, to exercise the breath;
And keep them in the pale of Words till death.

I would also add the spectre of meaningless figures:

> The conference documentation, generally regarded as conservative by most experts here, says there are 460,000,000 people in the world who are chronically malnourished. Half of these are pregnant women and children, and for this group malnourishment means stunted lives. Children's brains do not develop fully if they are malnourished and they lose forever a portion of the most basic of gifts, the ability to reason.
>
> A further 460,000,000 of the world's population live so close to the hunger line that in times of shortfall they may be temporarily over the line to an inadequate diet. For some, this is a yearly occurrence, for others it happens less often.

Has this writer ever seen a pregnant child? He has obviously never seen a hunger line as he unwittingly demonstrates that he does not know what it is.

Later in the piece, the author tells of the "likely outcome of this scenario". There it is! The choice word of the stage-managers who would control the scripts of our lives; the dramatic genre is tragic farce—"There is a possibility that some of the other suggestions for increasing agricultural production in the developing countries will bear a little fruit." Is this part of what the poet calls "the cold charities of man to man"?

Alongside the "unique accents and exotic settings", the editors of this newspaper see nothing improper in having a journalist playing on what Mencken called an immense and cacophonous organ, always going *fortissimo*. The language represents a lack of conviction and integrity by its spurious efforts to persuade by cliché alone. Taken with the language of advertisement the organization of the newspaper reflects an emptiness of life guaranteed not to disturb the comforts of the breakfast-table.

This journalistic language is different in degree but not in kind from that which both conceals and reveals the realities of political manipulation. It is directed at mob understanding and geared to economic management. I have taken the trouble to isolate it because by holding it up to examination the reader may respond to it critically. Unlike film or television or radio which normally have a more ephemeral impact, the permanence of print allows for private reflection, a more sustained attention, and the possibility of reply to the author's assumptions. If the reader is alive the word cannot dictate to him. In so far as nearly four million English-language newspapers were sold every weekday in Canada last year, we share a community of interest in reading just as much now as when Matthew Arnold noticed that in America "all classes read their newspaper." Fortunately, the common reader has the choice of deciding what is to have permanence as he tries to shape his own reality in the words and syntactical arrangements he uses—there are many uses for newspapers. Coleridge observed that the crisis of the Napoleonic wars "occasioned thousands to acquire a habit, almost of necessity, of reading," and that it was in the interests of an editor to retain this habit. This is still the case, and newspapers have both the opportunity to form the vital consciousness of a community and a responsibility not to betray a trust because they are indispensable. In order to assure a vitality in the press, the reader himself must always bring to its pronouncements that sharpness of judgment acquired through the critical awareness of language at its most vital.

V

Politics and journalism are not the only areas where the representation of the "real" world has the barren contours of a wasteland and the tired and shabby vocabulary of men on the moon. Demonstrating what Hazlitt called the "ignorance of the learned", the whole area of education may present a landscape where the mere man of clay, like Dickens's Dick Swiveller, will find himself "rambling through deserts of thought where there is no resting place, no sight or sound suggestive of repose, nothing but a dull eternal weariness . . . constant still to one ever present anxiety."

Some of the spokesmen for the "Humanities" do not seem to make language either more intelligible or humane. The following sentence, for instance, from a report of a University Committee on Academic Policy and Planning, is not only a triumph of jargon but a memorial to the failure of the humanities to make any impact in the "real" life of university affairs:

> Furthermore, a reallocation of teaching resources from upper-level
> seminars to 100 level courses would result in a reduction of flexi-
> bility from a Faculty perspective and would have an adverse im-
> pact in other areas of curricular change, for example, the introduc-
> tion of new programmes of study.

Reports containing passages such as this are discussed at Faculty
Council meetings and staff meetings throughout the country with
everyone imagining that he speaks the same language as
everyone else.

Here is a comment from a Dean of Fine Arts writing in defence
of a young artist, whose "visual commentary has shocked us into
greater awareness, and whose growth will hopefully bring further
challenges to those of us willing to grow with him." Awareness?
Of what? Nothing is supplied by the context. What does the Dean
hope for, or is he full of hope? Is it simply pedantic and carping
to complain of this nonsense occurring in a university which
should be the centre or the foundation of an educated public?
"They fail to recognize—as Av Isaacs did in exhibiting Prent's
work—the need of the young artist to try himself publicly and to
take his lumps, for on those lumps he will grow." It is not Mr.
Isaacs' "failure" which provided the shock of recognition. Why
should I be chivvied along by this grotesquely inept colloquialism
posing as art criticism?

When politics, education, and journalism mix, the product
may be a strange freak of nature, as in the following piece from
the *Times Educational Supplement*. This is a front-page editorial
and is presumably written by a staff writer who ought to know
what education is:

> There is, moreover, a point of substantial difference (and one well
> worth having a political argument about) between those who be-
> lieve that extended education is only needed by, and justified for,
> the specially intelligent, and those who believe for social and cul-
> tural reasons that most people can benefit by post-secondary educa-
> tion of some sort.
>
> Mrs. Thatcher clearly belongs to the former school, which sees

notning surprising in a long drain pipe of upper secondary and higher education fixed on top of the broad rectangle of compulsory schooling, while the Labour Party study group represents the latter view, in which the whole education profile is egg-shaped. Oddly enough, the more radical critics of the education scene—who attack the basic notion of compulsory education, and would presumably reject the Green Paper's plea for compulsory day release —seem to come closer to Mrs. Thatcher's élitist view than to the benevolent but soft-centred comprehensivism of the Green Paper. On balance the soft centre has the best of the argument at the present stage of educational development, provided a re-emphasis on further education is presented as an extension of the variety, quality and quantity of opportunity and, therefore, a liberal maximization of choice not the forced freedom of state paternalism.

This leader writer throws round his baleful eyes and witnesses "huge affliction and dismay". The tired vocabulary, the clichés, the unconscious pun, the lazy alliteration, all are sentinels for the prison formed by visual metaphors, the geometry representing a labyrinthine chaos.

I am not choosing to ignore the economic pressures within human society, they are forced upon me. But this is no reason to permit the language of the market-place to obscure the end of education—not mere reading, writing, and counting, but an unending process of leading men and women to a fullness in their individual lives wherein self-knowledge will include moral and emotional as well as intellectual development. Society has no meaning outside the lives of the individuals who compose it and the continuous waffle about the relationship of the University and Society is a frequent disguise for the inability to think outside an economic terminology.

It is the gross language of national product which makes the Draft Report of the Commission on Post-Secondary Education in Ontario so outrageously degrading. The dominant metaphors of the report reveal that the major intention is to save money: value is perceived in terms of class structures, and flexibility in such phrases as "consumer's choice", and the total vocabulary is marked by the greasy coin of the market-place, frequently debased. The theme of class structure is particularly interesting as it barely conceals the hostile anti-intellectualism of the bureaucracy to what it blandly calls "the professoriat".

Stating as beliefs that education must "be viewed as a humanizing process", that it must be "man-centred", that "depersonalization can permeate post-secondary education as it has already permeated other aspects of our lives", that "we must preserve and cherish the fragile, exquisite, special animal of this earth we call man" (Oh, for Chaucer's Harry Baillie who could recognize scoundrels—"Thou woldest make me kisse thyn olde breech, and swere it were a relyk of a seint"!), the Commissioners go on to demonstrate their command of the language:

> The challenge of our time is complex and compelling for humanity is at stake. The entire educational system, post-secondary particularly, has the potential of becoming a moving, changing responsive force in our society. The platitudes and metaphors of the past, overly facile analysis and simplistic solutions may have to be abandoned or created anew in somewhat different frames of reference. We must be prepared to seek a frame of reference which is human centred, which places its weight not upon the educational institutions *per se*, but upon the delivery of educational services to human learners in search of knowledge, skills and wisdom.

The position of that last word is the master-stroke of an empty style. Composed by "delivery" men, not a sentence without a cliché or with clear meaning, this passage (and the Report is full of examples) shows with incontestable force that the "beliefs" of the Commissioners are indeed platitudes. The Commissioners satisfied themselves that their "proposals are basically realistic and workable", in their firm dedication to the utilitarian. It is therefore not surprising that there should be no discussion of the humanities in their report when they speak of education as a "device". When they use such language as "consumer's choice", and "purchase", what is then the result of extending the metaphor?

> Student decisions as to what to "buy" would help our institutions (and the proposed alternatives to traditional institutions) to provide educational services that are more in keeping with what is really wanted. To accomplish this, of course, the established institutions

will have to be flexible. This flexibility, we suspect, will have to extend to the acceptance of student evaluation of their teachers.

Surely a curious context for "evaluation"? If "flexibility" does not mean spinelessness, I "suspect" that the authors do not know what they are supposed to be talking about: education. Nor do they seem to realize the nature of teaching.

No one is well served by responding to the aims of such documents as the Draft Report with such pleasantries as "laudable", or as "showing legitimate concern with the present and future", if at the same time he cravenly refuses to shout loudly and clearly that there is an indisputable connection between form and content. As with civil—very civil—servants under other despotisms, we make ourselves eunuchs, pledged to make education not better but very cheap.

Further political subversion of education in the guise of "relevance" is conducted by asking, in parrot-fashion, "interesting" questions. These are not questions which seek out a reality; they are rather a kind of state-administered third-degree investigation, yet another method of confrontation: "Why do we assume that learning must take place in an institution?" "What are the formal links, if any, between educational requirements and occupations?" "And why should initial certification or professional qualifications last for a lifetime?" "Is there any valid justification for the academic year?" "What are the true implications of University post-secondary education?" "Do our post-secondary institutions really contribute to a better, fuller life?" Where will the civil servants keep all the answers? In data banks, ready for processing? A contribution to the better, fuller life would begin with the perceptive critique of the language used by those who have to conduct those relationships of a university which are connected with the community. Such a critique would reject the clichés about the preservation of knowledge, the transmission of knowledge, and "direct service through the application of knowledge", in favour of something far less obviously utilitarian—the recognition that the study of the humanities, in particular the essentially collaborative and recreative study of literature, is central to both the understanding and the growth of human experience.

Before any of this comes to pass, however, there will doubtless be newer and newer "new education". "In the school of political projectors I was but ill entertained, the professors appearing in my judgment wholly out of their senses, which is a scene which never fails to make me melancholy." I borrow Swift's words and note that some educators are in a modern version of the Academy at Lagado. Here is part of the accompanying lecture notes for a "new media" (i.e. audio-visual) course known as "Arts 100 Communications". It is to be hoped that the pictures were good, for the description shows no understanding of the nature of language, confusing it with print in much the same way as children may see animation and print as the same thing: "Print, then, while a major medium and a dominant proxy-agent in the contemporary world, is not sufficient in itself to relate individuals to realities defined as infinite numbers of variable [*sic*] infinitely expressed." What kind of definition is that? Is the misprint a cunning application of the point?

Under the heading "value judgements", in a section of this video-tape explanation called "People-Print", the following disgrace appears, and is not untypical of many course descriptions in colleges and universities:

> Value judgements in the people-print combination gain their most significant impact from the mixing of characteristics of print and of people in print. The print itself, you will recall, introduces the qualities of linearity, of physical limits on space, of one-at-a-time expression. . . . The proxy role of *scanning* reality for us will tend, as a result, to become one of selecting reality . . . selecting according to the varied and value-loaded dictates of individual perception and judgement insofar as they are able to be presented in print.

Presumably, the video presentation of this course is literally "valueless". Presumably also, the content is sprayed on to the eyeball? Reading, in this account, is mindless "scanning" without any indication that both reading and writing might involve the progressive training of a mind to principles generative of new perceptions of value.

The dogma of trendiness takes many forms. The fashionable injection of "creative" writing courses into traditional curricula is a particularly unfortunate example of a fragmentation of reality by means of language. The implication of the term is that other courses are "uncreative". All that is meant, usually, is that certain individuals wish to be distinguished from their colleagues, especially those who seem to be the linear enemies of the flighty muse. Yet they may have some justification, for most of the pieces I have been quoting show that there is such a thing as degenerate or even destructive writing, the still-born produce of an unhealthy world.

Most of the energy in education is produced not by what has been jauntily described as the "anti-entropy business" of "new education", but by the energy and passion, the "life", of individuals who engage in collaboration with students. Any mutual inquiry which does not have behind it some intellectual rigour that may also be demonstrated in the written word may well turn into a sloppy and inconsequential chitchat for which the appropriate description might be "fun while it lasts". The easy relativity of the approach which undervalues the written word, and alarmist watchwords such as the following, undermine language. For all the technological bravado, this is an illustration of the sickness in the part "used to be call: soul":

> In a world of high-speed, complex, simultaneous, total-field change, the conventional pedestrian academic mode of analytic, linear segmentation and explication itself comprises a threat to our survival.

And yet the linear may co-exist with the simultaneous; an act of superb criticism demonstrated it. Coleridge brought his experience of literature, as it exists in life, to bear upon his judgment of the poetry of Wordsworth: "A poem is that species of composition" which proposes to itself "such delight from the whole as is compatible with a distinct gratification from each component part."

I wish to turn once more to the putative illiteracy of students; or, to speak with more precision, of the "student body". A student acquaintance of mine was recently involved in a discussion of the interrelationship of the feelings engendered by a sonnet and a play of Shakespeare. The plays "on the course" were *The Tempest* and *Antony and Cleopatra*, but with an admirable show of independence (for he had very little "purchasing power") the student chose to write about *Romeo and Juliet*. During the course of his essay the student did not seem very much concerned with the world of high-speed, complex, simultaneous total-field change; but then neither did he display the conventional pedestrian academic mode of linear analysis:

> The initial period of being in love is especially unrealistic. It is a period of intense fantasyzing and hopeful imagings. That is not a criticism but an observation. That is the case because, quite frankly, daily life is monotonous and boring. Love gives us a beautiful escape from normal life and opens the door wide to an eager imagination. The beaty of nature. . . .

Conventionally, and amid the hurly-burly of a life which may not be entirely dissipated by the marking of students' papers, it might be possible (if the piece is not plagiarized) to relate these remarks to the "theme", the "plot", the "characters", in *Romeo and Juliet* (good-naturedly, for the play is not "on the course") and after remarking on the spelling and the notions, hinting at the irrelevance and making a musty joke about the world not being his friend, give this essay a D—let's say a D+ for inspired malapropism. To do all this will be to miss the essential point about illiteracy.

The student does not know what he is talking about. He certainly does not know this play (or the other two). Yet his language betrays a considerable distinction from the bamboozling humbug of power, or the sensationalism and pretentiousness to be found in important areas of public communication. There is in this short passage I have quoted an attempt to write about the life he does know. What he does not know is how to write about it, and he is uncertain of how he knows what he knows. Just as his remarks seem unaccountably removed from the play, so his "observations" and frank acceptance of daily life as "monotonous and boring" reveal not only poor judgment, a resigned lack of discrimination, but blank emotional poverty and the need for experience. Does he know what he thinks as he sees what he says? Is this "study" of Shakespeare and the "grade" to be part of his formal education (remembered as English 200H) and yet to be what Yeats called "a preparation for something that never happens"? If the study of literature is to have any meaning, and if universities are to be for the living, then it is imperative that whatever is striven for by students be actuated in their language; that the possibilities of "realizing" their worth in language be rescued from the impoverishment and unconsciousness which, like infections, are displayed in the many, many such essays which are dutifully presented every year.

The activity known as "teaching" must always be a qualified success, if not a complete failure, because the shared process of inquiry which involves educing, or leading out, other minds and getting them accustomed to the strength which is the product of thought is one that can have no ending. Not only this, but the formal schooling of three or four years' duration seems to make no acknowledgement of what may be called intellectual gestation, what Wordsworth called "industrious idleness". Those engaged in this labour have undertaken a most onerous responsibility: not because they are making students more humane, not because they are continuing a cultural tradition, not because they are imparting mere information, and not even because they are trying to make criticism a creative and regenerative activity. Rather, the great challenging and sometimes melancholy difficulty arises because they are attempting to open, as love in a less "boring" world will open to "eager imaginations", another's creative perception of reality. The conviction of their own language (which not infrequently falters) must attempt to convey a recorded perception of a "real" world built with language exploited to the full capacity of meaning, and the artifacts of this world must be visited again and again. This is an act of love, an informing of community. The invitation of the polluting multitude to a healing paradise is not lightly given. The journey thither always requires effort, and has its own disturbing hardships and lonely terrors.

VI

May 16, 1975. I return to the tower as though emerging from dark vaults. The building is no longer snow-encircled or isolated.

Now the wheeling pigeons enjoy the spring sunshine and carelessly deface the structure, indifferent to architectural folly or academic pride. I look westwards across the suburban sprawl catching the glint of the Control Tower of Toronto International Airport, the stately solidity of the Niagara escarpment, and the splendour of the setting sun: the real world.

If I were to repeat Donne's passion-charged question in "The Sunne Rising",

> tell me,
> Whether both the India's of spice and myne
> Be where thou leftst them?

it must be asked at the Airport Information Desk with all the persistent charm or fractured cadence of a recent arrival from far places. The question is perhaps even too fanciful to put to the sun in a love poem, for my modern lover might well complain to her analyst: "We just don't speak the same language." To speak in this way will mark me either as a very new arrival, "unreal", or "far out". But creative artists are not uninformed about communications systems, as Pound perceived when he remarked that "poets are the antennae of the race." Their dwelling place is a kind of imaginative control-tower, their works a keep.

In spite of the new languages of different modes of communication with all their meretricious efficiency, I still need my old bawd of verbal expression to increase the range and depth of my emotional and intellectual experience. The company I keep with the language of literature involves me in a violent and amorous encounter, for it is the property of lunatics, lovers, spies, liars, prophets, explorers, exiles, and magicians. Every entry into the country of the creative artist, engaged in the human action of telling stories and making myths, is an adventure which increases experience of all but the complacent, "the average man", the unconscious unit. The engagement must be active.

There is a parallel between the attentive reader's approach to an author and the artist's relation with his "Muse". Traditionally goddesses, the daughters of Memory (Mnemosyne), the Muses represent the liberal arts, the memory of civilization. Coleridge's brilliant phrase "mobs have no memories" serves as a reminder that the "mass" media are the servants of the here and now. They dispense with the Muse in favour of novelty ("news") and a-musement. The artist has always been engaged in a passionate struggle with language and what begins as a gentle if unpredictable courtship of the Muse frequently ends in painful brawling. Robert Creeley's *Ballad of the Despairing Husband* shows how the Muse as "wife" will not be cramped into domesticity by the poet's conventional notions of form and content:

Oh wife, oh wife—I tell you true,
I never loved no one but you.
I never will, it cannot be
another woman is for me.

That may be right, she will say then,
but as for me, there's other men.
And I will tell you I propose
to catch them firmly by the nose

And I will wear what dresses I choose!
And I will dance, and what's to lose!
I'm free of you, you little prick,
and I'm the one can make it stick.

Was this the darling I did love?
Was this that mercy from above
did open violets in the spring—
and made my own worn self to sing?

The active engagement is emphasized by the persistence of this "worn self", the Orphic mouth of a vital community, a singing head floating down the river of time.

This persistence is well portrayed by the Nova Scotian author, Thomas Raddall, in a story called "Blind McNair". This story is framed by the sentence, "In Shardstown they sing ballads no more," and it is about bravery and treachery, cursing and love. The heart of the story is a singing contest in a blacksmith's forge, the social centre of the organic life of the village community. A brutal uncovering of the blind singer's eyes reveals "An image that could sing, sing forever and not be moved by earthquakes." McNair's further songs, one sung with "a strange violence, like the chanting of a curse'', the other an outline of a love song ''as old as the sorrows of the world'', are both songs of recognition in the context of the story. But there is a deeper sense of recognition which goes to the core of Raddall's vision of the community, an elegiac note reinforced by the wasteland and devitalization suggested by the very name of the community: ''For in Shardstown only the old men in the sunshine remember, and they sing ballads no more.''

I spoke earlier of teaching as a shared process of inquiry. Much of this process involves a dramatization of response, an evocation of the emotional range of literature by giving a tone to the voice, an attempt to catch the wonder and delight which love might make accessible to ''eager imaginations''. The importance of reading works of literature aloud, of hearing the words, cannot be sufficiently stressed. If there is any agreement that delight in richness and sweetness of sound is a requirement in a poet, if not the first, then the critical reader must try to recapture that delight. He must heighten his consciousness of literature by the active engagement of the ear as well as of the tongue and eye; and giving voice, the hearing of a tone, the sensing of a rhythm —which might even include the sense of dance—engage the author, reader, and audience in a communal shaping of the world. ''Once upon a time,'' Joyce's artist began to shape his reality, as do all spellbound children who gather round to hear the word; as did the men in Shardstown when it was a living community: ''It was strange; the big ox patient in the corner, and the tall red-bearded man above him, and the silence of gathered men, and the singer chanting in the midst, like something barbaric and old as the world.''

I am not speaking of a kind of aesthetic escapism, a self-indulgent wallowing in what is ''interesting'' to me alone, or of the ham performance of personalities. Nor do I mean mindless imitation, the attempt to recapture Wordsworth's northern ''burr'', Sir Thomas Browne's East Anglian, or Wendell Berry's soft Kentucky accent. Neither will revivals of ''elocution'' do (although even this would be better than reading as if one has a pencil between the teeth). Above all, I am not suggesting that reading aloud is a panacea for the evils of the world—the natural disappearance of famine and disease! Rather, I am trying to direct attention to the miserable inability of most people (not only students, but radio and television personalities, politicians and public men) to read anything without error. The slackness of co-ordination between tongue, ear, and eye is nothing less than sensory malfunction and deprivation. To adapt my suggestion of an amorous encounter, the first step to an increased sensitivity and a critical vitality must be the development of what might be called an erotic approach to reading. Such an approach suggests the active participation of the reader with the work, not a passive receptivity, and it hints at what might begin as a private experience. The "public" performance or "reading" before an anonymous and heterogeneous audience is no alternative.

The recent increase in public readings by poets at recitals, festivals, and happenings would be altogether more encouraging were the apologists for this kind of entertainment not so dogmatic in their insistence that such events are a return to the "truly-great bardic prophetic tradition". They are certainly not that. Rejecting the exponents of "linear communication with their insistently literary trains of 'flat earth' thinking", the poet Michael Horowitz suggests that public reading is a response to the "fresh conditions and stimuli of our expansively audio-visual culture". I would be less expansive. They do provide a poet with an opportunity to make some money (although it is probably still unwise to "pursue literature as a trade"); they do give a poet an opportunity to be heard and to perform. Such public readings do give an audience an opportunity to hear what voice and cadence and the rhythms of projection might offer, although it is true that some celebrated poets disappoint the preconceived notions of the audience, refusing all the accompaniment and orchestration of personality. But there is no possibility of dialogue or interchange except of a very limited kind. Without greatly enhanced memory, or a text, these readings are but another instance of the "now" culture, and they attract what I suggest is the "throw away" or "disposable" poem. The warm bath of social occasion is no substitute for the kind of attention which a community of response will provide and which will involve the test of several readings. Different voices, the shared experiences of the printed and sounded word, making musing possible. To offer a challenge: how does a reader approach Coleridge's "Rime of the Ancient Mariner" and include the beautiful and evocative prose of the marginal gloss?[1]

Nor is the public arena any guarantee for the social responsibility of the poet affirming him in a role as medicine man of society. After a poetry reading against the war in Vietnam, one American undergraduate wrote: "I feel curiously untouched at the end, as if we have come together for some ritual that none of us much cares for or sees much meaning for. . . . I feel that most of us came looking for directions for suggestions of what to do as the war drags on and glossy colored photographs of orphaned damaged children cease to affect even ourselves." This student's helplessness may only be alleviated by a trained critical response to the word, asking the appropriate questions, developing his critical awareness of the function of poetry. It will not be helped by propaganda or more volume on the loudspeakers.

In the words of the lonely Russian poet Anna Akhmatova, the poet as mouth is "witness to the common lot, survivor of that time, that place", and there are no national boundaries. In "Rage for Order" in *Lives*, the Irish poet Derek Mahon provides a fine illustration of the major social function of the literary artist in his attempt to bring order out of chaos by means of his careful attention to language. Hysterical women and stage-managers, for example, might choose to see the poet as far

> From his people
> And the fitful glare
> Of his high window is as
> Nothing to our scattered glass.

If the poet or artist seems preoccupied with "an eddy of semantic scruple in an unstructurable sea", he might not seem to belong to the "real" world, indifferent to riot and broken glass, the rhetoric of politicians, journalists, and educators. Yet Mahon insists that all division is partial and false; that "we", "I", "him", "me", are but masks of humanity emgaged in a "dying art":

> Now watch me
> As I make history,
> Watch as I tear down

To build up
With a desperate love,
Knowing it cannot be
Long now till I have need of his
Germinal ironies.

My own "high window" has provided no view of a promised land, but neither will it be provided from the Pisgah tip of the CN Communications Tower, the shadow of which has stretched across this paper. Caught up in the network, our expiring vitality may only, like the dying Falstaff, "babble of green fields" in a dehumanized, programmed, and mechanical world.

As I return to *Martin Chuzzlewit*, I can find a paradigm for the careful and regenerative use of language in the description of Tom Pinch's love for Mary Graham. With the cautionary remark that some readings are more germinal than others I urge that the passage be read aloud:

> It must be acknowledged that, asleep or awake, Tom's position in reference to this young lady was full of uneasiness. The more he saw of her, the more he admired her beauty, her intelligence, the amiable qualities that even won on the divided house of Pecksniff, and in a few days restored at all events the semblance of harmony and kindness between the angry sisters. When she spoke, Tom held his breath, so eagerly he listened; when she sang, he sat like one entranced. She touched his organ, and from that bright epoch, even it, the old companion of his happiest hours, incapable as he had thought of elevation, began a new and deified existence. (Chapter 24)

VII

I opened this paper with some very general observations on literacy and the artificial separation of the "student" or the "professor" from the commonplace sense of "reality". The examination of the language of some politicians, journalists, and educators displayed the urgency of the need for a critical view of language. I have used throughout (to adapt an electronic term) a "carrier wave" of illustrative examples to emphasize the critical perception of the artist. A brief encounter with one of the guides I have used will perhaps help to focus the relationship between literature and the real world and serve as a sharp reminder that we need to cultivate such critics now: we need the delicate particularity of their perception.

The criticism of Samuel Taylor Coleridge is never divorced from a vital consciousness of life in all its aspects—political, moral and religious—and he is continually testing his intellectual findings against his experience. At midnight on April 5, 1805, he recorded in one of his *Notebooks*:

> I will write as truly as I can from *Experience* actual individual *Experience*—not from Book-knowledge. But yet it is wonderful, how exactly the Knowledge from good books coincides with the experience of men of the World. . . . I yet believe that the saws against Book-knowledge are handed down to us from Times when Books conveyed only abstract Science or abstract Morality & Religion/whereas in the present day what is there of real Life, in all its goings on, Trades, Manufactures, high Life, low life, animate & inanimate that is not *in books*.

These notebooks, the confidential flux and reflux of Coleridge's experience, are a reservoir of his thought which is piped into the vibrant criticism of his prose works like the two "Lay Sermons", the *Friend*, and the aphoristic *Aids to Reflection*. These works are vital illustrations of his prescient awareness of the consequences and responsibilities involved in the massive growth of the literate public—the dangers of demagoguery and the need for the precise handling of truth. They show his continuous attempts to engage his readers in a process of self-education:

> accustom yourself to reflect on the words you use, hear, *or* read, their birth, derivation and history. For if words are not things, they are living powers, by which the things of most importance to mankind are actuated, combined, and humanized.

Coleridge's lifelong sense that "words are moral acts" forms what he might have called the "undersong" of all his writings, his expert journalism, political incisiveness, and the informing recognition that education involves the development of the "whole" man, his total psychological growth to maturity, or what he called "manliness".

The critical work *Biographia Literaria* is exactly one of those works which should be read aloud. The many notes on language, the parentheses and digressions, the very precisions and inferences, all call for a dramatic activity of the reader's mind. The criticism is rooted in Coleridge's "life and opinions", and directed to the education of "young men". This is the direction of the current beneath the surface of the work, towards those young minds which will strengthen with the formative importance of literature within their experience.

The heart of the book is Coleridge's defence of the poetry of Wordsworth against those critics who clearly demonstrate that they do not know what they are talking about. The analysis of Wordsworth's critical statements is naturally meant to involve the intellectual faculties of the reader, but by itself such criticism is merely "cold beneficence", a working good by halves. The reader is quickly shown that the appropriate defence is not the mere "head-work" of theory, but a drawing on the experience of the poetry as a living and felt product of the imagination. This defence is all the more skilful as Coleridge has to expose Wordsworth's own mishandling of language and inadequate criticism. A single but telling illustration will demonstrate the relation between experience and the critically imaginative response to another's act of the imagination.

Coleridge's notebooks are full of detailed observations. The very process of recording the details of a scene frequently involves the reader in considerable effort as he struggles to echo the rigour of Coleridge's own mental operations, and the attempt to capture the sensuous properties of a scene. For example, the complexity of the following passage is a reflection of a "reality", not the mere embroidery of anecdote:

Images of Calmness on ~~Grasmere~~ Rydale Lake, Jan. 14/~~new~~ fresh Delves in the Slate Quarry I *mistook* for smoke in the reflection/ An islet Stone, at the bottom of the Lake, the reflection so bright as to be heaved up out of the water/ the Stone & its reflection looked so compleatly one, that Wordsworth remained for more than 5 minutes trying to explain why that Stone had no Reflection/ & at last found it out by me/ the shore, & green field ~~with~~ a Hill bank below that Stone, & with Trees & Rock forming one brilliant picture without was such, that look at the Reflection & you annihilated the water/ it is all one piece of bright Land/ just half wink your Eyes & look at the Land, it is then *all* under water, or with that glossy Unreality which a Prospect has, when seen as thro' Smoke. (1804)

Ten years later, in *Biographia Literaria*, Coleridge describes, pictures, the special qualities of Wordsworth's presentation of natural scenes:

Like a green field reflected in a calm and perfectly transparent lake, the image is distinguished from the reality only by its greater softness and lustre. Like the moisture or the polish on a pebble, genius neither distorts nor false-colours its objects; but on the contrary brings out many a vein and many a tint, which escape the eye of common observation, thus raising to the rank of gems, what had often been kicked away by the hurrying foot of the traveller on the dusty high road of custom. (Chapter 22)

This is no passive reception of descriptive passages of poetry, but active and vital language in which there is a lyrical shaping of the reader's response if he will listen to the rhythm of the prose as part of its meaning. The opening sentence is more than a generalizing simile making an effect by its careful (but not mechanical) balance. Coleridge's discovery in that moment of small victory in 1804 has been turned to magnanimous praise in the forge of critical vitality. To adapt Coleridge's own phrase, I would say of his criticism here, "it is fresh and has the dew upon it."

The process involved in that notebook entry is a reminder that Coleridge did not regard himself as a teacher of "subjects", but as a "fellow-labourer" with students in a process of inquiry. His lifelong wish was to benefit his fellow men and such dynamic criticism as the above represents an approach to experience of which the ultimate goal and fulfilment is the community aspiring towards God. In Northrop Frye's phrase, Coleridge's criticism of life is a drive from "communication to community", and we still have need of such critics to "put us into a way of seeking". With language as the "armoury" of the human mind, with the "armed vision" that critical reading provides, with respect for our organs, a true country emerges from the narrow dimensions of mere political or geographical consciousness to a more fully realized imaginative state. It is the state suggested by Blake's giant figure of Albion, the fully human community, exclusion from which means the Ancient Mariner's "loneliness and fixedness", or the Nightmare "Life-in-Death".

NOTES

1   I should like to put on record that Marshall McLuhan is an excellent reader of poetry.

ACKNOWLEDGEMENTS AND SELECT BIBLIOGRAPHY

I should like to thank my fellow-travellers on the road for the companionship and wisdom they have shared and continue to share with me: Robin Biswas, Kathleen Coburn, Geoffrey Durrant, Elaine Feinstein, Joseph Gold, Mr. G. S. Griffiths, Desmond Maxwell, Richard Shroyer, and Eric Wright.

The following authors which inform the text must be considered as primary material:

Anna Akhmatova, *Poems*; Matthew Arnold, *Culture and Anarchy*; W. H. Auden, "In Memory of W. B. Yeats"; Amiri Baraka, "Black Art"; Donald Barthelme, "Report" in *Unspeakable Practices, Unnatural Acts*; William Blake, *Complete Poetry and Prose*; Ray Bradbury, *Fahrenheit 451*; Geoffrey Chaucer, "The Pardoner's Prologue and Tale"; J. C. Collins, *Ephemera Critica*; Cyril Connolly, *Enemies of Promise*; S. T. Coleridge, *Aids to Reflection, Biographia Literaria, Collected Letters, The Friend, Lay Sermons, Notebooks, On the Constitution of Church and State*; G. Crabbe, *The Village*; Robert Creeley, "The Ballad of the Despairing Husband"; Charles Dickens, *Martin Chuzzlewit, The Old Curiosity Shop*; John Donne, "The Sunne Rising"; Edward Dowden, *Fragments From Old Letters*; T. S. Eliot, *Four Quartets, On Poetry and Poets*, "Sweeney Agonistes"; Northrop Frye, *The Well-Tempered Critic*; Robert Graves and Alan Hodge, *The Reader over Your Shoulder*; William Hazlitt, "On the Ignorance of the Learned"; Robert Henryson, *The Testament of Cresseid*; Lyndon Baines Johnson, *A Time for Action*; James Joyce, *A Portrait of the Artist as a Young Man*; Thomas Kinsella, trans., *The Táin*; D. H. Lawrence, *Phoenix, Phoenix II*; F. R. Leavis, *Education and the University, The Great Tradition, Nor Shall My Sword, Culture and Environment* (with Denys Thompson); Dennis Lee, *Civil Elegies*; Malcolm Lowry, *Under the Volcano*; Derek Mahon, *Lives*; H. M. McLuhan, *The Gutenberg Galaxy, Understanding Media*; Herman Melville, *The Confidence Man: His Masquerade*; H. L. Mencken, "The National Letters"; Henry Miller, "The Air-Conditioned Nightmare"; John Milton, *Paradise Lost*, Books I & II; John Montague, *The Rough Field*; Flann O'Brien (pseud.), *The Best of Myles*; George Orwell, *Collected Essays, Journalism, and Letters, Nineteen Eighty-Four*; A. Pope, *The Dunciad*; Neil Postman and Charles Weingartner, *Teaching as a Subversive Activity*; Stephen Potter, *The Muse in Chains*; Ezra Pound, *ABC of Reading*; Thomas Raddall, *Tambour and Other Stories*; Theodore Roszak, *The Dissenting Academy*; George Sampson, *English For the English*; William Shakespeare, *Henry IV*, ii, *The Tempest*; P. B. Shelley, "Lines Written among the Euganean Hills"; Edmund Spenser, *The Faerie Queene*, Book I, *Veue of the Present State of Ireland*; George Steiner, *Language and Silence*; Jonathan Swift, *Gulliver's Travels*; Denys Thompson, ed., *Directions in the Teaching of English, Discrimination and Popular Culture*; William Wordsworth, *Poetical Works*; W. B. Yeats, *Autobiographies*, "John Kinsella's Lament for Mrs. Mary Moore", "Lapis Lazuli", "The Second Coming".

SECONDARY SOURCES

i) REPORTS

ADAMS, N. JOHN. "Trent Registrar's Recruiting Views Repudiated by University Head," *Globe & Mail* (Toronto), May 9, 1975, p. 5.

"The Changing Campus," from the text of the Report of the Minister of University Affairs of Ontario for 1970-71, *York Gazette*, 10 (November 1971), p. 2.

Council of Ontario Universities, Special Committee. *Notes of Fourth Meeting of Special Committee to Assess University Policies and Plans*, February 17, 1975, p. 3.

DOOLEY, D. J., President of the Association of Chairmen of Departments of English, *Letter to the Honorable Thomas L. Wells*, February 24, 1975.

Draft Report of the Commission on Post-Secondary Education in Ontario (Chairman, Douglas Wright), 1971.

GRAY, MALCOLM. "Literary Standard of UBC Students Found to be Low," *Globe & Mail*, January 24, 1975, p. 1.

JENSEN, R. C. "How a Tennyson Poem Affected the Course of World Events," *Kitchener-Waterloo Record*, April 22, 1975, p. 7.

KENNEDY, THOMAS. "Wrangling over Revenue from Resources Criticized," *Globe & Mail*, November 13, 1974, p. B1.

O'BRIEN, CONOR CRUISE. "Why I Voted Against Lynch's Bill," *Observer* (London), December 3, 1972, p. 15.

Ontario and Its Universities. Report of the Higher Education Seminar, York University/University of Toronto, 1973/74.

RUSK, JAMES. "World Hungry Not Fed by Rome's Rhetoric," *Globe & Mail*, November 9, 1974, pp. 1-2.

SALLOT, JEFF. "University Student Recruiting Called a Hunt for Warm Bodies," *Globe & Mail*, May 8, 1975, p. 1.

University of Waterloo Student Handbook. Art 100 "Communications".

"Wearing of the Green," *Times Educational Supplement*, February 2, 1973, p. 1.

"While the Hungry Wait," *Globe & Mail*, November 13, 1974, p. 6.

York University. Council of the Faculty of Arts, Committee on Academic Policy and Planning. *Report*, March 6, 1975, p. 3.

ii) ARTICLES

BRANDEN, VICKI. "Teaching the Unmotivated," *Saturday Night*, September 1973, pp. 19-22.

BROKL, ROBERT. "Some Hasty, Irreverent Thoughts on *A Poetry Reading Against the Vietnam War*," *NUC-MLC Newsletter*, vol. 1, no. 3 (1969), pp. 12-14.

COBBETT, WILLIAM. "To the Blanketeers. On the Utility of Knowing Grammar," *Cobbett's Weekly Political Register* (November 21, 1818), col. 249-78.

DI SALVO, JACKIE. "This Murder. Literary Criticism and Literary Scholarship," *NUC-MLC Newsletter*, vol. 1, no. 3 (1969), p. 11.

EHRENPREIS, I. "Yucktalk. Literary Style in the Oval Circus," *The New Review*, vol. 1 (September 1974), pp. 5-14.

GENT, LUCY. "English and the Hunger of the Imagination," *Times Higher Educational Supplement*, vol. 68 (February 2, 1973), p. 11.

GREEN, JOSEPH G. "Reflections on Mark Prent," *York Gazette*, vol. 4, no. 9 (April 10, 1974), p. 90.

HOROWITZ, M. "Blake and the Voice of the Bard in Our Time," *Books*, vol. 10 (Winter 1972), p. 18-24.

KAMPF, LOUIS. "The Scandal of Literary Scholarship." In *The Dissenting Academy*. Edited by Theodore Roszak, pp. 43-61. New York: Pantheon Press, 1967. vol. 1, no. 4.

KESSEL, BARBARA. "The English Teacher as Civilizer," *NUC-MLC Newsletter*, vol. 1, no. 4 (October 1969), pp. 1, 3, 20.

KNIGHTS, L. C. "A Liberal Education," *The Use of English*, vol. 9, no. 3 (Spring 1958), pp. 155-66.

LEE, DENNIS. "Country, Cadence, Silence," *Open Letter*, series 2, no. 6 (Fall 1973), pp. 34-53.

LUCAS, E. V. "Concerning Correspondence," *Cornhill Magazine*, vol. 67 (April 1898), p. 512.

MC LUHAN, H. M. "The Humanities in the Electronic Age," Humanities Association of Canada *Bulletin* (Fall 1961), pp. 3-11.

NISBET, R. "The Future of the University," *Commentary*, vol. 51, no. 2 (February 1971), pp. 62-71.

RICKS, CHRISTOPHER. "The Literary Style of LBJ," *Esquire*, vol. 66, no. 5 (November 1966), pp. 117-162.

SCHAAR, JOHN H., and Sheldon S. Wolin, "Education and the Technological Society," *New York Review of Books*, vol. 13, no. 6 (October 9, 1969), pp. 3-6.

THOMAS, JOHN. "The Sickening Servility of Kids in High Schools," *Saturday Night*, March 1971, pp. 17-20.

WHALLEY, GEORGE. "Sheet-Anchors and Landfalls," Humanities Association of Canada *Bulletin*, vol. 15, no. 2 (Autumn 1964), pp. 16-24.

WHITESIDE, THOMAS. "Annals of Television. Shaking the Tree," *New Yorker*, March 17, 1975, pp. 41-91.

iii) BOOKS

ASHLEY, L. F. *Children's Reading and the 1970's*. Toronto: McClelland and Stewart, 1972.

CARPENTER, EDWARD, and Marshall McLuhan, eds. *Explorations in Communication: An Anthology.* Boston: Beacon Press, 1966. (1960).

HOGGART, RICHARD. *The Uses of Literacy: Aspects of Working Class Life, With Special Reference to Publications and Entertainment.* London: Penguin Books, 1958. (1957).

HOLLOWAY, JOHN. *The Establishment of English.* Cambridge: Cambridge University Press, 1972.

PLUMB, J. H., ed. *Crisis in the Humanities.* London: Penguin Books, 1964.

ROBINSON, IAN. *The Survival of English: Essays in Criticism of Language.* Cambridge: Cambridge University Press, 1973.

SONTAG, SUSAN. *Against Interpretation and Other Essays.* New York: Dell, 1966.

STEARN, G. E., ed. *McLuhan: Hot and Cool. A Primer for the Understanding of and a Critical Symposium with a Rebuttal by McLuhan.* New York: Signet, 1969. (1967).

THOMPSON, DENYS. *Between the Lines or How to Read a Newspaper.* London: Frederick Muller, 1939.

———. *Voice of Civilization: An Enquiry into Advertising.* London: Frederick Muller, 1943.

WALSH, W. *Coleridge: The Work and the Relevance.* London: Chatto and Windus, 1967.

WILLIAMS, RAYMOND. *Culture and Society, 1780-1940.* London: Penguin Books in association with Chatto and Windus, 1963. (1958).

———. *The Long Revolution.* London: Penguin Books, 1965. (1961).

The Failure of the Machine and the Triumph of the Mind
PHILIP H. SMITH, JR.

Standing on the University of Waterloo campus in the evening sun last spring, I asked Phil Smith whether the reading-machine had yet appeared. Years earlier we had discussed the virtue of a machine that would not only scan but would be able to translate printed text into machine-readable form. We had once rhapsodized about the speed, the cost-saving, and the efficiency of such a procedure, and surely the task was simple enough. All such dreams were over, he said, and all our expectations had proved purely illusory. There was no point in wasting our time in idle speculation. At this point a university delivery truck drove up. To the best of my recollection, as they said on television through one memorable summer, the following conversation ensued. "The driver of that truck, any normal human being, is capable of such feats of knowledge and recognition, is such a storehouse of information, that a machine could not be imagined big enough and useful enough to begin to approach such mastery of transposable information. Why, the machine would not even recognize a broken letter, know one style of print or spelling from another, let alone distinguish a pun, and as for translation, which is simple enough for millions of people, it is a task of such subtlety and complexity that it can only leave us awestruck at its mystery when we contemplate teaching it to a machine. We just do it, but we can't begin to programme it," he said. Perhaps, I fantasized, it was not hardware at all that I needed for my work but a kind of artificial chemical brain, tuned to mine, kept in a case in my office and given books to read and summarize and document all day. "Aren't you describing a graduate assistant?" Phil asked. It seemed natural to tell him about this book and ask if he would write a final word for it along the lines of our conversation. His profound respect for language, acquired through years of discovering the limitations of machines, as he has designed tasks for them that they could perform, seemed to me the most fitting point of view to conclude our case. "We are in possession," he said, "of a great and magical gift, peculiarly ours. Don't fret about machines. Thank God for it." The following piece was his elegant answer to my request.

Editor

The director of a prosperous and renowned school of languages twenty years ago explained his venture into machine translation—the attempt to programme a computer to translate text from one language to another—by saying that the task should not be very difficult. "After all, a computer can do the job of a mathematician. Mathematicians are scarce and highly intelligent. Translators, on the other hand, are very ordinary people, not known for their brilliance, and not particularly well-paid. If a machine can replace a mathematician, surely it can replace a translator."

For the mid-1950s, this seemed fair enough. After all, everyone knew that the Giant Brains were solving problems unattempted yet by hand or mind, and science had no limits. Twenty years later, machine translation is still being attempted in a number of research centres in the world, and claims are made from time to time that this installation or that is "using machine translation" on a routine basis. But the computer translations never seem to be displayed publicly, and, by all the evidence, the amount of human translation being performed is still growing rapidly.

Brazil, it has been said, is the land of the future. "It always has been, and it always will be." The great scientific breakthrough of the future has, for the past twenty years, been the machine that could read printed text. I don't refer merely to scanning a text and sending a facsimile picture of it over a wire to another city, and I certainly don't mean "reading" text with comprehension or analytic ability. I mean simply a machine that might be shown a page such as the one you are reading and which would recognize that the first word in this paragraph begins with a capital "B", followed by a small "r", and so on, and recognize the same letters printed in bold-face, or in a flowing italic type, or in one of the Art Deco-type faces which are supposed to suggest the romance of the Gatsby era. At intervals of two or three years one of those companies in southern California whose name ends in "-tronics" or "-mation" advertises an "optical character reader", and sometimes the announcement is accompanied with talks, demonstrations, and slide shows. Just as regularly the news filters out in a few months that the company has ceased operating, or has gone broke, or that the machine simply cannot read printed text as it should. As a six-year-old child can.

What has gone wrong? Why are we left with the paradox that mathematical operations, which most of us cannot even comprehend, are regularly and rapidly performed by computers, while the childish task of reading text and distinguishing between the letters of the alphabet, to say nothing of translating between languages, remains beyond the capacity of the Giant Brains?

The problems have nothing to do with the size or speed of computers, as we once thought. As computers get bigger, faster, and cheaper to operate, solutions to our two simple problems of linguistic behaviour come no closer. Besides, "hardware" never was the limiting factor: the machines have been, at all stages of the attempt to translate languages or to read text, well beyond our poor attempts to programme them. No, the limiting factor, the stumbling block, has been our own inability to specify just what it is we do when we interpret the letters printed on a page, or understand a text in one language and render its equivalent in another.

It is a commonplace that a translator must do more than merely transfer words from one language to another, even obeying grammatical rules. He fails badly at translating a technical article if he does not understand the technology involved, nor can he translate a work of literature successfully if he knows nothing of the two cultures, those of the source and target languages. But how are we to teach chemistry to a computer, or immerse it in Russian culture (and our own) so that it will absorb the capacity to translate properly? We lack even the understanding of what it would mean to "teach a computer chemistry", and the idea of immersing a computer in one culture or another is ludicrous.

These two signal failures of "artificial intelligence"—there are many others—yield an astonishing lesson. The notion that such human drudges as translators could easily be replaced by the machines that supplanted geniuses like mathematicians has proved to be quite wrong. Any human being outside a mental institution, from the lowliest and poorest-paid to the most exalted, performs daily a kind of information processing which we do not understand, which cannot be emulated by the most sophisticated of modern computers, and the very nature of which eludes engineers, remaining in the province of philosophers: he uses language. He understands sentences in his native language, even though they be couched in layers of metaphor. He can generate an infinity of sentences, many of them probably never before generated by another human being, using a set of rules and a body of data which we have no idea how to codify. And, in the rich countries, he is usually able to read and write: that is, to decipher a very wide variety of designs and ascribe to them their "letter" values, and from that proceed to still higher levels of analysis until he has understood written utterances.

He does all this, to be sure, by using the grammar of his native language. But he uses a great deal more. Man does not speak in syntax alone, and underneath every syntactic analysis that we, as humans, make of a sentence lies our "understanding" of the sentence, which means that we apply to the resolution of syntactic ambiguities our knowledge of the way the world works. We may never even be overtly aware of many of the ambiguities in the sentences which we handle with ease. It takes a machine to point them out to us, as a familiar example will show. A group at Harvard has worked on the computer parsing of English sentences, in a system which yields all possible analyses for any sentence presented to it. It is reported that their computer has found three analyses for the common adage, "Time flies like an arrow." Analysis number one is the one we are acquainted with: a statement about the speed of time's passing. The second analysis finds an imperative sentence: telling someone to time the speed of flies, and do it quickly. And analysis number three is another declarative statement about a kind of flies, called "time flies", which are fond of arrows; sort of like saying, "Fruit flies like a banana."

There is no theoretical reason why we cannot put into a machine programme the necessary information about flies which will give us the proper analysis of this adage. I am not sure what the information would be, but I am certain that we could work it out, and even more certain that we could programme it: But the very next sentence that we tackle will probably contain a completely different ambiguity, one which as humans we would solve by applying some of the information we carry about with us all the time, such as the boiling point of water, or the fact that leaves fall in the autumn and not in the spring. To include all the necessary information in a computer programme is an immense task, to say nothing of the difficulty of dredging it up from the reservoirs of our brains. There may be clever new approaches to syntax, and there may even emerge thrilling new theories of linguistics, but I do not see anything on the horizon which begins to approach the problem of organizing into a computer system the staggering amount of information necessary—for language, as we treat it and use it as human beings, is nothing less than an embodiment of the totality of our experience.

Those who work daily with computers are still engaged largely in solving problems in mathematics and engineering, and they are well-pleased with their remarkable tools. It is those who have attempted to exploit the power of the computer in what seemed at first to be the less exotic tasks of processing language data who have been bruised and disillusioned. The dream of two decades ago, that computers could replace humans in the business of translating languages, or of reading text to the extent of distinguishing reliably between an "o" and a "c", seems to have faded, along with our innocence. But it has left in its place a much more solid respect for the uniquely human functions of manipulating language—of translating, of reading and writing, and even of speaking.